# COINS
# OF
# SOUTHERN INDIA

# COINS
# OF
# SOUTHERN INDIA

BY

**SIR WALTER ELLIOT**

K.C.S.I., LL.D., F.R.S.

GYAN

*Published by*

Gyan Publishing House
5, Ansari Road
Daryaganj, New Delhi-110002
Phone: 011-47034999, 9811692060
E-mail: books@gyanbooks.com

*Distribution Network*
gyanbooks.com
India, USA, Canada, UK, Australia, France



ISBN : 978-81-212-2664-6 (HB)
First Published, 1885

2nd Impression 2021

*Printed at:* Gyan Press, Delhi.



**Coins of Southern India**
Author: Walter Elliot

# AUTHOR'S PREFACE.

THE appearance of this contribution to the INTERNATIONAL NUMISMATA ORIENTALIA has been much delayed by the failure of my sight, which has latterly proved a serious hindrance in the revision of the press, and more especially so in the re-examination and description of the coins themselves.

The difficulty of correcting proofs by means of the ear alone must be obvious, and will suffice to explain many of the typographical errors that would have been removed had the slips chanced to pass under my own eye.

In describing some of the coins here noticed, I had to trust chiefly to memory, which, notwithstanding the cheerful aid rendered by members of my own family, and by several friends, often left me in doubt and perplexity.

The plan I have followed in this essay has been to give a slight historical sketch of the principal southern rulers who issued dynastic coinages, as far as the limited means at my disposal would admit. Where the data for these were wanting or defective, I have indulged in greater detail, especially where the received history, such as it is, appeared to be inexact, or the chronology faulty or open to question. My speculations on these points may be amended and adjusted as the progress of the South Indian Archæological Survey brings more comprehensive evidence to light.

Residing in a distant part of this country, I have had to depend for the leading facts, in a great measure, on my own library and on my own original collection of coins. Aided by these, it has been my aim merely to give such a sketch of the monetary system of the Hindu principalities of the south, as will assist future numismatists to enter more fully into the coinage of the different dynasties. Hitherto specimens of earlier coins have rarely been met with, not because they were wanting, but because when found, as they are, in considerable numbers, they are at once converted into articles of modern use. When, however, the demand for them now manifested has given to them an extrinsic value, in excess of the market price of bullion, they will find their way more readily into the hands of collectors.

In conclusion, I must express my gratitude to MR. EDWARD THOMAS, the superintending editor of the INTERNATIONAL NUMISMATA ORIENTALIA, for the constant aid he has afforded me, notwithstanding his own important and absorbing pursuits, not only in the shape of frequent advice and annotations, but in the arrangement and description of the plates, which are almost entirely his work. I have also to thank GENERAL G. G. PEARSE, C.B., for his liberality in placing the contents of his own valuable collection at my free disposal, and for the ready assistance he has afforded me in arranging my own specimens when I was unable to do so from the failure of my sight and on all other occasions when I consulted him; DR. CODRINGTON and MR. J. GIBBS for similar contributions of the early coins of Western India; and MR. P. RAMASWAMI RAJU, Professor of Tamil in London University, for his readings of the legends on the Pandyan coins. Nor must I omit to acknowledge the aid I have received from my old Tamil instructor, SAMUEL PILLAY, late of the Vepery Mission, Madras.

I have interchanged frequent communications with BISHOP CALDWELL while in England, with DR. GUNDERT of Calw in Wurtemberg, and DR. ROST of the India Office Library, to all of whom I must now express my grateful thanks. COLONEL YULE has kindly undertaken to superintend the correction of the map.

WALTER ELLIOT.

WOLFELEE, HAWICK N.B., *November* 15, 1884.

# ALPHABETS OF SOUTHERN INDIA.

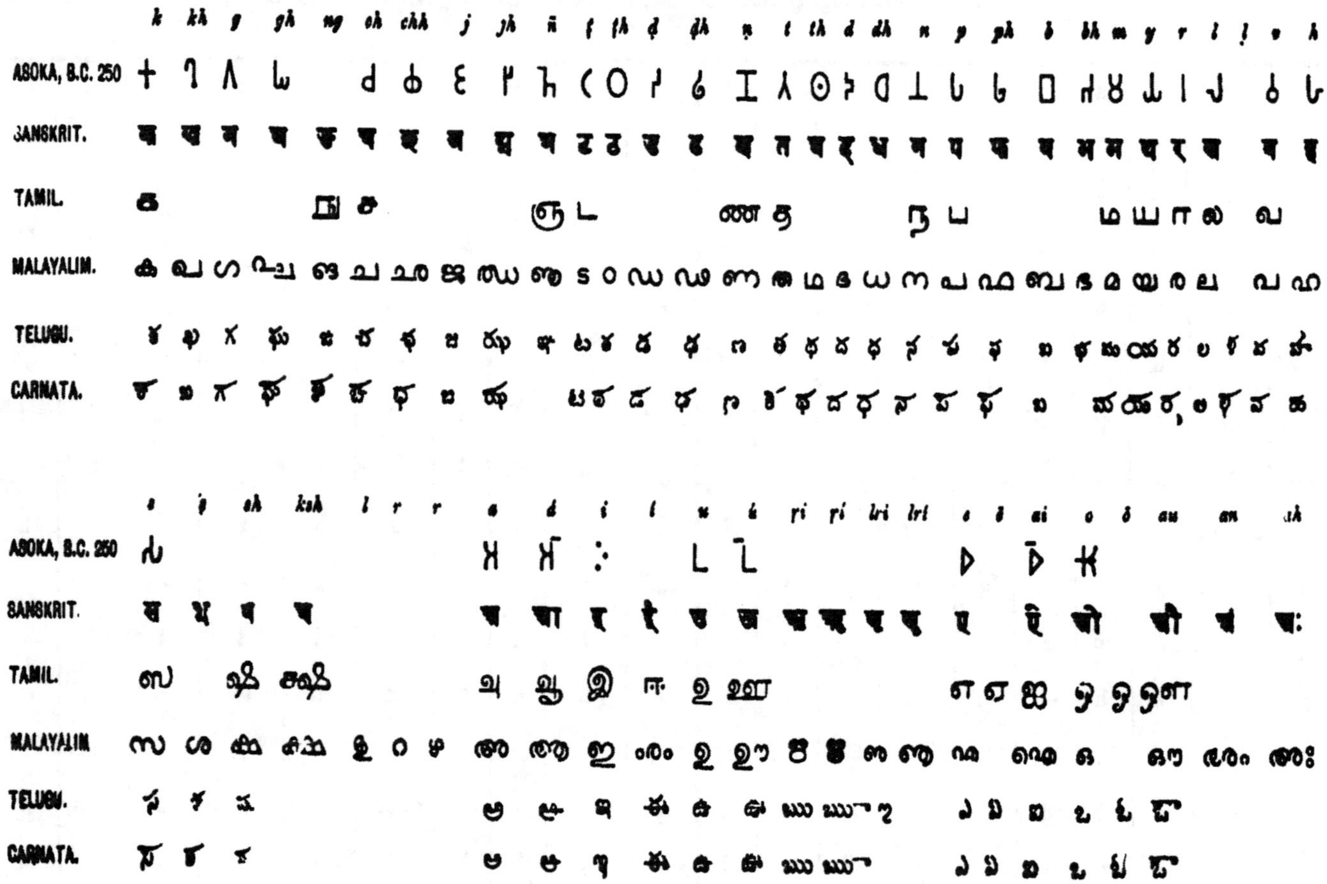


---

"The following comparative view of the Devanágarí and the Tamil alphabets exhibits the relations which the one bears to the other" (Caldwell, Dravidian Grammar, page 13).

**Vowels.**

Sanskrit: *a, á : i, í : u, ú : ṛi, ṛí : lṛi : — ê : ai : — ô : au : ṅ : h.*
Tamil: *a, á : i, í : u, ú : — — : — : e, ê : ai : o, ô : au : — : h.*

**Consonants.**

Gutturals, Sanskrit: *k, kh : g, gh : ng.*
Tamil: *k, — : —, — : ng.*

Palatals, Sanskrit: *ch, chh : j, jh : ñ.*
Tamil: *ch, — : —, — : ñ.*

Linguals, Sanskrit: *ṭ, ṭh : ḍ, ḍh : ṇ.*
Tamil: *ṭ, — : —, — : ṇ.*

Dentals, Sanskrit: *t, th : d, dh : n.*
Tamil: *t, — : —, — : n.*

Labials, Sanskrit: *p, ph : b, bh : m.*
Tamil: *p, — : —, — : m.*

Semivowels Sanskrit: *y, r, l, v.*
Tamil: *y, r, l, v : ṛ, ḷ, ṉ.*

Sibilants and Aspirate, Sanskrit: *ś (or ś), sh, s, h.*
Tamil: — — — —

**METHODS OF TRANSLITERATION** *suggested by different authorities, for the purpose of reproducing* **IN ROMAN TYPE, THE CRITICAL EQUIVALENTS OF THE SEMITIC ALPHABETS,** *with the compromise suggested for* **THE INTERNATIONAL NUMISMATA ORIENTALIA.**—(Cols. 8, 9.)

| | 1 | 2 | 3 | 4 | 5 | 6 | 7 | 8 | 9 | | 1 | 2 | 3 | 4 | 5 | 6 | 7 | 8 | 9 |
|---|---|---|---|---|---|---|---|---|---|---|---|---|---|---|---|---|---|---|---|
| | Sir W. Jones. | Mirza Ibrahim. | Mr. F. Johnson. | M. A. Chodzko. | Dr. Wright. | Dr. Fuerst. | Mr. Lane. | Persian. | Arabic. | | Sir W. Jones. | Mirza Ibrahim. | Mr. F. Johnson. | M. A. Chodzko. | Dr. Wright. | Dr. Fuerst. | Mr. Lane. | Persian. | Arabic. |
| ا | a | a | a | e, a | ' | | | a | | ع | ع | a | ع | 'a | ʻ | | ', ạ | ' | ' |
| ب | b | b | b | b | b | b | b | b | b | غ | gh | gh | gh | gh | ġ | ġ | gh | gh | gh |
| پ | p | p | p | p | p | — | — | p | — | ف | f | f | f | f | f | f | f | f | f |
| ت | ṭ | t | t | t | t | t | t | t | t | ق | ḳ | ok | k | q | ḳ | ḳ | ḳ | ḳ | ḳ |
| ث | th *or* ṣ | s | s | s | ṯ | t, θ | th | s | th | ك | k̤ | k | k | k | k | k | k | k | k |
| ج | j | j | j | dj | ǵ | ǵ | j | j | j | گ | g | g | g | g | g | — | — | g | |
| چ | ch | ch | ch | tch | c | — | — | ch | — | ل | l | l | l | l | l | l | l | l | l |
| ح | ḥ | h | h | hh | ḥ | ḥ | ḥ | ḥ | ḥ | م | m | m | m | m | m | m | m | m | m |
| خ | kh | kh | kh | kh | ẖ | ẖ | kh | kh | kh | ن | n | n | n | n | n | n | n | n | n |
| د | d | d | d | d | d | d | d | d | d | و | v, w | v | v, w | v, oû | w | v, w, û | w | v, w | w |
| ذ | ż | z | z | z | d | ḏ | dh | z | đ | ه | ḥ | h | h | h, é | h | h | h | h | h |
| ر | r | r | r | r | r | r | r | r | r | ي | y | y | y | y, ì | y | y, i | y | y,i,e | y |
| ز | z̈ | z | z | z | z | z | z | z | z | ـَ | a | ă | a | e | a, è, e | a *or* e | a *or* e | a, ă | a |
| ژ | j | j | j | j | j | — | — | zh | — | ـِ | i | ĕ | i | i | i, ì | i *or* y | i | i, e | i |
| س | s̤ | s | s | s | s | s | s | 's | s | ـُ | u | ū | u | u | u, o, ö | o *or* u | u *or* o | u | u |
| ش | sh | sh | sh | ch | ś | ś | sh | sh | sh | ـَا | ā | — | ā | â | ā | — | á | á | á |
| ص | ṣ̈ | s | s | s | ṣ | ṣ | ṣ | ṣ | ṣ | ـِى | ī *or* e | — | ī | — | ī | — | ee | í, é | í |
| ض | z | z | z | z | ḍ | ḍ | ḍ | ẓ | ḍ | ـُو | ū *or* o | — | ū | ô *or* ou | ū | — | oo | ú, | ú |
| ط | ṭ | t | t | t | ṭ | ṭ | ṭ | ṭ | ṭ | ـَو | au *or* aw | — | au | ôou | au, ō | — | ow, ó | au, ó | au |
| ظ | z̈ | z | z | z | ẓ | ẓ | ḍh | ẓ | ẓ | ـَى | ai | — | ay | — | ai, ē | — | ey, ei | ay, ai | ay, ai |

*The diacritical dots may be omitted at option, but preferentially where the original text accompanies the romanized version.*

No. 1.—Persian Grammar. London, 1828. No. 2.—London, 1841.
No. 3.—Persian Dictionary. London, 1852.
No. 4.—Grammaire Persane. Paris, 1852.
No. 5.—Arabic Grammar. London, 1874-75.
No. 6.—Hebrew and Chaldee Lexicon. London, 1867.
No. 7.—Arabic Lexicon. London, 1863-74.
No. 8.—The International Numismata Orientalia—Persian, etc.
No. 9.—*The International Numismata Orientalia*—Arabic.

# CONTENTS.

# ILLUSTRATIONS.

# ERRATA.

Some errors have crept into the Map, which was not submitted for final revision, but only the two following are mentioned.

pp. 4, 14, 37, 89, 108, etc. The province of Tondamandalam between the Eastern Ghâts and the Pálar river, corresponding with the modern districts of North and South Arcot, is omitted. The Tondaman, prominently inserted in Tanjore, head of the petty chief of Pudukotah, did not exist at the same early period.

p. 108. The western boundary of Cholamandalam, Kutakeri or Kotakarei, is synonymous with the modern Kodagu or Coorg.

p. 5. *For* 'Kabburga' *read* 'Kalburga.'

p. 24. *For* 'Gougaḍh' *read* 'Jougaḍh.'

p. 39. *For* 'Musulipatam' *read* 'Masulipatam.'

p. 44, line 22. *For* 'specimens' *read* 'coins.'

pp. 53, 57. *For* 'Ala-ud-din' *read* ''Alá-ud-dín.'

p. 59, line 19. *After* 'Not worth a cash' *add* 'Gund. Mal. Dict. p. 245, s.v.'

pp. 91, 93. *For* 'Anégundi' *read* 'Anagundí.'

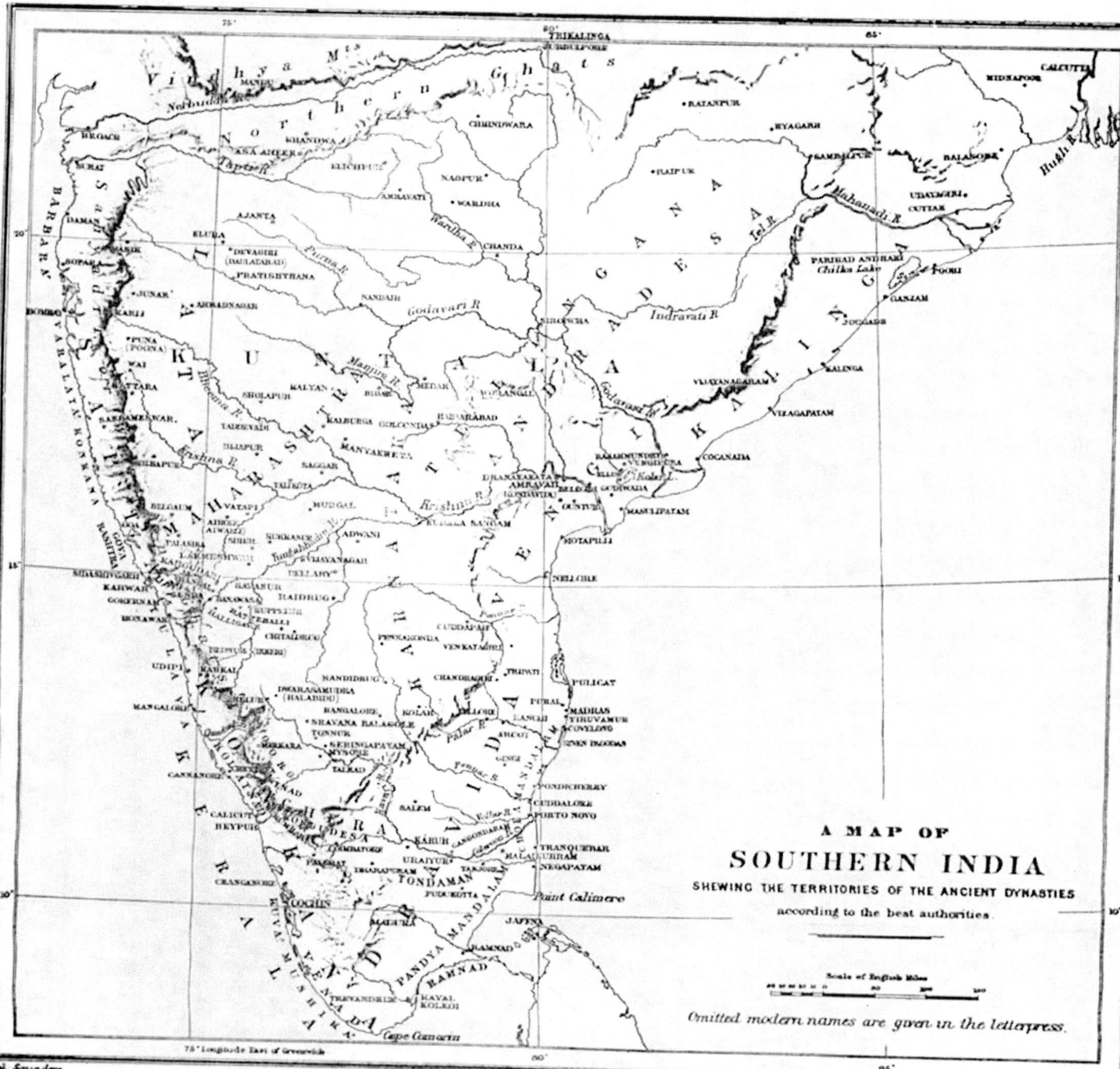


Ed. Saunders

London Trubner & Co.

Stanford's Geog¹ Estab¹ London

# COINS OF SOUTHERN INDIA.

## INTRODUCTION.

THE part of India to which the following Section of the International Numismata Orientalia refers is that lying to the south of the Narbada (Narmáda) river, and the Vindhya Mountains, now known as the Dakhan, to distinguish it from Hindustan proper, a term which, in its restricted sense, is confined to Northern India. Between them lies an extensive tract of hill and forest, the Highlands of Central India, which forms not only a geographical, but also an ethnographical boundary, separating the Aryan from the Dravidian races. The latter, although not the first occupants of the land, preceded the Aryans. They appear to have arrived by successive immigrations from their Trans-Himalayan seats, driving out or enslaving the aboriginal inhabitants, and each new swarm pushing the preceding arrivals onwards until they settled into their several localities, where they now form the Tamilian, Canarese, Telugu, and other communities. In the course of these displacements, some, unable to find a resting-place in the plains, betook themselves to the Highland region, where they have preserved their primitive character in feature, language, and manners, with little change.[1]

Before being restricted to their present limits, the Dravidians, as may be inferred from scattered communities of their race still subsisting in the Sub-Himalayan region, the Rájmahal Hills, etc., appear to have been spread over Northern India, whence they were ejected by another race of intruders from the north-west. The Aryans, after establishing themselves in the Punjab, eventually became the predominant power in the Gangetic valley, but they do not appear to have crossed the Vindhyan barrier in force, or to have gained a permanent footing in the Dakhan.[2] This did not hinder them from maintaining a friendly intercourse with their southern neighbours. When the traditionary Agastya, overcoming the obstacles interposed by the mountainous regions, penetrated into the south,[3] he found a people enjoying advanced institutions

[1] They are comprehended under the general Sanscrit term of *Dakshindpathqjamanas*, of whom a list is given in Wilson's Sanscrit Dictionary, *sub voce*, p. 395. The only one of these now found existing, under the names therein given, as an independent clan, are the Sávaras, who occupy a district to the west of Ganjam. To these may be added the Khonds, Gonds, Bhils, Santals, and other rude tribes.

[2] The Sanscrit word *Dakshina* (vulgo dekhan) signifies *right* as distinguished from *left*. The Aryans, coming from the west, applied this term to the country on their right hand, which thus became synonymous with *south*. In like manner the country before (*púrva*) then became *púrba*, and *purab—east*; and the inhabitants *púrbyas* or easterns. Another word for east, *práchi*, supplied the Greeks with their name of *Prasii* for the people of the Gangetic valley.

[3] Hence the additional name or title given to him of Vindya-Kuta, Vindhya-humbler'. Wilson, Dict. p. 773.

and a literature of their own, which enabled them to appreciate the elegance of the Sanscrit language, and to profit by the Aryan learning, of which it was the depositary. At the same time they imparted, not unacceptably, to their visitors, all that they knew themselves.[1] Nor did the mutual advantage of these new relations end here. Thenceforward Sanscrit continued to be sedulously cultivated in conjunction with native literature, and in after-ages, when the existence of the former was imperilled by the wars and political convulsions that overwhelmed its original seat, it not only found an asylum in the South,[2] but was transmitted in its most approved condition to modern times.[3] But although the Dravidians were not the earliest settlers, and although they have not been exempt, and that in no small degree, from external influences, it is from them that the civilized part of the Dakhan derives its characteristic features in language and institutions. Among the latter may especially be noticed its monetary system, and the coins in which it is expressed. These occur in great variety in all parts of the country, according to the range of the dynasties from which they originated. But here a preliminary difficulty at once presents itself. The history of these Powers has never been written. Nor is this all. In some instances the territorial names of the countries over which they reigned have been changed and their limits altered. The sites of some of their capitals are unknown, or are only recognized by inscriptions (fortunately not rare), and by the coins found among their ruins. Even these, when discovered, are too often without legends or dates, by which they can be assigned to their proper authors. The principal and most important of the states of the Dakhan arose in the northern part of the country, the physical character of which was favourable to their territorial aggrandizement. The natural aspects of the southern districts, on the other hand, kept the people distinct from their northern neighbours, and their relations were confined in a great measure to transactions among themselves. The most remarkable feature of North Dakhan is an extensive table-land rising on the north from the Valley of the Tapti, and bounded on the west by the Sahyadri Mountains. Most of our maps exhibit well-defined ranges

[1] That Dravidian literature had been highly cultivated by native students at an early period cannot be disputed. But the preference of European scholars for the study of Sanscrit has kept its merits too much in the shade, although it has not been possible to ignore them altogether. Professor Max Müller admits that there are grounds for believing that the *Taittiriya* or *Black Yajur Veda* had been studied and annotated by the non-Aryans of Drâvida, from which he draws a gratuitous inference adverse to its antiquity (Sans. Lit. 2nd ed. p. 334); and he refers to Dr. Weber's notice of a northern pandit quoting with respect the comments of *Dâkshinâtyas* on Vedic subjects. According to Burnell, the science of grammar (*vydkaraṇa*) was cultivated in the south from a very early period, not as derived from Sanscrit, but as communicated from a divine source, in other words, as being of indigenous origin (Aindra Gram., 1876, pp 5, 15, 53, 56, 67, etc.). It has further been held that the Sanscrit phonetic system was derived (in part at least) from the south, and that the original Aryan alphabet was "superseded by the more exact and appropriate system of the south" (E. Thomas, in Prinsep's Essays, vol. ii. p. 50; and Dynasty of the Guptas, p. 31, *note*), and certainly the harsh sounds of the cerebral consonants agree better with the rugged tones of the Turanian dialects than with the polished utterance of the Aryan tongues. Dr. Gundert has pointed out the not inconsiderable number of Dravidian roots adopted into Sanscrit, a fact persistently ignored by northern pandits (Zeit. Morg. Gesch. vol. xxiii. p. 517), to which Dr. Caldwell adds his testimony in the Second Edition of his Comparative Grammar, p. 454, *et seq.*

[2] "It must never be forgotten," Burnell observes, "that under the barbarian kings of Southern India . . . Sanskrit literature flourished more than it perhaps had ever done before, and that not only did this foreign civilization reduce Southern India to order but even extended thence to the Malay Archipelago." And he adds, in a note, that the Javanese civilization was derived from Kalinga, and from Southern rather than Northern India. —Preface, Burnell's Vamçabrahmana of the Sama Veda, p. xxxix.

[3] Several of the standard texts have been edited with much acceptance by southern scholars, and the most approved commentaries on the Vedas were the work of the celebrated minister of Vijayanagar, the last notable Hindu kingdom of the south. Burnell's Aindra Gram. 1875, pp. 5, 15, 53, 67, etc.; Sir W. Jones on Vaivaswata, As. Res. vol. i. p. 230, 8vo. edition.

of hills on the north, the east, and the south, but they are not really continuous like those on the west. On these three sides the plateau is defined by an abrupt slope or scarp, rising occasionally into detached groups of hills and rocky ridges unconnected with each other,[1] but, sometimes, as at Kambákam-drúg, Nagari-nose, and other places, attaining a considerable height. The eastern limit stretches in a southerly direction as far as Venkatagiri and Tripati, whence it slopes towards the south-west until it meets the Sahyadri chain at the place where it is broken by the remarkable gap, Pálghât. These natural limits are pierced by passes called ghâts, through which the roads are carried that afford access from the low country (or *Páyan-ghât*) to the upper plateau (or *Bálá-ghât*). Hence the boundary-lines have received the names of the northern, eastern, and southern ghâts. It was on this elevated table-land of Kuntala, as it was originally called, that the principal Hindu kingdoms known to us were established on the subjugation of the aboriginal settlers. Here, for about fourteen or fifteen centuries, the Andhras, the Chalukyas, the Yádavas, and other dynasties ruled, until the Mahommedan conquest swept over the land, and continued in the ascendant. With the destruction of Hindu States the name of Kuntala fell into disuse, and was replaced by three principal territorial designations, viz. Maharashtra, Karnataka, and Andhra, derived from the languages spoken by the inhabitants. A line drawn from the city of Bidar to Sadáshivgaṛh on the Malabar coast, curving first somewhat to the north, and then pursuing a south-west course, marks approximately the division between the Maháraṭṭa and the Canarese inhabitants. A second line, carried nearly due South from the same point, a little west of Nandidrúg, Adwáni, and Kolár, separates the Telugu-speaking people of Andhra from the Karnatak, a term which by a strange perversion has been transferred to the Tamil country, now known as the modern Carnatic. Of the maritime country on either side of Kuntala,[2] the Konkan on the west has generally followed the fortunes of the dominant power above the ghâts. The corresponding strip on the east side consisted of two provinces, Kalinga, reaching from the Mahánadi to the Godávari, was the first settlement of the Andhras, and Vengi, which, extending from the Godávari to Nellore, belonged to the Pallavas, an aboriginal or very early race, subjugated by the Chalukyas, first in the table-land, and afterwards in Vengi. Both fell under the sway of the Chalukyas of Rájamahendri; and the name of Vengi, like that of Kuntala, became obsolete, while Kalinga still retains its name, although it is now rarely used. Subsequently it was added to the kingdom of Orissa. The rest of the Dakhan, from Nellore and the ghâts to the sea, is the ancient Drávida-désam, the land of the Tamilians, the typical as well as the oldest section (certainly in India) of the Dravidian family. From time immemorial it has been known as the country of the Chola Chéra and Páṇḍyan princes, dynastic titles assumed by different families which have successively risen to eminence. The northern

[1] Manual of Geology of India, 1879, vol. i. p. iv, introduction.

[2] The Konkanas generally (Saptakonkana) were—1. Kéraḷa; 2. Tula or Tulunga; 3. Goa or Gova ráshtra; 4. Konkana proper; 5. Karátaha; 6. Varalatta; 7. Barbara. But the lists vary, and some show Kuva and Mushika, as the two most southerly districts, but they are, in fact, subdivisions of Kéraḷa.

portion, or Cholamandalam,[1] extended from the Káveri to the Púlár, to which was added by the conquest of the Kurumbarnádu the district of Toṇḍamandalam, as it was thenceforth called. From the Káveri to Cape Comorin, Paṇḍya mandalam, and the Chera country comprised all the territory westward to the sea; but on the dismemberment of the latter, then the most powerful of the three, in the fourth century, its eastern portions were formed into two minor states, Seralum or Chéra proper, the capital of which was Talkád and Konganadu, the chief city of which was Karúr (Caroor), near the Pálghát; while the western districts on the sea-coasts became known as Kéraḷa, now constituting the kingdom of Travancore.

The following is a tabular statement of the principal dynasties of the Dukhan, the coins of which may be expected to be identified.

### A.—Hindu Dynasties of South India.

I. The Andhras of Kuntala.
II. The Pallavas of Bádámi, Vengi, and Kanchi.
III. The Kadambas of Kéraḷa.
IV. The Chalukyas of Kuntala. 489–1189 A.D.
V. The Chalukyas of Rájamahendri and Vengi. 605–818-20.
VI. The Chola-Chalukyas. 820–1150? A.D.
VII. The Raṭhors or Raṭṭas of Mányakhéṭa (Málkheḍ). 660–972.
VIII. The Kalachuris of Kalyan. 1128–1183.
IX. The Yádavas of Devagiri (Daulátábád). 1187–1311.
X. The Yádava Hoysala Ballála of Dwarásamudra or Halábidu. 1047–1310.
XI. The Kakátíyas of Anumakonda, or Orugal (Worangal).
XII. The Cholas }
XIII. The Chéras } of Drávida-désam
XIV. The Paṇḍyas }
XV. The Paṇḍya-Cholas.
XVI. The Kongu, or Ganga Cheras.
XVII. The Yádavas of Vijayanagar, Bijanagar, or Anagundi. 1334.
XVIII. The Yádavas of Maisur.

This list does not include two minor dynasties, viz. the Siláháras of Kolhápur and the Vema Reddis of Kondaviḍu, of which few details were forthcoming.

[1] The transliteration of this name causes much perplexity, owing to the peculiar sound of the Tamil letter ழ, which has been rendered by *l*, *r*, *j*, *zh*. There being already two *l*'s and two *r*'s, Beschi describes it as another *r*, formed by pressing the tip of the tongue to the extreme back of the palate, producing a sound, which, in despair, he compares *voce vitulæ matrem vocantes*. The initial is pronounced sometimes as *s*, sometimes as *ch*. Hence comes the sóṛa, sóḷa, chóḷa, chóṛa mandalam of different writers. The early Portuguese and Dutch voyagers always wrote Choramandala and Choramandel, and as the former, like the English, often pronounce the *ch* hard, the modern Coromandel is easily accounted for.—Caldwell, Comp. Gram. pp. 28, 29.

## B.—The Mahommedan Kings of the Dakhan.

I. The Báhmanies of Kabburga. 1347–1525.
II. The Adil Sháhis of Bijapur. 1489–1660.
III. The Nizam Sháhis of Ahmadnagar. 1490–1607.
IV. The Kutb Sháhis of Golconda. 1512–1671.
V. The Ismáil Sháhis of Elichpur. 1484–1568.
VI. The Berad Sháhis of Bidar. 1492–1669.
VII. The Fáruki of Kandesh. 1379–1396.
VIII. The Ghori? of Malwa and Mandu (Capital Dhár). 1387–1568.

The coinage of these Mahommedan princes does not enter into the scope of our present paper.

Of all these dynasties, long enduring and widely ruling, as some of them were, we possess numismatic examples in appreciable numbers of the Andhra, Chalukya, and Bijanagar princes only in North Dakhan. Those of Drávida are more numerous, although examples of the earlier princes are still scanty.

Coins of the Mahommedan rulers are also rare, but are known to exist in larger numbers in private hands, and may hereafter possibly be fully illustrated.

During the last two centuries many local governors, Zamindars, Poligars (Pálayakars), and district chiefs,[1] taking advantage of the weakness of the paramount power, assumed the right of issuing money coined by themselves, and thus have flooded the country with gold, silver, and copper in endless variety, the later issues becoming more and more degraded, till all resemblance to the type from which they professed to be derived was lost.

It thus happens that of the great number of uncurrent coins which are constantly discovered, very few are worth the attention of the numismatist. Specimens of value for their rarity, or the light they throw on the past, are doubtless not of unfrequent occurrence, but they seldom find their way into the cabinet of the collector. Gold and silver pieces are speedily converted into jewels. The copper, of which vast quantities are collected by itinerant pedlars, are sold as old metal, and amongst the heaps of these, which have been occasionally inspected, it requires a practised eye and much patience to select a piece worth preserving from the mass of dirt and verdigris with which they are associated.

The prizes that have occasionally rewarded such quests show what may be expected when more have been rescued from the goldsmith's crucible and the brazier's melting-pot.

[1] Such were the Rájas of Sunda, the Bedar chiefs of Shorapur, and Bednur or Nagar, the Reddis of Condavir, the Poligars of the Ceded Districts (Ballári and Kadapa), the Zamindars of Ramnad and Shevagahga, the Nawabs of Savanur, Ginji, and Kadapa, the Nayaks of Tanjore, Trichinapali, and Madura, etc.

Of such as have hitherto escaped that fate, a few are preserved in museums, where they have excited little attention. More have passed into private hands and been dispersed.[1] Few have been hitherto published.[2]

The series now to be described consists of a Collection formed in India during several years, from 1825 to 1859, supplemented by a few examples communicated by the Bombay Branch of the Royal Asiatic Society, and such as could be found in the British and Indian Museums, and a few in private cabinets. They are arranged in three Classes :—

**A.**—Die Coins of lead, copper, and mixed metal, found in the north of Kuntala, especially in the Deltas of the Godávari and Krishna.

**B.**—Coins of Drávida, and the Western coast, exhibiting the progress of the normal native currency, from the prehistoric *purána* (described by Mr. Thomas in Vol. I. p. 52) to the artistic issues of the Vijayanagar mint.

**C.**—Coins of Eastern Drávida and Coromandel, imitated apparently from a northern type, intermingling by degrees with those of Class II., and becoming gradually degraded till they exhibit the scarcely recognizable symbols of the latest native coinage.

[1] Prof. H. H. Wilson, As. Res. vol. xvii. p. 559.

[2] The following list contains all with which I am acquainted:

I. A single plate in Marsden's Numis. Or. 1823-5.

II. A single plate, No. civ. in More's Hindu Pantheon, 1828.

III. A nominal list of Col. Mackenzie's Collection, without figures or description, and comprising 55 gold coins, 33 silver, 47 copper, and a few lead types, of which a few are described in the next (Wilson's Cat. ii. ccxx. 1828).

IV. Select coins from originals and drawings in possession of the As. Soc. by H. H. Wilson, with figures. As. Res. vol. xvii. 1832, plates iv. and v.

V. Incidental notices of single coins, by James Prinsep, in Jour. As. Soc. Bengal.

VI. Numismatic Gleanings. Madras Jour. Lit. and Sc. vols. xix. or xx. O.S. or vols. iii. and iv. N.S. 1857-9.

VII. Occasional notice in J.R.A.S. Bombay, from 1844 to 1870.

VIII. Occasional mention in Proceedings J.A.S.B., and

IX. In Indian Antiquary.

# A.—NORTHERN DIE COINS.

## SECTION I.

## ANDHRAS.

The first class contains the earliest die-struck coins.[1] They belong chiefly to the Andhra dynasty, of which both the era and the original seat are involved in much obscurity. It is certain that the princes of this race were established in the Valley of the Krishna and the Delta of the Godávari about the beginning of the Christian era, whence they extended their sway across the Table-land to the opposite coast, and as far north as Bombay and Nasik. But they are also stated to have flourished previously on the banks of the Ganges, and the evidence in support of this assertion requires to be carefully examined in virtue of its bearing on the character and description of their coins. The materials available for this purpose are:—

I. The Lists of Hindu kings found in the Puránas.

II. Statements in the works of Greek and Roman writers.

III. Contemporary historians.

IV. The Coins themselves.

I. The historical part of the *puránas* professes to give the succession of all the princes who have ruled over India from the beginning. The earlier portion, relating to the avowed past, closes with the Great War, and is purely mythical. The rest purports to be a prophetic narrative of what will take place subsequent to that event. This part begins by stating that seven dynasties will reign over the kingdom of Magadha, of which the last and the longest is that of the Andhras. The fourth is the well-known race of the Mauryas, the epoch of which has been fixed by the identification of its founder Chandragupta with the Sandracottus or Sandracoptas, who was the ally of Seleucus Nicator. An approximate date is thus obtained from which to calculate the era of those that follow.

The results so obtained, as will be seen hereafter, do not synchronize with calculations based on other more reliable data, and there is also reason for discrediting the list of princes as they stand in the several *puránas* on account of the irreconcilable differences they exhibit, as may be seen by the accompanying comparative tabular statement.

[1] Ind. Ant. vol. ix. p. 61.

# ANDHRA DYNASTY ACCORDING TO THE PURÁṆAS.

| | Matsya Puráṇa. | Years. | | Years. | Vishnu Puráṇa. | Váyu Puráṇa. | Years. | Brahmandu Puráṇa. | Years. | Col. Wilford's List as in "As. Res." Vol. IX. | Years. |
|---|---|---|---|---|---|---|---|---|---|---|---|
| 1 | Şişuka | 23 | Şişuka | 23 | Sipraka | Sindhuka | 23 | Ch'hismaka | 23 | Sri Karna Deva or Sipraka | 23 |
| 2 | Krishna | 18 | Krishna | 18 | Krishna | Krishna | 10 | Krishna | 18 | Krishna | 18 |
| 3 | Simalakarṇi | 18 | Şri Şátakarṇi | 18 | Srisátakarṇa / Santakarṇa | Sri Şátakarṇi | 56 | Şri Şátakarṇi | 18 | — | — |
| 4 | Púrnotsanga | 18 | Purnotsanga | 18 | Purnotsanga | — | — | Purnotsanga | 18 | Purporisanga Sri Karṇa | 56 |
| 5 | Srivaswáni / Skandhastambhi | 18 | Şátakarṇi | — | Şátakarṇi | — | — | Şátakarṇi | 56 | — | — |
| 6 | Şátakarṇi | 56 | Şrivaswani | — | — | — | — | — | — | — | — |
| 7 | Lambodara | 18 | Lambodara | 18 | Lambodara | Lambodara | — | Lambodara | 18 | Lambodara | 18 |
| 8 | Apílaka | 12 | Apílaka | 12 | Ivilaka / Divilaka | Apilaka | 12 | Apilaka | 12 | Apilaka | 12 |
| 9 | Sangha or Meghaswáti | 18 | — | — | Megʰaswáti | — | — | Sandasa | 18 | Sandasa Meghaswati | 18 |
| 10 | Şátakarṇi or Meghaswáti | 18 | — | — | — | — | — | Avi | 12 | Atamán or Putumán | 24 |
| 11 | Skandhaswáti | 7 | — | — | — | — | — | Skandaswati | 7 | Hala or Haleya | 25 |
| 12 | Mrigendra | 3 | — | — | — | — | — | Bhavaka | 5 | Pulaka | 5 |
| 13 | Kuntalaswáti | 8 | — | — | — | — | — | — | — | — | — |
| 14 | Swátikarṇá | 1 | — | — | — | — | — | Pravillasena | 12 | Pravillasena | 21 |
| 15 | Pulomávi | 36 | — | — | Patumat, or Paduravi, or Patumabi | Patamávi | 24 | Sundara Satakarṇi / Chakora Sátakarṇi | 1 / 6 | Sundara Sri Karni / Chakora Sri Karni | 1 |
| 16 | Gorakshâswasti | 25 | Arishṭakarṇi | 25 | Arishtakarman / Arishtarṇa | Nemikrishna | 25 | Mahendra Sátakarṇi | 3 | Mahendra Sri Karṇi. | |
| 17 | Hála | 5 | Hála | 5 | Hála | Hala | — | Kuntala Sátakarṇi | 8 | Kuntala Sri Karṇa. | |
| 18 | Maṇḍalaka | 5 | Maṇḍalaka | 5 | Pattalaka or Talaka | Puttalaka | — | — | — | — | — |
| 19 | Purindrasena / Sundaraswatikarná | 5 | Purindrasena | 5 | Pravilasena | Purishasena | 21 | Swatishena | 1 | — | — |
| 20 | Rajádaswáti / Chakoraswatikarná | ½ | Satakarṇin / Vikarni | 1 / ½ | Sundara Sátakarhin / Chakora Sátakarnin | Sátakarṇi | 3 | — | — | — | — |
| 21 | Sivaswáti | 28 | Sivaswati | 28 | Sivaswati[1] | Chakora, Ch. Sata K. / Sivaswati | ½ / 28 | — | — | Sivaswami | 28 |
| 22 | Gautamiputra | 21 | Gotamiputra | 21 | Gomatiputra / Gautimiputra | Gotamiputra | 21 | Yantramali | 34 | Gautamiputra | 21 |
| 23 | Pulomat or Padumi | 28 | Pulomat | 28 | Pulimat | — | — | Sátakarṇi | 29 | — | — |
| 24 | Sivasri | 7 | Sivasri Satakarṇi | 7 | Sivasri / Satakarṇin or karṇi | — | — | Avi | 4 | Madasri | — |
| 25 | Skhandhaswáti | 7 | Sivaskandha | 7 | Sivaskandha | — | — | Sivaskanda Satakarṇi | 8 | Sivaskanda Sri Karṇi. | |
| 26 | Yajnaşri | 9 | Yajnasri | 9 | Yajinaşri Satakarṇi | Yajnasri | 29 | Yajinaşri Sátakarṇi | 19 | Yajnasri Karni. | 29 |
| 27 | Vijaya | 6 | Vijaya | 6 | Vijaya | Vijaya | 6 | — | — | Vijaya. | |
| 28 | Vadasri / Chaṇḍasriśátakarṇi | 10 | Chaṇḍraşri | 10 | Chaṇḍraşri | Dandasri | 3 | Dandasri | 3 | Chaṇḍra Şri | 3 |
| 29 | Pulomat | 7 | Pulomat | 7 | Pulomarchis or Puloman (Wilf.) | Pulovápi / Puloman (W.) | 7 | Puloman | 7 | Puliman | 7 |
| | Total | 435 yrs. 6 m. | | | | | | | | | |

The double names are variant readings from other MSS.

[1] Wilford interposes another name, Vataka, between Chakora and Sivaswati.

From this Table it will be seen that none of the lists agree absolutely with each other, either as to the succession of the names, or in the specified duration of the reigns. Neither do any of them establish conclusively that the dynasty contained thirty princes, nor that it lasted for the fixed period of 456 or 460 years. One name may probably have dropped out of the Matsya list, which if recovered would easily make up the full *nominal* tale.

Although such discrepancies and omissions in these lists militate generally against their reception as reliable authorities,[1] it must be remembered that they relate to matters of remote antiquity, that they probably were compiled at a comparatively recent period from older documents, which have perished, and that they have suffered equally from errors of transcription, the omission, displacement, and misreading of names and figures, to which MSS. on perishable materials like bark and palm-leaves are especially liable. Nor should a fertile source of confusion be overlooked in the practice, so frequent among Indian princes, of taking different titular designations during the course of their careers and assuming corresponding vernacular titles, by one or other of which they were subsequently distinguished during and after their own lifetimes.[2]

Allowance being made for these drawbacks, the lists exhibit a certain congruity in themselves, the average duration of reigns is nowhere in excess of probability, whilst they receive occasional confirmation from independent sources.[3]

II. Of this nature is the support derived from the works of Classical writers. These rest mainly on the statements of Megasthenes, who, about the year 295 B.C., was sent by Seleucus Nicator as ambassador to Chandragupta, Emperor of the Prasii, at whose Court, in the City of Palibothra, he resided for a considerable time. Unfortunately his work, τὰ Ἰνδικά, is lost, and his narrations are only known from fragments embodied in the writings of others. These have been diligently collected, and critically arranged by Schwanbach. Among them is found the oft-quoted extract, from the elder Pliny (vi. 17, 19), in which he refers to the Andhræ. In describing the lower course of the Ganges, he adverts to the

[1] Of the eighteen *purânas*, four only contain dynastic lists, representing all the indigenous history of which the Hindus can boast. These are:—

The Matsya.
The Vishnu.
The Bhágavata, and
The Váyu.

In these the events of the past are told in the form of dialogue, up to the close of the Great War of the Mahâbhârata. The narrator then assumes a prophetic style, and foretells the succession of princes who are to rule in the future. The dates of these compositions are unknown, but the best critics consider that in their present form they cannot lay claim to high antiquity. Colonel Wilford pronounced them to be modern compilations from valuable materials no longer in existence (As. Res. v. 244. 8vo. ed.). In which he has been followed by M. Burnouf, the translator of the Bhágavata; by Prof. Wilson, who has made the Vishnu accessible in an English Version, and by Colebrooke. According to these authorities, the *purânas* date approximately, some from the ninth or tenth century, and others as late as the sixteenth or seventeenth. The Vishnu is assigned to the eleventh or twelfth century, and the author of the Bhágavata is said to have lived at the Court of the Ballala king of Devagiri, in the thirteenth century [*circa* A.D. 1210-20]. Burnouf, vol. i. pref. lvii-viii and xcviii; Wilson, pref. l-li, and *passim*, Colebrooke's Essays, vol. i. p. 93. On the other hand, Col. Vans Kennedy thinks they were written in their present form at a very early period, and hence from their great age are called *purânas*. Mr. E. B. Powell, Principal of the Madras University, from the internal evidence of astronomical facts, contained in the Vishnu Purâna, assigns to it an origin west of the Indus. Madras Journal Lit. and Science, vol. xvii. p. 1.

[2] As. Res. vol. ix. p. 133, 8vo; Cunningham, Bhilsa Tope, pp. 92-93, also 108-109.

[3] Prof. H. H. Wilson, Preface to Vishnu Purâna, vol. i. p. cviii.

Brachmanæ,[1] "a general name for many races, among whom are the Maccocalingæ. . The [people called] Calingæ are those nearest the sea," above or beyond whom certain others are particularized. Then he adds, "The end of that tract is the Ganges. . ." Returning to the river, he continues, "The last part of its course is through the country of the Gangarides Calingæ; the country is called Parthalis. Seventy thousand infantry, a [a numeral probably omitted] thousand cavalry, and seven hundred elephants fully equipped for war serve as guards to the king. . . There is an island in the Ganges of great extent, inhabited by a single tribe called Modogalinga." After whom he names some others, and continues, "Whose king possesses an army of 50,000 foot, 3000 horse, and 400 elephants . . . but a still more powerful people are the Andaræ, who have many villages, thirty fortified and walled towns, and their king has a standing army of 100,000 infantry, 2,000 (?) cavalry, and 1000 elephants."

From these statements it would appear that the valley of the Ganges, on both sides of the river, from the frontier of Magadha to the sea, was possessed, in the third century B.C., by the Kalingæ and the Andáræ, the former consisting (apparently) of three distinct communities, inhabiting different but contiguous localities. Ptolemy, writing in the middle of the second century A.D., does not specify the Andaræ, but in his lists of names in India beyond the Ganges,[2] he makes mention of Triglypton regia, and in the notes on the map of the tract in which it is placed, he gives the duration of the day and the distance from Alexandria of Trilingum,[3] both names being placed together on the map, as if they were one and the same people, on the east side of the river, and near the shore of the Gangetic Gulf, from which they are separated by the Cirradæ (Kirátas). This is nearly the position assigned to the Andre-Indi, in the Peutingerian Tables,[4] except that the latter are closer to the left bank of the Ganges, and between it and the Catabeda, or Calincius River, which Ptolemy makes to intervene between the Trilinga regia and the Ganges. It may therefore be inferred that the ancient geographers considered the Andhras and Kalingas to be cognate races, and assigned to them a northern habitat, two centuries before the Christian era. This

[1] . . Multorumque gentium cognomen Brachmanæ, quorum Maccocalingæ . . Gentes Calingæ proximi mari, etc. . . . finisque ejus tractus est Ganges. . . novissimâ gente Gangaridum Calingarum; regio Parthalis vocatur. Regi LXX. Mill. peditum, equites mille, elephanti D.CC. in procinctu bellorum excubant. . . . Insula in Gange est magnæ amplitudinis gentem continens unam, Modogalingam nomine. Ultra siti sunt, etc. Rex horum peditum L. mill. equitum III. mill. elephantos CCCC. in armis habet. Validior deinde gens Andaræ, plurimis vicis, XXX. oppidis, quæ muris turribusque muniuntur, regi præbet peditum C. mill. equitum II. mill. elephantos mill. etc.—Schwanbach, p. 161-163; Plin. Lib. vi. cap. xvii. xix. Elz. 1635.

Megasthenes is really the only reliable authority on ancient India who speaks from personal knowledge. At the Court of Sybartes, Satrap of Arachosia, he had already become familiar with Eastern affairs, and he traversed the whole country in his journey from Philadelphia to Magadha, where he had ample time and opportunity for inquiry and observation. His veracity, it is true, has been impeached by Strabo, Eratosthenes, Diodorus, and others, not one of whom had seen India; but Arrian is of a contrary opinion, and the indefatigable compiler Pliny, in the above passage, quotes his statements without question. In defending his accuracy Schwanbach rightly distinguishes between his statements as an eye-witness and those derived from native informants. Some of those for which he has been most vituperated are now proved to be well founded. The wild men who could not be brought to Sandracottus, because they would have died of starvation, whose heels were upturned, and toes bent back, are exactly the wolf-children of Oudh described by Col. Sleeman; and the monstrous snakes that swallowed deer were pythons, which are well known to do so (see Report Brit. Assoc. 1870, part ii. p. 115; see, too, H. H. Wilson, Notes on Ctesias, p. 29, and note to Lieut. Wilcox's Journey, As. Res. vol. xxii. p. 456).

[2] Lib. vii. cap. ii. p. 178.

[3] Lib. viii. tab. xi. p. 211. Mercator in his notes on the map writes the name "Triglyphon," p. 28.

[4] Segmentum, viii.

may explain the origin of a term which occurs in several inscriptions of the seventh and eighth centuries, in which the Rájas of Chedi are styled "Lords of Tri-Kalinga"[1]—a name which Professor Kern[2] has found in the *puránas*, and which General Cunningham[3] connects with the names in Pliny, pointing out that the Mahábhárata refers to the Andhras three times, on each occasion in conjunction with different peoples. The Sanscrit term Tri-Kalinga may therefore be taken as representing the three separate communities into which the Kalingas were divided. Moreover, the Dravidian equivalent of the three Kalingas is found in one of the names employed by Pliny, viz. that of the local Modu-Galingas.[4]

The use of the name of Tri-Kalinga did not cease with the departure of the Andhra-Kalingas from Bengal. Wilford[5] in his essay on the Kings of Magadha identified the Sri Karṇa Deva of a copper grant found at Benares in 1801, where he is styled "Lord of Tri-Kalinga" with the old Andhra dynasty. That document, as well as several others in which the same title occurs, has now rightly been assigned to the Hai-haya or Kalachuri dynasty of Chedi in Malwa. In the last of these,[6] the name of Karṇa occurs three times. The history of the Chedi dynasty has been investigated by Prof. FitzEdward Hall, and also by General Cunningham in volume ix. of his Arch. Reports, pp. 99, *et seq*. The symbol on the seals[7] attached to their grants is the *quasi*-Buddhist emblem of elephants, pouring libations over a seated goddess, hence called Gaji Lakshmi, often found carved on the lintels of ancient temples. Coins with this device have been found in the valley of the Krishna.[8] It also occurs on coins of the Bactrian King Azes, of much earlier date.

III. Of the third class of evidence, that of Contemporary Inscriptions, the earliest example hitherto met with is in the celebrated edicts of Asoka. The sixteenth tablet of the version at Sháhbázgarhi, in the Yusufzai country, contains a list of contemporary potentates, including the names of Alexander, Antiochus, etc., followed by an enumeration of the best known Indian kingdoms, the last two being the *Andhras* and *Pulindas*, proving that the former of these nationalities was recognized as a substantive power by the greatest monarch of his time, who reigned B.C. 259 to B.C. 235.[9]

[1] J.A.S.B. vol viii. p. 455.

[2] Wilson's Vishnu Purana, vol. ii. pp. 132, 156, 166, 187. In all these the Kalingas are classed with Northern tribes and places; as Magadha, the Málas of Málbhûm or Midnapur, the Angas or Vangas of Eastern Bengal and Bhagalpur, to the Kirátas, who are placed next the Andari and Trilingas in the Ptolemaic and Peutingeri Maps. Much reliance, however, cannot be placed on the strings of names.

[3] Anct. Geogr. p. 519.

[4] *Mudu* = "three" in Telugu and Galinga—initial *k* becoming *g* in the middle of a Dravidian word (Caldwell, p. 32). Tri Kalinga by an obvious ellipse may easily pass colloquially into Trilinga, a *form from* which native grammarians have deduced the modern name of the Telugu dialect.

The late F. W. Ellis in his essay on the Telugu language quotes the Andhra Dipika, a standard lexicon, which, in giving examples of the rhetorical figure *tadbhava*, cites among others the following:—

| SANSCRIT. | PAISACHI. | DRAVIDIAN BY TADBHAVAS. |
|---|---|---|
| Trilingah — | Telingo — | Telungu.<br>Telugu.<br>Tenugu. |

See also Burnell, South Ind. Paleo., 1st ed. p. 20, *note* 1.

[5] As. Res. vol. ix. p. 104, 8vo. ed.

[6] J.A.S.B. vol. xxx. pp. 317-336; see also vol. viii. pp. 354, 481, and Oriental Amer. Journ. vol. vi. p. 516.

[7] Wilford, As. Res. vol. ix. pp. 104-108; Beng. Journ. vol. viii. p. 354, Plate.

[8] Num. Gl. 23; Madras Journ. vol. iii. N.S. pl. x. fig. 68.

[9] Cunningham, Arch. Rep. v. 20.

On the south gate of the Sánchi Tope, a memorial of an offering made by Ananda, son of Váśishthá,[1] in the reign of Ṣátakarṇi, has been found by Gen. Cunningham, who attributes it to a younger son of Gautamíputra.

But the most interesting of the Northern inscriptions is engraved on a rock at Girnár in Káthiáwaḍ, to commemorate the repair of a tank, the dam of which had been breached by a flood. Originally constructed in the time of the Mauryan kings, it was now restored by order of Rudra Dáman, the Kshatrapa (or Satrap) ruler of Gujarát, in the year 72 (?), who is stated, *inter alia*, to have "obtained glory, because he did not destroy (the) Śátakarṇi, Lord of the South (Dakshinápati), on account of their relationship, although he had twice conquered him." The era of the so-called Sáh dynasty, to which Rudra Daman belonged, being still undetermined, the Andhra king referred to cannot be identified.[2]

As was to be expected, inscriptions become more frequent in the Dakhan. The rocky hills around Nasik, Junár, Kárli, etc., in the Púna district, contain numerous Buddhist cave-temples, on the walls of which the names of their founders and the particulars of their gifts are engraved, but only a few contain matter of historical interest. Those at Nasik have been carefully copied and translated, and one of the longest among them records the grant of a village by "the Great Queen Gautamí," in "the nineteenth year of her grandson, Sri Puḍumayi Váśisṭhiputra." She is described as "a daughter of royal sages, the mother of (the) Śátakarṇi Gautamíputra (who was) the destroyer of the Sákas, Yávanas, and Palhavas, . . . who exterminated the race [*vansu*] of Khagárátha, and established the glory of the Śátaváhana family [*kula*], etc. She, the Great Queen, the mother of the Great King, and grandmother of the Great King, in the nineteenth year of Śrí Puḍumayi, bestows," etc. And this is followed by a later decree of Śrí Puḍumayi himself, here styled "the Lord of Navanara," in which he modifies the preceding acts of "the Lord of Dhanakaṭa" (his father), at whose instance the village had originally been given.

In the same cave a further edict records the gift of two pieces of land, the one conferred by (the) Śátakarni Gautamíputra, the Lord of Dhanakakata himself, the other by his Queen Vasisṭhí.[3]

The name of Puḍumayi is found in two other caves (Nos. 3 and 27), spelt Puḷumai in No. 3, but in both he has the title of Vasishthíputra. Cave 24 furnishes another royal name, (the) Śátakarṇi, Śrí Yajna Gautamiputra.[4] A few more names of lesser note occur, such as that of Krishna, Raja of (the) Satavấhana family (*kula*), residing at Nasik, in No. 6, but

[1] Bhilsa Tope, pp. 264, 272, pl. xix. No. 190.

[2] Lassen places the event in 59 B.C. (Muir, Sansk. Texts, vol. ii. p. 142, 1st ed.); Prinsep, though with hesitation, in 189 B.C.; Dr. Bhau Dáji inclines to 200 A.D. (Journ. Bom. Branch Roy. As. Soc. vol. vii. p. 117-120). Mr. Newton in his Coins of the Sáh Kings places Rudra Dáman about A.D. 40-45 (*Ib.* vol. ix. p. 17), which Mr. Thomas is inclined to regard with favour (J.R.A.S. vol. xiii. N.S. p. 524). This inscription has attracted much attention, having been edited and translated by Prinsep (J.A.S.B. vol. viii. pp. 334-348); by Prof. H. H. Wilson (Prinsep's Essays, ed. Thomas, vol. ii. pp. 57-67); by Prof. Eggeling (Burgess, Second Rep. p. 129), and by Bhagwan Lál Indraji and Dr. Bühler (Ind. Ant. vol. vii. pp. 257-263).

[3] Trans. Inter. Orient. Cong. 1874, pp. 306-325; Journ. Bom. Branch Roy. As. Soc. vol. vii. pp. 37-41.

[4] Rája Gautamíputra Swami, S'rí Yajna S'átakarṇi or Gautamíputra II. (Trans. Or. Cong. 1874, p. 340).

without royal titles, and therefore probably a relation only of the royal house. He has been considered by many as the second in the *purána* list, which is obviously incorrect, as the Andhras had not then settled in the Dakhan. If he was a Satavāhana, he would, as will afterwards appear, be one of the later, or Andhrabhṛitya section. The name of Maha Hákusri, found in what is called the Chaitya Cave (No. 10), may refer to the similar name in the remarkable sculptures at Nánaghát, now to be described.[1] At the ancient site of Junar (not without some grounds supposed to be the Tagara of Ptolemy and the Periplus), the inscriptions in the numerous caves are of little historical importance. But a cave at the head of the Nánaghát pass, on the road leading from Junár to the Konkan, calls for more special notice. It appears to have been a work of charity, excavated as a resting-place for pilgrims ascending the pass, the vestibule being furnished with seats for the use of weary travellers. Within this, on the front wall, are sculptured six life-size figures, now much defaced, each with a name carved above it. Within is an inscription[2] of some length, but in bad preservation. It imports that certain sacred offerings were given by Vedisiri or Vedasri, who is supposed to have constructed the cave; but his connection with the figures sculptured on the wall is not apparent, there being no complete translation of the text.[3] They seem, however, to represent the members of a single family. The title of the first is, "The auspicious Rája Satavanana, the prosperous."[4] Next are two figures, a woman and a man, superscribed "Devi Náyanikaya, the Queen," and "Śrí Śátakarṇi." Then, following them, "The Chief (*virah*) of the Mahárāshtras," or it may be "of the great Warriors"; and then two young men, styled respectively, "*kumára* (or prince) Hákusri," and "*kumára* Śátaváhana."

In 1839 Dr. Bird opened the largest tope at Káṇheri (Kennery), in the island of Salsette, and found two inscribed copper plates, which, unfortunately, have disappeared without having been critically translated. Attempts made by Dr. Stevenson and Pandit Bhagwán Lal to restore the imperfect transcripts left by Dr. Bird have yielded results irreconcilable with each other—to the strange extent, that names read by the former cannot be traced at all by the latter. The same date, however, has been read by both, viz. the year 245, but there is nothing to show what era is referred to.[5] Prinsep thought it might be equivalent to A.D. 189; but beyond proving the dominion of the Andhras in that region, this memorial, as we now possess it, must depend for its value upon new discoveries.

A few other Andhra names have been preserved, which, though not perhaps those of reigning princes, may be worth noting for comparison with the legends of any coins that may be discovered hereafter. Such are Dása Karni, Chivari Karna, Naga Kanda, the nephew

[1] Trans. Or. Cong. pp. 343-344; Journ. Bom. Branch. Roy. As. Soc. vol. vii. p. 43.

[2] J.R.A.S. vol. iv. p. 287; Journ. Bom. Branch, Roy. As. Soc. vol. xii. p. 404, and vol. xiii. pp. 310-312.

[3] Probably owing to the dilapidation of the tablet. Mr. Burgess submitted a large fac-simile of it in its present condition.

[4] Rája Srimukha S'átaváhana Srimán.

[5] Journ. Bom. Branch Roy. As. Soc. vol. v. p. 32; Arch. Surv. West. India No. 10 (1881), p. 58.

of Śrí Yadnya, Śáta Karṇi, (son?) of Gotamíputra, at Kanheri, Raja Vírasena, the Abhíra of Nasik,[1] etc.

The inscriptions in several cases also record benefactions made by a member of the family of the Kshatrapa ruler of Gujarát, which bear on the history of the Andhras by the support they give to the assertions in the Girnár record of Rudra Dáman. They are found in five of the Nasik Caves, and in the great Chaitya Temple at Kárli. The donations are all made in the name of Ushavadáta, the son of Díníka, describing himself as son-in-law of Kshatrapa Nahapáṇa, the Kshaharata, Rája or Ruler of Gujarát. They consist of villages, cows, money, which he confers with a lavish hand on priests and Brahmans; in one instance the gift being that of his wife Dakhamitra, the daughter of Nahapáṇa. From this it would appear that Ushavadáta was Governor of the subjugated province of Nasik, under his father-in-law. It may further be inferred from the munificence of his gifts, from the length of time necessary for the construction of the cave-temples bearing his name, and from a military expedition he was ordered to conduct to Máláya, that his charge must have been extensive, and that his rule lasted for a considerable time. The tablets at Kárli and Junár merely give Ushavadáta's name and family.

IV. The last remaining source of evidence is that derived from coins. These are found in considerable numbers in the deltas of the Krishṇa and Godávari. The most common are of lead, rudely executed, more or less coated with white oxide; others are of copper mostly alloyed. They bear a general resemblance to the type described by Prinsep and Wilson, under the name of Indo-Scythian or Barbaric Coins.[2] Few have legible epigraphs, but some of them, which seem to be more recent, are better executed, and exhibit legends with the names of the later princes in the list.

Another type, differing remarkably from those above noticed, occurs in the Western or Maharashtra districts. They are of a coarse alloy, and like the last mentioned pertain exclusively to the latest names in the series.

The information gleaned from the foregoing sources of evidence may be summed up in few words. In the third century B.C. a Dravidian colony, probably the latest migration of the race, is found occupying the Lower Valley of the Ganges, and consisting of several communities, of whom the Andhras[3] and the Kalingas were the most conspicuous.[4] The earliest reliable

[1] Journ. Bom. Branch Roy. As. Soc. vol. v. pp. 22, 24, 26, 28; Trans. Or. Cong. 1874, pp. 326-342.

[2] J.A.S.B. vol. iii. pl. xviii. p. 227, figs. 2, 3, 5, 22, and pl. xxv. p. 436, figs. 1, 2, 3; vol. iv. p. 626, pl. xxxiv. p. 684, pl. xlix. figs. 23-8; Ariana Ant. p. 414, pl. xv. figs. 27-33.

[3] The Peutingerian Tables place the ANDRE INDI to the North of the Ganges, plate xiii.

[4] The normal constitution of these Turanian colonies appears to have been somewhat of a Republican character. An aggregation of clans, independent as regards their internal economy, but united by a common interest. Colonel Dalton found something of the same kind among the Kóls, and a more perfect example is afforded by the Kurumbar communities of Tondamandalam in the Carnatic, described in Ellis's Treatise on Mirási Rights. Dalton, J.A.S.B. vol. xxxv. pt. ii. Ellis, Replies to Queries on Mirási Rights.

mention of them by Greek writers represent the Andhras as living under a monarchical form of government, and as being the most powerful section. Native accounts assign to them a succession of thirty princes, who ruled for a period of 456 years, first in the north and then in the Dakhan, but the details given on this authority are inexact. Of their alleged supremacy in Magadha during this long period there is no proof beyond the assertion of the Paurանik writers; while more trustworthy evidence shows that they could not have occupied so important a position during the period stated. The probability is that they took advantage of the anarchy consequent on the disruption of the Mauryan empire after the death of Asoka, and obtained a temporary footing in the eastern portion of it, from which they were dislodged by the arrival of later intruders, and driven to seek for a resting-place in the direction previously taken by colonists of their own race, of whose prosperity in their southern settlements they could not be ignorant. As seems to have been the general practice in these early times, they moved about bodily with their slaves,[1] their flocks and herds. Following the line of coast, the Kalingas settled in the country north of the Godávari, where their name is perpetuated in that of the province, as well as in that of the seaport of Kalingapatam; while the Andhras, after resting awhile on the shores of the Chilka Lake, in some old maps called Parikad Andhari (and where a pergunna, entitled Andhari, still retains their name),[2] and proceeded further south, establishing themselves on the Krishṇa, and made the city of Dhanakakaṭa their capital. This is supposed to be the modern Dharaṇakota, the ruined site of which, marked by the extensive mounds characteristic of old fortifications, is seen on the Krishṇa a little above Amráwati. Thence they spread over the greater part of Kuntala, till their territories extended from sea to sea, and from the Godávari on the north to the frontiers of Cholamandalam on the south, and Banawási on the south-west.

A pressure powerful enough to dislodge a whole people and drive them from the region in which they had taken root must have been no common one. Such a force is found in the restless spirit which animated the Scythian hordes about two centuries before the Christian era, and made itself felt through Central Asia.[3] After they had overrun part of Persia and Affghánistán they entered India, took possession of the Gangetic Valley, and even penetrated beyond the Vindhyan Mountains.[4]

There is thus no ground for the statement of the *puránas*, which assigns the Empire of Magadha to the Andhras, in succession to two shorter dynasties following the Mauryas.

[1] The Telugu serfs or Agrestial slaves are called Múlas, a term of doubtful origin (Caldwell, p. 549), but it may with some probability be deduced from the aboriginal people of Mál-bhúm, now part of Midnapur, a Gangetic province, forming part of the earlier location of the Andhras. Vish. Pur. vol. ii. pp. 156, 166.

[2] Hunter's Orissa, *Official* Map, A.D. 1871. So also Rájendra's Map, vol. i. p. 201.

[3] Cunningham Arch. Rep. vol. i. p. 139; vol. iii. p. 29 *et seq.* and p. 42; vol. v. pp. 20-1, 62; Bhilsa Tope, p. 125; Ariana Ant. pp. 134, 303; J.R.A.S. N.S. vol. v. p. 182; vol. vii. p. 380; Journ. Bom. Branch Roy. As. Soc. vol. ix. p. 143.

[4] Inscriptions dated in the reign of Kanishka, the most powerful Indo-Sycthian prince, have been copied at Mathura by Gen. Cunningham (*supra*), of the last century B.C.; and coins, evidently of the Indo-Sythic type, have been found in considerable numbers at Jougaḍh, in the Puba Kondah Taluk of Ganjam. Mad. Journ. of Lit. and Science, vol. iv. N.S. pp. 76-8. To the same cause may not improbably be assigned the introduction of several of the predatory tribes in India, as the Gújars, Ramúsis, Bedars, Marawars, noted for their warlike qualities and fondness for the chase.

The recently discovered inscriptions of Kanishka at Mathura prove that the Scythian power had been firmly established in Magadha during the last century B.C.; and as Kanishka was followed by more than one successor of his own race, their rule must have been prolonged into the first century of our era.[1] This view is also incompatible with the chronology of the *purânas* by which the epoch of the Andhras has been commonly computed.[2] According to that mode of reckoning the sum of the reigns assigned to the princes of the three preceding families,[3] or 294 years, is deducted from the known date of Chandragupta, B.C. 317, and the commencement of the Andhra dynasty is thus placed in B.C. 23, and its termination, after a duration of 456 years, in A.D. 437—a conclusion irreconcilable with their recognition as an existing power by Asoka's edict, and the absence of any mention of them in the annals of the Dakhan, which have now been ascertained with tolerable accuracy from the latter part of the fifth century; on the other hand, they can only be relegated to an earlier date, antecedent to the time of Kanishka, by rejecting the *paurânic* list altogether.

A solution of the difficulty, however, is obtained by supposing the earlier Andhras to have been contemporaries of the Mauryas and their successors of the other earlier dynasties before they obtained a footing in Magadha.[4]

On this theory it is possible to derive a probable date for their migration to the Dakhan, which will harmonize better with other authorities.

Assuming, as before argued, that the Andhras were contemporary with the Mauryan dynasty, and accepting the statements of the *purânas* that they flourished under a succession of thirty princes for four centuries and a half,[5] we obtain an average[6] of fifteen years for each reign. This affords a clue by which to estimate, approximately, the time of the Andhra migration to the Dakhan.

Now, looking down the list of names in the Tabular statement, at page 8 (*ante*), the eye is arrested, about the middle of the column, by that of Kuntala Swâti Karṇa, as being the only instance in this series, of a personal formed on a territorial designation—a circumstance significant of some remarkable incident in the career of the individual, which may not unfairly be taken to have reference to the establishment of his people in the province of Kuntala. Now, as he stands thirteenth in the most complete list, his era, at the average of fifteen years to a reign, would be 122 B.C., which gives 261 for the duration of their empire in the Dakhan. In another list (that of the Brahmandu) he appears in the sixteenth place, which would bring him to 77 B.C., and the Dakhan rule to 216 years A.D.

Vague as these calculations are, they afford grounds for assuming, in the absence of more reliable data, that the Andhra migration took place about a century before the Christian era, and that their power survived for two centuries after it.

[1] Cunningham, Arch. Rep. vol. ii. pp. 42-46.

[2] Wilson, Vish. Pur. vol. iv. p. 203, where the end of the dynasty is placed A.D. 419.

[3] The Indo-Scythian dynasty of Kanishka. See *note* 4, p. 15.

[4] Prinsep makes a similar suggestion with reference to the Sata or Satrapa princes of Gujarât. J.A.S.B. vol. vii. p. 347.

[5] Wilson, Vishnu Pur. vol. iv. p. 199.

[6] The exact average is 15·2 years per reign.

On the events that happened during this later period in the Dakhan, history is silent. Some light is obtained from the inscriptions before described, which show that the fortunes of the dynasty culminated in the reigns of the twenty-first and twenty-second kings. Gautamíputra, the latter of these, was the most conspicuous of the later Andhras. He offers the first example of a name taken by the reigning prince from that of his mother; a practice followed by many of his successors.

This has been considered by some to be a remnant of the Turanian law of inheritance, under which property was transmitted through females, as is the case to this day on the Malabar coast.

General Cunningham suggested that it arose from the Queen's desire to do honour to her *puróhit*, by adopting the name of his *gúru*. This he afterwards rejected for an explanation proposed by Dr. Bühler, who attributed it to the practice of polygamy in Rájpút families, where it is followed to distinguish the offspring of different mothers.[1]

But none of these suggestions are satisfactory, no such customs having prevailed among the Andhras or other people of Dravidian race. With more probability it might be connected with something memorable in the character or history of the Queen-Mother herself, a view which derives support from an examination of the place in the list to which her name must be relegated. This, it will be seen, presents a somewhat unusual appearance, and, taken with the first occurrence of these metronyms, lends colour to a suspicion that there may have been some interruption to the succession, not unlike a break in the old line.

For the reigns immediately preceding the 22nd (*viz.* from the 18th to the 21st) are represented as having been unusually short, the 20th and 21st lasting only from one to five years and six months respectively, which, although not incompatible with the known uncertainty of human life, is also indicative of unsettled times, in connection either with hostile invasion or intestine disorders. The language of the inscriptions contains allusions which may apply to both these conditions. Rudra Dáman, in the Girnár tablet, claims to have twice conquered the Andhra king, and to have been withheld from destroying him by motives of clemency and family ties. Again, the long inscription in the Nasik cave (No. 26) points to a turn in the tide of fortune, and credits Gautamíputra, not only with the expulsion of the invaders, but with dispensing the public revenues, "levied only according to law," as if such had not been the case previously. This may have been caused by the disorders to which all states, especially those in the East, are liable under the scourge of foreign invasion, and still more if the indigenous population should take part with the invaders. The normal inhabitants of Kuntala appear to have been the people called Pallavas—a bold, hardy, warlike race, who never failed to assert their independence when a favourable occasion offered, as will appear more fully hereafter. In the inscription they are mentioned in the same breath with the Sákas and Yávanas, by whom we understand the Scythian and Indo-Bactrian invaders from

[1] Stupa of Bharahát, p. 129.

Gujarát. Sákas or Sacæ is a common equivalent for Scythians, and in the Nasik caves the term occurs more than once.[1] And Yávanas is now a general term for foreigners, but at first was more particularly applied to Greeks; and here with especial force to the conquerors of Gujarát, whose silver coins of the so-called Sáh type are evidently taken from Greek models. The expression, "he left no trace of the race of Khagáratha," has probably further reference to the expulsion of the Sákas. The tribal name of the Satrapa ruler is not mentioned, but in No. 16 (p. 335) Nahapáṇa is styled the Satrap King Kshaharáta Nahapáṇa, a title approaching closely to Khagáratha Nahapáṇa.

In support of the other hypothesis that the old Andhra dynasty underwent a change, there is the assertion that Gautamíputra "established the glory of the Śátaváhana race or *Kula*," a name not before known in connection with the old royal family.

On the above grounds, slight and isolated as they are, we may be permitted to found a hypothesis, which may give them some coherence.

The power which gained possession of Gujarát in the century before the Christian era, pushing its advances onwards, effected a lodgment in the Dakhan, about the same time that the Andhras were advancing along the valleys of the Godávari and Krishṇa.

Nahapáṇa obtained his position in Gujarát by conquest, either on his own account, or as the delegate of some Scythian or Parthian lord paramount.

The Satrapa rule was long firmly established in Gujarát, and their hold on the Dakhan provinces was no transient one.

Ushavadátha, the governor, on the part of the first Satrapa, constructed some of the Nasik Cave-temples, and conducted a military expedition into Máláya (Malwa) or Malabar? (No. 19, p. 328). Rudra Dáman was 5th or 6th in succession to him.[2]

I assume that the relations between the two powers[3] were sometimes friendly, sometimes the reverse, and that at length they ended in a serious war, in which the Andhras were defeated, and a period of anarchy ensued. A bold adventurer, whether a relative, or a subject of the reigning family, took advantage of the confusion to seize on the throne. Having driven out the foreigners, and restored order in the provinces, he established the Sátaváhana branch of the Andhra dynasty firmly on the throne, of which it continued in possession for about 115 years, until its extinction in the person of Pulomat, the thirtieth Prince of the line. This supposed revolution may explain the origin of the term Andhra*bhritya*, or servants of the Andhras, in contradistinction to the Andhra*játiya*, or the true Andhras. That the mother of Gautamíputra took a prominent part in the transaction seems probable. She describes herself as "Queen Gautamí, the presiding genius

[1] Nos. 14 and 2, though with some doubt in the former as connected with the names of Ushavadátha, owing to the fracture of the stone.

[2] Bombay Journal, vol. vii. p. 20; Burgess, Arch. Report, pp. 130-3. There is a break in the line of Satraps between the Khagáratha, Nahapáṇa, and Chastana whose name stands first in the inscription of Jusdun (Bombay Journ. vol. viii. p. 234) without any family designation, and the relation in which they stood to each other, whether of family or office, is not apparent.

[3] J.R.A.S. vol. xii. pp. 23-50.

of powers . . . . the daughter of royal sages, the mother of the Śátakarṇi," etc. And when in addition her name is found so remarkably associated with that of her son, and adopted by others as a household word, while no notice whatever is taken of her husband, we may conclude that there was some good cause for the distinction.

The foregoing supposes that Gautamíputra's exploits were confined to the expulsion of the Sákas from his own territory. Gen. Cunningham[1] takes a much larger view of his importance, and by a calculation, founded on Asoka's celebrated edict, identified him with the famous Sáliváhan or Sátaváhan, the founder of the great Sáka era, from which all the chronology of Southern India is calculated. If his data are well founded, there is much to be said in favour of this view.

The practice first seen in the case of Gautamíputra is repeated in the names of several of his successors, as we learn from the cave inscriptions and from coins, by the help of which we are enabled to construct the genealogical list given on the next page:—

[1] Cunningham, Arch. Rep. vol. v. p. 20. The Sanscrit word Saka has two meanings (Wilson's Sans. Dict.): 1st, with the first syllable short = "a prince, an era," "a country," or in the plural, "the people of a country, Scythians, Sacæ"; 2nd, Sáka (long), "A power, an era." These terms, with the name of the Prince Vikramaditya, which is nothing more than a title meaning "the Sun of heroism," and assumed by numerous princes, go far to account for the confusion that exists upon the subject.

Many celebrated native princes adopted eras of their own, which after flourishing for a time passed away. Such are those of the Guptas, the Balabhis, Sri Harsha, etc. A popular mnemonic verse enumerates six (J.B.A.S. vol. x. p. 128), the three last being future. Of the others, the Yudhishthira Saka is obsolete; that of Vikramaditya, current in Northern India, dates from a king of Ujjayani, said to have expelled the Indo-Scythians in 57 B.C., whence he has the epithet of *Sakári* (= foe of the Scythians), and afterwards to have been slain in battle with Sáliváhana in 78 A.D.—statements carrying contradiction on their face, for the interval of 135 years between these events is fatal to the idea of a personal collision. Sáliváhana is the presumed founder of the third Sáka era, par excellence, in use south of the Narbadá. It commences with the installation or *abhisheka* of its founder, after the supposed defeat of the Ujjayani prince above mentioned. Thus both traditions appear to be founded on successes gained over the northern invaders of Hindustan.

The obscurity in which the subject is shrouded has frequently exercised the ingenuity of the learned. Dr. Bhau Daji, in 1862, at first came to the same conclusion as Gen. Cunningham and fixed on Gautamíputra (J.R.A.S. Bombay, vol. viii. p. 118), but finally agreed with Mr. Justice Newton (*ib.* vol. viii. p. 238) in favour of Nahapána, deeming it improbable that an era so widely adopted could be derived from the exploits of a humble prince, whose capital was Paithán on the Godávari (*ib.* p. 233). Mr. Fergusson, on the other hand, considers Gautamíputra to have been the most important sovereign of his time, but the chronological theory adopted by him placed his reign in the fourth century (J.R.A.S. N.S. vol. iv. p. 127). Afterwards in an unpublished memoir (1875) he came to the conclusion that the Sáka was founded on the *abhisheka* or inauguration of Kanishka, the great Indo-Scythian king, and had nothing whatever to do with a victory over Scythians. At the same time he relegates the origin of the Vikramaditya era to a much later period. The latest opinion, that of Dr. Oldenberg, coincides with Mr. Fergusson's (Ind. Ant. vol. x. p. 215). I am inclined to agree with Mr. Fergusson that the Saka era had nothing to do with the Scythians, unless the Gujarát kshatrapas are included under that designation; and I share in the doubts expressed of an actual Sáka-conquering prince of Ujjayani at that early period.

One of the Sákas set aside was that of the Sri Harsha, king of Ujjayani, a prince of great fame; but it is not probable that he would have abolished so remarkable an established era of his supposed predecessor. It is further observable that no date founded on the Samvat Sáka has hitherto been found earlier than the ninth century, or A.D. 811 (J.R.A.S. Bombay, vol. ii. p. 371). Dravidian tradition is consistent in assigning the origin of the Sáka to Sátaváhana, ruler of Pratishthana, which Col. Wilford (As. Res. vols. ix. and x.), on the authority of Col. Mackenzie, accepts. Others represent him as a Sámana, which may be either a Jaina or a Buddhist, and in describing his advance to attack the enemies of his country (Taylor's Cat. Rais. vol. iii. p. 42), as made from the Godávari northwards. Jaina writers generally describe him as an author and a man of learning. The coincidence of his name, the Sátaváhana, with that of his race in the Nasik temple inscriptions, go far to prove that the Southern traditions are deserving of credit, and therefore affording support to Gen. Cunningham.

| No. | Name | Queen-Mother |
|---|---|---|
| 22 | Sivaswáti ... ... ... ... <br> Sátakarṇi ... ... ... ... | Gautamí (?) the Great Queen. |
| 23 | Gautamíputra ... ... ... ... | Vasishṭhí. |
| 24 | Puḍumayi, Pulomat <br> Váśishṭhíputra I. | |
| 25 | Sivasri Sátakarṇi ... ... ... | Maḍhari. |
| 26 | Sirisena, or Siva Skanda ... ... <br> Sátakarṇi, Maḍhariputra ... ... <br> Sivala Kuru ... ... ... ... | Gautami II. |
| 27 | Yajnasri Gautamíputra II. ... ... <br> Vidiváya Kuru ... ... ... | Vasishṭhí II. |
| 28 | Vijaya... ... ... ... ... | Váśishthí III. (?) |
| 29 | Vadasri Chandasri. <br> Sátakarṇi. <br> Váśishṭhíputra II. | |
| 30 | Pulomat. | |

Of these names Nos. 22, 23, 24, are obtained from Nasik Cave (26) inscription supported by coins. The 25th and 26th rest on a coin recently discovered at Kolhápur, and an inscription at Kánheri.[1] That of Yajnasri, the 27th, is also found on coins with the addition of the metronym Gautamíputra, confirmed by the Nasik Cave (24), in which the reading is Gautamíputra, so there must needs have been a second princess of that name. Gen. Cunningham has a coin, of which he kindly sent me a sketch, on which is the figure of an elephant, with the epigraph

*Rájna Váśiṭhiputasa Siri Chanda satása,*

which introduces a third Queen Mother, named Váśishṭhí.[2]

From this it would appear these female names are more of the nature of titles, which took the place of the individual proper name of the reigning Queen.

[1] Rep. Or. Inter. Cong., J.R.A.S. Bombay, vol. xii. p. 409.

[2] Chandra Sri, which is written Vada Sri in the Radcliffe MS. of the Matsya Pur., has been supposed to be the author of the inscription at Nánaghát, which, as imperfectly read, purports to record the gift of 7000 cows by Saráhariya (or. Subhamiya), probably the Queen-mother. After the invocation at the commencement, occur the words—

*Kumdra varaṇa Vada (or Vendi) siriṇa,*

which would imply that at the time Vadásri was only a prince and had not succeeded to the throne. In the last line the words—

*Mahá rathine Andhija Kula sadhanasa*

have been read, which should remove any doubt that might exist whether the Nánaghát sculptures represent individuals of the Andhras.

The last nine reigns from the great Queen inclusive embrace a period, according to the years assigned to each, of 116 years, to which, on Gen. Cunningham's assumption, if we add 78 A.D., the conclusion of the line is carried to 194 A.D., or deducting Gautami's own reign of twenty-eight years to 166 A.D. Calculating these nine reigns at the average of 15·2, the date of their termination would be about 213 A.D.

How that termination was brought about is unknown. The two or three centuries before and after the Christian era seem to have been a period of turbulence and change, presenting opportunities to the aboriginal races for throwing off a foreign yoke. The two most ancient indigenous peoples of whom reliable information survives, are the Rattas in the West and the Pallavas in the East of Kuntala.

It was from them that the Chalukyas wrested that province in the fifth and sixth centuries. The Raṭṭas threw off their yoke in the eighth century, and established an independent dynasty at Mányakhéṭa, now Malkhair, which subsisted for a considerable time. At a subsequent period they rose against the Mahommedans, and still maintain their sturdy independence, not only in their own Mahárâshtra, but in other parts of India. The Pallavas, driven from Bádámi, established themselves successively for a time at Vengi and at Conjevaram in the South, and ultimately became fused in the mass of the population. Their name now only exists in tradition, or is preserved in some local association.

From whatever cause, and at whatever period, the Andhras took up their abode in the Dakhan, they have left memorials of their power, showing that it lasted for no inconsiderable time. The classical name of the Telugu province is Andhradesam, and the Andhrika literature abounds in works composed in Sanscrit or in Telugu, which are still studied and highly appreciated. One of the early names of Kuntala was Karṇátaka, which, although now erroneously given to the Drávida or Arcot province, is applied by all natives to the part of the Dakhan east of Maharashtra and north of the line of Ghâts, throughout which the Kanarese language is now spoken. The term was probably derived from Karṇa,[1] the dynastic name or title of the Andhra princes, who, besides its employment in the form of Sáta Karni, had frequently the terms Karṇa or Karṇi, Sata, Swata, etc., varying (as Professor Wilson observes)[2] to suit the metre, joined to their proper names.

Further, the two branches of the Godávari, where the river divides to form the Delta, are still distinguished by the names of the two great Queens, the Northern as the Gautami, and

[1] Grammarians assign a different etymon, and derive the word from *karna*, "black," in allusion to the black soil, called *regaḍ* and cotton-soil, which abounds in many parts of the province. To this it is objected that the *regaḍ* is not peculiar to Kuntala or even to the Dakhan. According to the Geological Survey, "Tracts are found scattered throughout the valley of the Krishṇa, and occupying the lower plains and flats of Coimbatore, Salem, Maḍura, Tanjore, Ramnad, and Tinnevelly. There is but little in Mysore. . . The great alluvial flat of Surat and Broach consists of that soil. It occupies the depression between Ahmedâbâd and Káṭhiâwâḍ, connecting the head of the Gulf of Cambay with the Run of Cutch" (Manual of the Geology of India, ch. xviii. p. 432).

The name of Karṇa still survives in many places, as, for example,
Karṇi-pura District.—Ind. Ant. vol. i. p. 206.
Karṇaghar, an ancient city in Sagao, near Jabalpur, mentioned by Prof. Hall.
Karṇavati River, now Kayan, or Kane of the maps, sometimes written Kiranavati. The Kainus of Arrian.—Cun. Ancient Geog. p. 487; Cun. Arch. Rep. vol. ii. pp. 446, 453-4; *ib.* 1864-5, p. 453.

[2] V. Pur. vol. iv. p. 201.

the Southern as the Vásishthí channel. The Telugu term applied to the agricultural serfs (see p. 15, *note* 1) has before been referred to as brought by them from their native country in Bengal. It may be added that the Telugu people are known as Vadagas or Northerners by the other Dravidians, from whom they were further distinguished by their finer physical development as the tallest and handsomest section of the race.

Other monuments of Andhra rule are found in their religious edifices. Professing the faith of Buddha, they signalized their devotion by the construction of *Stúpas*,[1] of which that at Amrávati, on which the name of Puḍumayi has recently been read, was probably unsurpassed in the East, and by the excavation of numerous Cave-temples, among which that at Kárli is conspicuous.

The coins of the Andhra monetary system have already been noticed with reference to the historical evidence deducible from them. They differ from those of the rest of Southern India, and have a character peculiarly their own. The prevailing metal of which they are composed is lead. A few occur of copper, and some of alloy of copper and tin, but none of gold or silver. As yet they have only been collected in the deltas of the Krishṇa and Godávari, and recently a few have come from the Western Mahraṭṭa State of Kolhápur. The greater part of the Andhra dominion is now included in the territory of the Nizam of Haidarabad, where the facilities for numismatic research are small, so that it would be rash to conclude that the Andhras had no gold or silver money, although the large find of leaden pieces somewhat favours that presumption.

Professor Wilson has remarked on the prevalence of silver billon and copper in the Græco-Bactrian currency, while that of the Indo-Scythian consisted exclusively of gold and copper; the latter in large quantities. And he quotes Arrian's statement that the Indians with whom Alexander came in contact were without gold [ἀχρυσιοι, Arr. Ant. 347–9].

The characteristic of the Andhrian coinage was the employment of lead with but a small proportion of copper.

General Pearse has called my attention to a passage in Pliny to the effect that India has neither brass nor lead,[2] receiving them in exchange for precious stones and pearls, which may afford some explanation of this peculiarity.

The lead is generally very pure, a careful analysis detecting only a trace of copper, probably accidental in some specimens. One class of coins was found to consist of a kind of speculum of an alloy of lead and tin, and another of an impure lead ore, which gave them the appearance of a coarse alloy.

They are stamped with symbols of a Buddhist character. The obverse has figures of a lion or horse with the name of the sovereign, but his effigy, never. The reverse

[1] Two have been demolished within my own recollection, one at Gudiwáḍa, by the Department of Public Works, about 1842, the other near Cocanada, by the Pittapur Zemindar, in 1848 (Mad. Journ.); Ind. Ant. vol. xii. p. 34; some others are yet standing at Batiprola, Juggiapetta, etc.

[2] India neque æs neque plumbum habet, gemmisque suis ac margaritis hæc permutat.—Nat. Hist. xxxiv. 17, Elz. Ed.

has often the Buddhist cross or wheel to which the name of Ujjain symbol has sometimes been given.[1]

The pieces vary greatly in size, they are generally round, sometimes square. Some are only struck on one side, the reverse being plain or exhibiting marks of the substance on which they had rested (wood or stone) to receive the impact of the upper die.

Many of the smaller pieces appear to have been cast in moulds, with the figure of an elephant rudely represented by three convexities, with or without legs, these in the latter case mere stumps, thick or thin, long or short. On the die-struck specimens, the elephant is sharp and symmetrical, facing mostly to the right, the trunk pendant or raised over the head.

On the larger lead pieces is a stately maneless lion, the reverse with Buddhist emblems, or plain; while on the thicker alloyed specimens from the Krishṇa the animal has an ample mane, is short-legged, one paw uplifted, and on the reverse a vase (the *Drona*) between two candelabra. It is doubtful, however, whether these latter truly belong to the Andhra dynasty. The coarse, thick, impure lead-pieces from Kolhápur form a third type. They have the effigy of a bow and arrow on the obverse, and a many-arched *chaiṭya* with other emblems on the reverse.

Good representations of the former, leaden, etc., will be found in Madras Journal, vol. iii. N.S. pp. 234–249, plates ix. x. xi.; and of the latter, from Kolhapur, in Bombay Journal vol. xiii. p. 303, plates iii. iv. Descriptions of coins without plates will also be found in Bombay Journal, vol. xii. p. 407; Ind. Ant. vol. vi. pp. 276–7; Ind. Ant. vol. ix. p. 61.

The monetary value of the several pieces, and the relation in which they stand to each other can only be surmised. The unit appears to be the smaller leaden kind first mentioned. It is found in the largest numbers, and though varying in weight may be taken to average about thirty-five grains. From this a scale, ascending by a process of reduplication, will be found to include the most prominent examples hitherto found, as thus:—

35 — 70 — 140 — 280 — 560.[2]

From the disappearance of the Andhras, about the end of the second or beginning of the third century, to the rise of the Chalukya empire in the fifth, we have no numismatic record of any important or leading power.

The country from the Mahánadi and the Narmadá to the Godávari seems to have been parcelled out among many local chiefs, the forerunners of the Doralu and Racnawars of modern times, who enjoyed a quasi independence.

[1] This symbol, which is associated with Ujjain, in virtue of the old Asoka letters bearing that name, has been lately identified with the original local Sun-worship of India.—Num. Chron. 1880, Article on the "Indian Swastika and its Western Counterparts." Mr. Thomas tells me it occurs also on some of our early English *Sceattæ*, where it also clearly refers to the Sun-parallels of Stonehenge, etc.—Ruding, Supplement, plate ii. fig. 17, and pl. xxvi. fig. 13.

[2] But the scale does not provide for all the varieties which range from 20 to 40—50 to 60—70 to 90—100 to 140—180 to 200—250—after which the two heaviest I possess are 559·9 and 602·[illegible]. These, the only examples I possess, were found in a deserted site at the village of Chittala, in the Yernagudem Talook of the Godávari district.

Traces of these may still be recognized in the settlements at Rutnapur, in the Ryagarh province of Nagpur, and the hill districts of Orissa and Ganjam, where a few specimens of local coinage have been met with, like those at Gowgadh in Ganjam Yellamanchali, etc.[1]

With these may perhaps be associated the maned-lion coins, doubtfully attributed to the Andhras in a former paragraph. Others may be looked for, as these little-frequented districts are more fully explored.

NOTE.—Since the foregoing was written Dr. Bühler has sent me the proofs of an essay, in the preparation of which he assisted, on the "Discoveries"[2] made by Pandit Bhagwánlál Indraji, at Sopara and Paḍana.

In the course of these investigations the Paṇḍit, when excavating a tope at Sopárá, came upon a copper casket, in which he found a silver coin, represented in the subjoined woodcut, critically reproduced by an experienced artist from an electrotype copy of the original. The coin weighs thirty-four grains, and exhibits a strong resemblance to the pieces of the Sah dynasty. Thus the anticipation hasarded above, that gold and silver coins of the Andhra dynasty might still be in existence, has been realized.

The obverse of the piece in question, bears the head of a king, with an inscription which Bhagwánlál reads "Yajna Satakarṇi, the king Gotamíputra,"[3] thus corresponding exactly with No. 27 in the genealogical table given above. The inscription on the reverse is very imperfect. The Paṇḍit makes some ingenious attempts to restore it, which result in the doubtful tentative reading, "Yajna Satakarṇi Gotamíputra, prince of Chaturapana." This he compares with another inscription above a water cistern recently discovered at Nanaghat, read as "Chatarapana Satakaṇi (Satakarṇi) Vasathi (Váśishṭhí)," and he suggests that this Chaturapana may be the father of Yajna Śrí, for reasons which he gives at length.

Following these indications Dr. Bühler refers to the inscription, No. 11, of the Junior Series in Burgess' Reports, vol. v. pl. v. recording the gift of a fountaiṇ, which the Paṇḍit reads, "Of the Queen of . . Vasishṭhaputra Śátakarṇi, (who is) descended from the race of Kardamaka kings, (and) the daughter of the Mahakshatrapa, Ru . . ."

From these facts Dr. Bühler deduces the following conclusions:—1st, that Váśishṭhaputra Satakarṇi was an Andhra king, and that his queen was the daughter of a Kshatrapa; 2nd, that Váśishṭhaputra Satakarṇi of Kánheri (No. 11) is the same person as Chaturapana Vasishṭhaputra Śátakarṇi; 3rd, that his queen was the daughter of the Mahakshatrapa Rudra, the mother of Siriyana, and commonly called Gotamí, *i.e.* Gautamí; 4th, that the relationship of Rudra Daman with the Dakshanapati was, on the above identifications, either through his son-in-law, Chaturapana, or through his grandson, Siriyána, or at least that Siriyana's mother was some near relation of Rudra Daman's. According to these views the genealogical table given at p. 8 would read thus:—

[1] Madras Journal, vol. iv. N.S. p. 76. [2] Bombay Journ. Roy. As. Soc. vol. xv. p. 273. [3] Plate ii. fig. 7, p. 288.

No. 26. Chaturapana Váśishṭhiputra Śátakarṇi = Gautamí II., daughter of Mahakshatrapa Ru. . .
No. 27. Siriyána Gautamíputra II. =

These identifications do not appear to me altogether satisfactory; but if they are admitted, they do not invalidate the theory before given, of the revolution that brought in the Andhrabhṛitya line, which may have been as well owing to the other causes there mooted, as to the Kshatrapa invasion; while the postponement of the success achieved by Rudra Daman over his relative may be taken to have helped the catastrophe which soon after extinguished the Andhra line.

Although the last name in the pauranic list is Pulomat, for which there is no other authority, it is possible that the name Purisadatta, lately discovered by Dr. Burgess on the Jaggayyapeṭṭa *stúpa*, may have been that of a subsequent pretender of the Ikshváhu race, endeavouring to maintain or resuscitate the name of the time-honoured line (Ind. Ant. vol. xi. p. 256; Dr. Bühler on Inscriptions from the Jaggayyapeṭṭa *stúpa*).

Perhaps also to this time, and to a similar connection with the Andhra Śátakarṇis, may be assigned that "Háritiputa Śátakaṇi of the Veṅnukaḍaḍutu (?) family," whose name is preserved in the Páli inscription at Banawási (Arch. Survey, 1881, Ins. 14, p. 100).

[Sir Walter Elliot has asked me to describe such coins in this Southern series as chance to bear Nágarí or North-Indian characters.—E.T.]

| OBVERSE. | REVERSE. |
| --- | --- |
| Head, the King with a close-fitting helmet, possibly swathed in muslin. The symbol of the Sauras or sun-worshippers is seen in the front. | The conventional Sáh device, but the Ujain symbol of the sun appears on the left. |
| सर यञ सातकनस रञो गोतमि पुतस | सर यञ सातकनस . . . नस गोतमि पुतस |
| *Siri yaña sátakanisa Raño Gotami-putasa* | *Siri yaña sátakanisa . . . nasa Gotami-putasa* |

A critical difference may be detected in the style of the Hindí characters on the obverse and reverse. The former follow the forms of the square alphabet employed by the Andhras, the latter partake of several of the modifications incident to the Western style of writing, to be seen on the *Kshatrapa* Girnár inscription (Prinsep's Essays vol. ii. pl. xxxviii. pp. 40, 53), where the downstroke of the letters क *k*, ञ *ñ*, र *r*, and the *u* in पु, are curled backwards, as in the legends of the Sáh coins proper. The formation of the स *s* also varies in a marked degree.

I am unable to follow Pandit Bhagvánlál's reading of *Cha-tu-ra pa-na-sa*. In the electrotype before me, there does not appear to be space enough left for *four* conjectural letters in sequent order; but if we could be assured of his first suggestive reading of the initial consonant, there would be much reason to identify the missing name with चष्टन *Chashṭana.*

The coins of Nahapana and Chashṭana th display numismatic peculiarities which may have important bearing upon the age and location of the new type figured above. I therefore reproduce my previously-published readings of their coins, which I have tested anew from the electrotypes supplied to me by Mr. Newton some years ago, as also from an earlier example of the coinage of Chashtana (No. B.).

### *Nahapána.*

A. Silver. Weight 31 grains. *Trilingual.* Mr. Newton, late Bombay Civil Service.

| OBVERSE. | REVERSE. |
| --- | --- |
| King's head to the right, with rough hair, in free Scythic fashion, bound with a fillet. Very coarsely executed. | A broad-barbed arrow, and a crude definition of a thunderbolt. |
| Legend, in imperfect Greek, with traces of the title — τυPANNουντος. The suggestion for this somewhat hazardous reconstruction is derived from the parallel legend on Scythian coins of more northern sites, which run ΤΥΡΑΝΝΟΥΝΤΟΣ, etc.[1] | Legend, in Bactrian-Páli characters, reading from the right, commencing below the point of the spear, נהפנש *Nahapanasa*, following which, reading from the inside, but in the reverse direction, in Indian-Páli letters, नहपनस *Nahapanasa.* |

Sir Walter Elliot has adverted, in previous pages, to the inscriptions of Nahapána found in Western India. Mr. Burgess has lately collected, in his Archæological Reports, all the most recent *data* on this subject, and likewise revised the earlier and less perfect transcripts and translations, so that we now seem to have all the available epigraphic evidence before us.

It appears that there are no less than seven inscriptions extant (at Násik, Junnar, and Karle) of this king, set up, on the one part, by his son-in-law and Viceroy, Ushavadatta (*Rishabhadatta*[2]), the son of Díníka, "*a Ṣaka*" by race; and, on the other, by his daughter Dakshamitrá; and also, in one case, by "Ayama of the Vatsa-gotra, prime minister to the King, the great Satrap, the Lord Nahapána." He is ordinarily styled in these documents "the Kshaharáta king, Kshatrapa Nahapána," which designation of *Kshatrapa*[3] or *Mahakshatrapa* was adopted by Chashṭana and was continued as *the* Dynastic title of the succeeding Sáh kings of Surashtra. The most advanced date in Nahapana's Inscriptions is 46, defined simply as *vase*, "in the year," as if it referred to some well-established method of reckoning. If we test these figures by the Mauryan epoch of 312 B.C., or the parallel Seleucidan era of 311 B.C., we have the option of three resulting dates, under the Indian home system of omitting hundreds,[4] viz.:

B.C. 312 — 100 = 212 — 46 = 166 B.C.
B.C. 312 — 200 = 112 — 46 = 66 B.C.
B.C. 312 — 300 = 12 — 46 = 34 A.D.

The Scythian dates of Vasudeva, etc., from Mathura, gave a general return by the same process of reckoning—of B.C. 2 to 87 A.D. But I am not sure that I should not now prefer the previous century for both classes of rulers.

[1] J.R.A.S. vol. xv. N.S. p. 74; N.C. N.S. vol. xiv p. 161.

[2] "*Ṛishabha* Devaji was the first Jain Tírthánkara—*the* Prathama Jina."—Colebrooke's Essays, vol. ii. p. 187; As. Res. vol. ix. p. 305; Indian Ant. 1873, p. 134; Vishṇu Puráṇa, ii. 104. See also the Sáh Inscriptions in the caves of Junágaḍh—Burgess's Report, 1874, p. 140, and the mention of "Kevalins"—as proving the Jaina influence in those parts.

[3] The title of Χατράπης "*Chatrapa*," first appears in the Bactrian series, in the sub-Azas group. Prinsep, vol. ii. pp. 210-11; see also p. 223.

[4] Bühler, Rupnáth Inscr. Ind. Ant. vol. vi. p. 149; Cunningham, Arch. Reports, vol. v. 1875, p. 181; vol. xiv. 1882, p. 122; Bactrian Coins and Indian Dates, J.R.A.S. vol. ix. N.S. p. 1; Burgess's Report, 1874-5, p. 32; Albirúni, Reinaud, p. 145.

*Chashtana.*

B. Silver. Weight 34 grains. Col. Watson, Bombay Army.

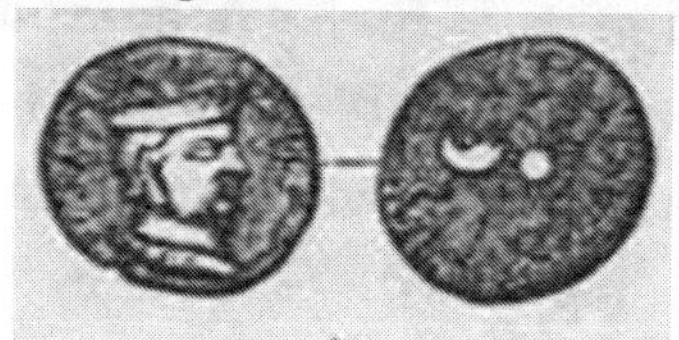

**Obverse.**

King's head to the right, with flat (Spanish style of) cap, and well-defined features.

Legend, in Bactrian characters (?), only partially legible.

**Reverse.**

The sun and the moon

*Legend.*

श्री रञो चचपस ष्यमोतीक पुच

*Şrí rajno Kshatrapasa Syamotika putrasa.*[1]

On the left side, a Bactrian ᚹ *s*.

It seems that he had not as yet claimed the title of मह *Maha* "great," prefixed to the *Kshatrapa* in No. C.

C. Silver. Weight 23 grains. Legends, in *three* different characters.

**Obverse.**

King's head to the right, with flat cap and well-executed profile. The secondary prototype of the Sah Mint device.

Legend, in imperfect Greek, with apparent portions of the word—*τυρΑΝΝοῦντοι*.

**Reverse.**

A *chaitya, tope* or tumulus, composed of superimposed arches, with a demilune capital. Serpent below; above a well-defined boldly-rayed sun to the right, with a corresponding moon to the left.

Legend in Indian-Páli—

रञ महचचपस . . . तिकपुचस

*Rajno mahakshatrapasa* [*Syamo*]*tika putrasa*

चष्टनस } repeated in Bactrian Páli. { גטנש

*Chashṭanasa* *Chaṭaṇasa*

The inscriptions bearing the name of Chashṭana, though not contemporaneous, may prove of considerable value in determining the system of reckoning followed by his successors, the Sah kings of Surashtra. We are still unable to fix with absolute precision the *starting* date-point, but the preference apparently remains with the wide-spread *Samvat Vikramáditya*, 57 B.C.[2]

[1] *Sayam* seems to have been a favourite Scythic name. It occurs in the series of Indo-Scythic coins with Hindi legends, lately published by me, of which the following is a full list, with the associate tribal subdivisions.

| | |
|---|---|
| *Şakas* | Me. |
| " | Pa. |
| " | Bhri. |
| " | Bhu. |
| " | Sayam. |
| " | Senam. |
| *Kushana* | Kidara (Hodi ?). |
| *Gaḍahas* | Kirda (Kardi ?). |
| *Bhanḍhis* | Básanam (Bastán ?) |
| " | Bhadri. |
| *Mahis* | Pu. |

—Indian Antiquary, Bombay, 1883, p. 6. The general type of this class of coins may be seen in Prinsep's Essays, plate xxx. figs. 16–20, and in J.R.A.S. o.s. vol. xii. plate vii. figs. 16–20.

[2] Prof. Max Müller, following-up Mr. Fergusson's suggestion (J.R.A.S. vol. xii. N.S. p. 271), has lately reiterated all the arguments tending to prove that the Vikramáditya Samvat of 56·7 B.C. was an after-invention, or in other words altogether unauthentic (Note G. "The Renaissance of Sanskrit Literature"). He has been answered from India, in the terms of his own challenge, "to show that something less than 600 of the Vikrama era" can be produced in documentary evidence,—in Mr. Fleet's article in the Indian Antiquary (Nov. 1883, p. 291), where it is demonstrated that the recorded dates of 421 and 486 on the Gurjara copper plates must clearly refer to the Vikramáditya era.

It is evident from the coincident tenour of the subjoined inscriptions, not only that we must reject the personal, or *quasi*-regnal date of 72, in favour of a dynastic or otherwise recognized era, which follows on, in the terms of the Jasdan epigraph, to the similarly undefined year 127.

Any disturbance of these *written* dates, *inter se*, is happily disposed of, by the concurrent *figured* dates on these coins, which we can now read with some certainty, and which practically run on all fours with the more fully-defined lithic writing.

*Inscription at Junágaḍh.*

This work (the embankment of the Sudarṣana lake) gave way on the 4th day of the dark fortnight of the month of Márgaṣirsha of the 72nd year of Rájá Mahákshatrapa Rudra Daman, whose name is oft repeated by the great, the grandson of Mahákshatrapa Chashṭaṇa of well-accepted (propitious) name . . . the son of . . ., etc. (Arch. Rep. 1874–5, p. 129; Indian Antiquary, 1878, p. 261.)

From the subsequent terms of the inscription, it would seem that this embankment had been previously repaired or extended by Pushya Gupta, on the part of the Great Maurya Rája, CHANDRA GUPTA, and also subsequently by Tushaspa, "the Yavana Rája of ASOKA Maurya.[1]

The most important passage in this inscription, however, in relation to our present subject, is the reference to the Andhras, which is couched in the following terms:

"He who has obtained glory because he did not destroy Sátakarṇi, the lord of the Dekhaṇ, on account of his near relationship, though he twice really conquered him." (Ind. Ant. 1878, p. 262.)

If we could rely upon the conjectural restoration of the name of Chashṭaṇa on the coin at p. 25, it would throw much new light upon the family relations.

*Inscription at Jasdan.*

In the year 127 Bhádrapada, dark-half 7 of the moon, this *Satra* (tank) of Rájá Mahákshatrapa Bhadramukha Swámí Rudra Sena, the great-grandson of the son of Rájá Mahákshatrapa Chashtaṇa; the grandson of the son of Rájá Kshatrapa Swámi Jayadáman, the grandson of Rájá Mahákshátrapa . . . Rudra Dámá, (son of) Rájá Mahákshatrapa Bhadramukha Swámí Rudra, etc. (Dr. Bhau Dáji, Journ. Bombay Branch Roy. As. Soc. vol. viii. p. 235.)

The subjoined list of Andhra coins, bearing legends in one of the first removes from the old *lát* character of Asoka, was compiled by me, some years ago, with a view to its final insertion in the present work of Sir Walter Elliot. If there are but few additions to the general series, there are, as far as I am aware, equally few rectifications to be made in my original decipherments.

The Asoka Inscription at Ganjam, in the earliest *lát* alphabet at present in evidence, prepared us for the use of a similar style of writing among a race, who passed on their way to southern conquests along the seaboard of the eastern coast, or along the traditional route of Ráma. And the near identity of the forms of the letters on the Andhra coins with

[1] Paṇdit Bhagvánlál, in his revised translation (p. 257) of this inscription, refers to the apparent date of 72 of this King's reign, and adds: "But it seems altogether improbable that Rudradáman should have reigned for so long a time, and it is still less probable that he should have had a still longer reign. . . . It seems therefore necessary to assume, as has been done by former translators of the inscription, that the figure of 72 refers not to the years of Rudradáman's reign, but to the era used on the Kshatrapa coins. This explanation is confirmed by the fact that the coins of Rudradáman's son, Rudrasimha, are dated between the years 102 and 117 of the same era."

the fixed prototypes of B.C. 250, rather suggests for the Dynasty itself an epoch earlier than has hitherto been conceded to them by modern inquirers.

This is an era of much importance in Indian history, which seems to be further elucidated by recent interpretations of the celebrated Aira inscription at Udayagiri[1] (sun-rise hill) in Cuttack, a new and revised translation of which has been contributed to the recent Oriental Congress at Leyden, in the following outline terms:—"It is sufficient here to mention a communication of the first importance made to the Aryan Section by Prof. Peterson, of Bombay, on behalf of Paṇḍit Bhagvánlál Indrají. The Paṇḍit has succeeded in deciphering the well-known inscription of Udayagiri, formerly ascribed to King Aira or Vera, but which has hitherto baffled all attempts to read it. He shows that the real name of the king is Khárávela, who ruled over Kalinga, and belonged to the Cheta family and to the Jain faith. The king gives a long account of his doings during thirty-eight years; and though some of the details still remain uncertain, it is clear that he mentions a Western (that is, Andhra) king Sátakani, and dates the extension of certair works at the close of 'the 165th year of the Maurya kings.'"

Assuming that the latter era dates from the *Abhishek* of Chandra Gupta, as accepted by the Jains, or 312 B.C., this would fix Khárávela's public works in 147 B.C.[2]

No. 1. Lead. Size, the full 9 of Mionnet's scale. Weight, 220 grains.

OBVERSE.

A crudely-outlined representation of a primitive semicircular bow and broadly-barbed arrow.[3]

The broad arrow is rendered in an identical form at Udayagiri.

At Sanchi the arrows vary, and have no barbs.

REVERSE.

A *chaitya*, or typical form of a *tumulus*, formed of four rows of inverted semicircles surmounted by a half-moon;[4] to the *right*, a sacred tree—an object alike of the simple adoration of the forest tribes, and afterwards of the more matured reverence of the Jainas and their imitators the Buddhists—with seven leaves or branches; at the foot, an oblong box-pedestal, within which is a free definition of *a serpent* in the form of a wavy line, with intervening dots.

*Legend.*

रञो मढारी पुतस सिवाल कुरस

*Raño Maḍḍrí- putasa Sivála-kurasa* (*kula*).

[1] The first translation of this Inscription was made by Prinsep in 1837 (J.A.S.B. vol. vi. p. 1080), from eye facsimiles traced by that most accurate Palæographer, Captain M. Kittoe. A revised translation was undertaken in 1877, by Babu Rajendra Mittra, from plaster impressions (J.A.S.B. 1877, vol. xlvi. p. 165), who remarked on its general tenor as follows:—"The author of the record was one Aira, a usurper, who overthrew the dominion of an ancient king of Kalinga and, himself becoming the sovereign, repaired the city walls, etc. . . . The most important fact mentioned in the record was the overthrow, by this usurper, of King Nanda of Magadha, and this carried him back to the middle of the fourth century B.C. It was not distinctly stated which of the nine Nandas he overcame in battle; but assuming the potentate meant to be the last of the line, the time would be a few years before the invasion of India by Alexander the Great in 327 B.C." Since this was written, I have received from the Paṇḍit himself his article on the Násik caves, extracted from the Bombay Gazetteer. At p. 73 he gives some further notices of this Inscription.

[2] Wilford, As. Res. vol. ix. p. 173; Jacobi, Kalpa Sútra, p. 8, 109; J.R.A.S. vol. xiii. N.S. p. 548.

[3] The same typical form of bow and arrow occurs repeatedly on the earlier specimens of the ancient *punched* or hall-marked coins. Indian Weights, Numismata Orientalia, Part I. plate, fig. 12, etc. and the accompanying Plate I.

[4] J.R.A.S. o.s. vol. xii. (1854), p. 1.

No. 2. Lead. Size, 7 of Mionnet's scale. Weight, 228 grains.

**Obverse.**

Device a rude strung bow and broadly-barbed arrow, ready set for use.

*Legend.*

रञो वासिठी पुतस विदवाय कुरस

*Raño Vásitho-putasa Vidavdya-kurasa.*

**Reverse.**

A conventional *chaitya* consisting of three layers of inverted semicircles with inner dots, surmounted by a *chakra* or wheel, perhaps the typical figure of the sun. To the *left*, a sacred tree with seven broad-spread leaves. At the foot, an oblong pedestal, in which is figured a serpent, the wavy intervals being filled in with dots.

I place this piece in the tentative list of the issue or descendants of Vásiṭhi,[1] earlier than those bearing the name of the children of Gautamí, on strictly numismatic grounds.

No. 3. Lead. Size, 9 of Mionnet's scale. Weights range from 180 grains to 196. The execution of the dies is inferior to the preceding. Numerous specimens and examples are available.

**Obverse.**

The usual crude bow and arrow.

*Legend.*

रञो गोतमी पुतस विदवाय कुरस

*Raño Gotami-putasa Vidavdya-kurasa.*

**Reverse.**

*Chaitya* device as above, but the symbolic tree is attached to the main device, and rises directly from the end or outer upright line on the right of the pedestal.

Many of these coins are what is technically termed "double-struck," *i.e.* the dies of a successor or adverse contemporary have been repeated *over* the original impression, without any re-fashioning or possibly much re-softening of the metal of the piece itself.

These indications are often of much value in determining the relative priority of the conjoint rulers. In the present instance they distinctly authorize us to place the children or issue of Madári before those of the more prolific or possibly more powerful ancestress Gautamí.

The first of these coincidences is exemplified in No. 13 of the original plate iv., Bombay Branch Royal Asiatic Society, 1877, where the outer or natural edge of the piece retains a portion of the normal legend in the letters

तञो मढार पुतस

*Raño Madári putasa:*

while the second impress of a new die, in its false centering, overlaps the lower surface with the letters of a broken legend in the words

कुरस रञ गोतमी पुत

*kurasa. Raño Gotamí puta . . .*

To exemplify further the custom of renewed or revised impressions upon the fully *issued* or so to say current coin, I may add that in one case a piece of the Gautamí-putras of type No. 3 has clearly had the identical legends of the original *obverse* re-struck or repeated over the obvious surface of the old *reverse.*

[1] घराम '*beauty,*' وشتي beautiful. 'ושתי 'Αστιν, Οὐάστιν Esther i. 1, Jos. Ant. xi. 6, 1 वासित 'perfumed.'

It is difficult to determine by what process this was effected, as Sir W. Elliot has a very sharp and perfect specimen of coin No. 3, which shows indubitable signs of having been *cast*—the marks of the moulds are set irregularly at the edges, and two definite orifices have been left at the sides to receive the metal, the superfluous quantity of which still adheres to the piece.

General Pearse has lately acquired a group of five coins which seem to connect themselves in a measure with the above pieces, in the metal and general appearance of the joint issues, in the retention of the same forms of letters, and in a certain degree of the character of the devices themselves.

The new coins, however, bear strange names, and cannot strictly be classed with the Andhra series, but rather seem to belong to some potentates who succeeded to a section of the dominions of that race as they made their way onwards to the Western coast.

No. *a*. Lead. Weight, 250 grains. Plate II. infra.

OBVERSE.

A chaitya with two rows of invented semicircles at the base, and a larger open or cupola arch above.

*Legend.*

रञ मदेंन दस

*Raño Madenna dasa.*[1]

REVERSE.

A sacred tree, in a four-square pedestal, or pot, with curious devices at the sides.

No. *b*. Lead. Weight, 278 grains.

OBVERSE.

Central device similar to No. *a* above.

*Legend.*

रञ वदक देंन दस

*Raño Vadaka donna dasa.*[2]

REVERSE.

Device, in the first instances, similar to the above. Later examples complicate the pedestal or box below the tree into twelve squares, and enlarge the size of the $\overset{\omega}{o}$ symbol, which is transferred from the left to a more prominent position on the right of the central device.

No. 4. Copper. *Small Coins.* Size, 4 of Mionnet's scale. Weight, 28 grains.

OBVERSE.

Archaic bow and arrow.

*Legend.*

रञो वास . . . तस विदवाय कुरस

*Raño Vdsi[ṭho-pu] tasa Vidavdya- kurasa.*

REVERSE.

*Chaitya*, with the sacred tree represented as growing on the apex or summit.

[1] *Md* is one of the titles of *Lakshmi*, Vishṇu Puráṇa, Hall's edition, vol. v. p. 387. *Dena* looks like a form of Hindi دينا 'to give,' the Marathi देणें *denen* means 'a gift'—and *Dasa* (=Dás, Doss) 'a slave.' In S. India *Ddsa* implies 'a worshipper of Vishṇu.'

[2] In one instance the ˙ or *anuswdra* is repeated over the वृ *n*. *Vada* forms part of the name of Vadaṣri, p. 8, and in the coin *a*, above; it is stated, in the Vishṇu Puráṇa, "to be a Veda of the Magas or Heliolaters in Ṣáka-dwipa." Hall's ed. vol. v. p. 383.

In the field of one specimen, a monogram possibly composed of the letters तचा *tachá* or तवा *tavá;* on the other example, a letter like a Chaldæan-Pehlvi ע, א (*a*).[1]

No. 5. Lead. Size, 7. Weight, 230 grains.

Obverse.

Device similar in some respects to the reverse of No. 1, but the *chaitya* or tumulus in this case is solid, surmounted with the usual half-moon, while the standard tree is replaced by a conch shell, the favourite symbol of Nemi, the 22nd Jaina *Tírthankara*, and equally of the Hindú god Vishṇu, balanced on the other side of the field by a lotus or water-lily, the type of the 21st Jaina. The conventional serpent appears at the foot, but free and clear of the main device.

*Legend.*

रञो गोतमी पुतस सिरि यञ सतकणस

***Raño Gotamí-putasa Siri Yaña Satakaṇasa.***

Reverse.

Four leading circles at right angles, each composed of a central dot and two concentric outer circles, the upper pair and lower pair are severally connected by a semicircular line. This combination, varied by the junction of the four balls of a simple cross, is conventionally recognized as the Ujjain symbol, to which reference has already been made.[2]

In the last and succeeding Numismatic instances male rulers seem to have re-asserted their rights of kingship, while still in a measure recognizing the traditional law of the supremacy of maternity. So that the gradations, in this instance, seem to have followed *a.* the Scythic female head of the camp; *b.* the ruling warrior king. Ultimately, the Sáh kings—who affected patronymics—progressed into, or more probably reverted back to local *Republicanism.*[3]

No. 6. Lead. Size, 5. Weight, 86 grains.

Obverse.

Small *chaitya*, with three inverted semicircles, and free serpent at the foot.

*Legend.*

रञो वासिठ पुतस सर यसतस

***Raño Vásiṭho-putasa Siri Yasatasa*** (No. 7 *a* ?)

Reverse.

The conventional Ujjain symbol.

[1] See Journal Royal Asiatic Society, N.S. vol. iii. (1868), p. 264. It may be as well to add that the occurrence of such a letter on the local coinage need not necessarily reduce the age of the pieces so inscribed to the modern limits assigned to extant Pehlvi inscriptions. The letters of these alphabets are found on very early specimens of the Parthian coinage.

[2] See Journal Asiatic Society of Bengal, vol. vii. plate lxi; Numismata Orientalia, 'Ancient Indian Weights,' part i. plate, figs. 5, 6. Dr. Schliemann, in his work on Mycenæ, enlarges upon the identity of the Greek *Triglyph* with the Indian *Swastika* cross, and there is also a singular approach to this circular Indian design in many of the patterns found on his buttons or *whorls*, the only appreciable difference consisting of the centre *dot*, which fills-in the space between the four circles in the latter. See Nos. 428, 404, 406, 411, etc. A great variety of the forms of the *Ujjain* pattern may be seen in vol. vii. plate lxi. Journal of the Asiatic Society of Bengal, and a series of many cognate devices are figured in General Cunningham's Bhilsa Topes (1854), pl. xxxi. xxxii. The *Swastika* device, apart from its use as a running pattern, was not, however, limited either to Eastern or Western acceptations, as may be seen in the examples in Fabretti's work on Etruscan Antiquities, 1st Supplement, plate iii. Nos. 29, 30; 3rd Supplement, plate xxix. fig. 38; and on vases in the British Museum.—[Since this was written, I have gone more fully into the question of Indian religious symbols—both in the pages of the Indian Antiquary (March—May, 1880) and in a more comprehensive article on 'The Indian Swastika and its Western Counterparts,' in the London Numismatic Chronicle, vol. xx. N.S. pp. 18-48. Dr. Schliemann (Ilios, 1880, p. 353) adopted my views implicitly, and they are found to accord with the deductions independently obtained by our prominent Danish Numismatic authority—Dr. Ludwig Muller.]

[3] J.R.A.S. vol. xii. O.S. p. 39, and vol. i. N.S. pp. 458-471.

## SIMILAR COINS—VARIANTS OF No. 6.

No. 7. One coin of this class gives distinctly the letters सिवसर *Sivasara*, No. 24 of the Puráṇik list at page 8, which reading is further confirmed by one of Mr. Sewell's specimens, which contributes the outlines of the letters—

. . तस सिवसिर
*Pu tasa Sivasira.*

No. *7a.*

*Legend.*—. . . . . . सठ पुतस सिरि वदसतस
*Rano Vásiṭho-putasa Siri Vadasatasa.* Vadasri or Chanda, No. 28 of the Puránik list, p. 8.

No. *7b* of Mr. Sewell's collection reproduces, in a more definite form, the imperfect specimen of Sir W. Elliot's plate xi. 100, and retains in legible letters the name of Pudumavi, No. 29, list, p. 8.

रञ वसुठपुत . . . . युमवस
*Raño Vasiṭho-puta . . . Puyumavesa.*

No. 8. Lead. Size, 4½ Mionnet's scale.

OBVERSE.

A well-executed figure of an *elephant*, to the left.

*Legend.*

रञो गोतमी पुतस सिरि यञ सतक
*Raño Gotami- putasa Siri Yaña Satakanasa.*

REVERSE.

The usual four double rings joined by a cross. Some examples add a *Swastika* on the obverse field, to the right of the *chaitya*.

No. 9. Lead. Size, 4. Weight, 70 grains.

OBVERSE.

A boldly sunk die bearing a well-designed figure of a *horse* to the left.

*Legend.*

रञो गोतमी पुतस सिरि यञ स
*Raño Gotami- putasa Siri Yaña sa . . .*

REVERSE.

The conventional Ujjain symbol.

No. 10. Copper or bronze. Size 4. Weight (average), 35 grains.

OBVERSE.

A well-outlined figure of an *elephant* in free form, with trunk erect; without trappings.

*Legend.*

सिरि सतकणि
*Siri Satakani.*

REVERSE.

Four single circles joined by cross-lines.

No. 11 *Variant.* The *elephant* is decorated with rich head-gear.

यञ सतक
*Yaña Sataka.*

N.B.—The forms of the letters of the legends clearly indicate that these two coins, as well as those which follow, belong to a later date than the specimens previously described.

No. 12. Lead. Size, 6. Weight, 133 grains.

OBVERSE.

A well-executed figure of a *horse* to the right, with a half-moon in the field above.

*Legend.*

रञ ग . . . . . . सतकणस
*Raño G*(otami-putasa) *Satakaṇase.*

REVERSE.

Device indistinguishable.

No. 12*a*. New coin, Mr. Sewell. Size, 5. Weight, 112 grains. From Gudiváḍa.

OBVERSE.

*Horse* to right.

Legend.

ञ सिरि चद . .
(Ra)*ño* *Siri* *Cha*(*n*)*da.*

REVERSE.

The Ujjain symbol.

No. 13. Lead. Size, 3. Weight, 35 grains. Two specimens.

OBVERSE.

A crude figure of an *elephant* to the left.

*Legend.*

सरिवण *Sarivaṇa* or *Salivana*, perhaps a repetition of the name, but not necessarily indicative of the personality of the great monarch.

REVERSE.

The Ujjain symbol.

No. 14 Lead. Similar coins. Three specimens.

*Legend*—सर रुद
*Siri Ruda.*

The द is on one occasion given as ड, and the *R*, if required for *Rudra*, has to be supplied to the existing context.

## PART I SECTION II.

# COROMANDEL COAST DIE COINS.

### (a) KURUMBARS. (b) PALLAVAS.

Along the Coromandel Coast, from Nellore as far South as Cuddalore and Pondicherry, a class of thin copper die-struck coins occurs, which, although not directly connected with the Andhra type, may be appropriately considered next. They are found in considerable numbers in or near dunes and sand-knolls in the vicinity of the *kupams*, or fishing hamlets that stud the shore, together with Roman oboli, perforated Chinese coins, bits of lead and other metal, beads, fragments of charcoal, etc.

These are collected by the wives and children of the fishermen after gales of wind or heavy rains, and purchased from them by the itinerant pedlars, called Labis and Merkuyars, in exchange for useful necessaries, by whom they are sold to braziers and coppersmiths. The discovery of articles of this description in such localities indicates the existence of a considerable maritime trade in former times, probably during the first four or five centuries of the Christian era.

The Roman coins are all of the smallest value, and are generally worn smooth, but on two or three the names of Valentinian and Eudocia have been read.

Gold coins of earlier dates, found in Nellore, Madura, Cuddapah, etc.,[1] may have come by land from the opposite coast, where intercourse with the West was more frequent, and Roman relics are more numerous; but these poor copper pieces could only have been dropped by mariners and traders frequenting the places where they now lie.

Those of native origin are small, irregularly rounded pieces of thin copper, bearing generally the device of a bull, with occasionally some letters in the Cave-character on the obverse; and on the reverse a tree, ship, star, crab, fish, etc. But their most remarkable characteristic is the elegance and delicacy of form with which the animals are designed, indicating a considerable advance in art; and in this respect contrasting favourably, both with the Andhra money on the one side, and with the Choḷa and Paṇḍyan currencies on the other.

[1] Madras Journal Literature and Science, vol. xiii. p. 214; other finds have been recorded on the Malabar or Western Coast, Coimbator, Sholapore, etc.

In addition to these, a few specimens of another description, which apparently belong to this series, have come to my notice, but they are very rare. They are between the size of a sixpence and a shilling, rather thicker, of billon or some white metal containing tin, and bear on the obverse, some the figure of a bull, others of a horse, of the same elegant design as those of the copper. The only two I ever possessed had the reverse plain.

Colonel Frederick Clerk had three or four of the same description, with one or two letters like those on the copper. My own specimens have, unfortunately, been lost, and Colonel Clerk's were dispersed at a sale shortly before his death,[1] and I have failed in all my endeavours to trace them.

In vain do we look for some independent power with which to identify this class on sure grounds, or even with any tolerable show of probability. Nothing is known of any dynasty or paramount ruler in that part of India, anterior to the time when the Choḷa princes began their career of conquest about the eighth century, which made them masters of great part of the South of India, and culminated in the overthrow of the eastern Chalukya kingdom in the twelfth.

There were, it is true, two smaller states enjoying a certain independent existence in the Arcot district during the period to which these coins must be assigned, which deserve a passing notice. These were:—

(*a*) An aboriginal or very early pastoral race, living in associated communities, under the general name of Kurumbars.

(*b*) A Pallava principality seated at Conjeveram.

## (*a*) THE KURUMBARS.

For some hundred years before the seventh century the country, from the base of the table-land to the Pálar and Pennár rivers, was occupied by a section of the pastoral race, traditionally designated as Kurumbars, of whom little is known.

Fragmentary notices of their social organization, and the ultimate fate of that part of them with which we are now concerned, may be gathered from Mr. F. W. Ellis' Essay on Land Tenures,[2] and from traditionary statements preserved in the McKenzie Collection of MSS. They appear to have formed a sort of Confederate State, "under chiefs of their own, each of whom resided in a fortified stronghold, having a district of greater or less extent under its jurisdiction, denominated a *kóṭṭam* (from *kóṭṭai*, a fort or castle), the largest of which was recognized as the head of the Union. Of the kottams there were twenty-four,

[1] On Tuesday, July 29th, 1873. In Sotheby, Wilkinson, and Hodge's Catalogue, p. 27.

[2] Replies to Seventeen Questions relative to Mirasi Rights, and with two Appendices, etc. Folio. Madras, 1818.

Catalogue Raisonné of Oriental MSS. in the Government Library, by the Rev. W. Taylor, 3 vol. 8vo. Madras, 1857-1862. Also Second Report of Progress made in the examination of the Mackenzie MSS., etc., by the Rev. W. Taylor, in Madras Journ. Lit. and Science, vol. vii. Madras, 1838.

each consisting of one or more *nâḍus* or parishes, and each nadu subdivided into several *naṭṭams* or townships.

They are farther stated to have been engaged in trade, and to have owned ships, and carried on a considerable commerce by sea. Their wealth attracted the cupidity of their neighbours, and they suffered from hostile inroads, but defended themselves with courage and success, till at length, about the eighth or ninth century, they were attacked by an army, under a general named Ádoṇḍai or Tondamán, the son (illegitimate according to some) or brother of the ruler of Cholamandalam. He encountered an obstinate resistance, but after sustaining some reverses, subdued the whole province, and incorporated it with the Chola territories, changing the name to Tondamandalam. The fierceness of the struggle was probably intensified by religious hatred; the one side being Jainas, while their conquerors were votaries of Siva. The Kurumbars were so completely exterminated, that it became necessary to replace them by introducing an agricultural colony from a distance.

Ellis, following the accounts handed down by their enemies, and preserved in Tamil narrative, represents them as a "pastoral, half-savage tribe," and again as a "Nomadic race"; whilst the native writers paint them as crafty, cruel and tyrannical.[1] But such characteristics, assigned on the testimony of their enemies, are incompatible with an organized social system having territorial institutions, of which no similar examples are found in the adjacent countries, and dwellings defended by permanently fortified castles, the ruined sites of which are still shown. Moreover, there is reason to believe that they had some knowledge of metallurgy, and were acquainted with the use of bronze, implements of which metal are occasionally found. It is also expressly stated that Ádondai transported the bronze gates found in the capital of the Confederacy at Pural[2] to ornament the great temple at Tanjore.

The attainment of this degree of civilization may be accounted for by the circumstance of the Kurumbars being Jains—a sect prevailing from a very early period in the South, and probably also throughout other parts of India. Judging from the remains that have survived the ravages of time, and the rage of persecution, its votaries had reached a high degree of intellectual culture.[3]

Their literary[4] compositions are still esteemed, and their works of statuary and architecture even now bear testimony to their proficiency in the higher walks of art.[5]

The ruined sites of mines, long abandoned, in various parts of the country are believed to be relics of Jaina skill. Such are the excavations for copper, found by Mr. V. Ball, in

[1] F. W. Ellis, Mirasi Rights.

[2] The site of Pural is now known as the Red Hills, twelve miles north of Madras, where an extensive necropolis of Kistvaens and circles may still be seen.

[3] Dr. Caldwell considers the earliest cultivators of Dravidian literature to have been Jainas (Comp. Gram. pp. 122-124-128). Dr. Burnell also assigns a high antiquity to Jaina literature (South India Palæography, pp. 12, 47-8; Ind. Ant. vol. i. p. 310).

[4] *e.g.* The Amara Kosha, the works of Hemachandra, the Sâbdaminidarpaṇam of Kesava, etc., etc.

[5] As the colossal statues of Srivana Bélagolo, Karkal, and the smaller images of the Tirthankaras or Saints, exquisitely carved out of basalt . . . Such too are the numerous temples of polished black stone, with pillars elaborately sculptured or elegantly chiselled, as if formed by a turning lathe, many of which have been appropriated by other sects, and turned into ill-disguised Brahminical shrines. The very Digambara idols, clothed in modern dress, have been made to do duty for Hindu gods, as described by Dr. Stevenson and Fergusson at Pandarpúr (J.R.A.S. vol. vii. p. 5; J.A.S.B. vol. xxxv. part i. pp. 186-290, also pp. 170, 184).

Chotia Nagpur, which the rude inhabitants can only say were the work of an ancient race called *Séraks* [1] (quasi-*Srávaks*), whom Colonel Dalton states to have been Jainas.[2]

The long-forgotten Kolár gold mines, now re-opened by British capital and enterprize, are within the limits of Tondainádu,[3] and those of Wynád may not improbably have been the work of Jainas also. The name of one of the last subscribing witnesses to the copper-plate grant in the possession of the Jews of Cochin, according to the Jewish version, is supposed to refer to the Kurumbenádu rulers, and in the epithet attached to his name, which may be rendered "Mountain-splitter," they find the Chieftain of Kurumbar, or Jungle-dwellers, so called, either from his mines at Tamracheri,[4] or from a pass he opened through the Ghâts.

The foregoing considerations throw no light on the direct authorship of the coins in question, but they go to prove the existence of a civilized community, capable of producing exceptional specimens of skilled manufacture, about the required period, and occupying a tract which extended inland from the particular line of coast on which the coins are found.

It may be added, that the Kurumbars who form the subject of the foregoing observations are but a small section of a great tribe, which occupied a larger extent of territory, formerly designated Kurumba-bhúm—a name now obsolete—the limits of which can only be guessed from the localities in which the scattered remnants of the tribes are now found to linger. Individuals of the race have risen to eminence, and even founded Royal dynasties, as will be noticed hereafter in treating of the Yádavas.[5]

[1] Proc. R. As. Soc. 1869, p. 170.

[2] V. Ball, Jungle Life in India, 1880, pp. 167-171; Proc. As. Soc. B.; Dalton, Ind. Eth.; and J.A.S.B. vol. xxxv. pt. 2, p. 164.

[3] Ellis states expressly that the Upper (=Western) part of Tondai, which did not come within the scope of his essay, consisted of four of the 24 kóṭṭams, the extent of which is unknown, and all traces of their nádus lost (page xi); but in a previous page (iv) he had explained generally that they included the North-East districts of Maisúr, comprehending the Parganás of Kolár, Bara Balapur, part of Penakonda, and the Subah of the Sirá, the first of which contains the whole of the gold-field forming the 22nd kóṭṭam, in which is also situate the fortress of Nandidrúg (A. pp. iv-viii). For a long time I was led to attribute the higher works of art found in the Dakhan mainly to the genius of Buddhism, but more intimate acquaintance with Tamil records induces me to modify this view and to recognize the claims of Jaina skill. The Bauddhas do not appear to have gained the same hold of the people of the South that they obtained over those of the North. The term *Sramana* in Tamil writing, read as applicable exclusively to Buddhist priests, is now shown by Mr. Beal to be a title of religious teachers in other sects as well (Ind. Ant. vol. ix. pp. 122, Notes to Ellis' Kural; see also Drs. Caldwell and Burnell, *supra*). Viewed in this light the origin of the Panchalar, or five castes of skilled artificers, should be considered as an escape of Jaina artificers from destruction, by assuming a semblance to their Saivite persecutors; this agrees better with their secret forms of worship, which has no similitude to that of Buddha (Journ. Ethnol. Soc. vol. i. N.S. pt. 18, p. 111, where the figure of the idol is certainly Jain; Taylor's Cat. vol. iii. p. 418). The narrative of the feud between Bauddhas and Jainas should probably be understood as between the latter and Saivas (*ib.* p. 423).

[4] Dr. Gundert, Mad. Journ. vol. xiii. p. 140.

[5] I add a figure of a piece of bronze found in Tondamandalam, near Puṛal, the ancient capital, as a specimen of Kurumbar skill. It appears to have been the end or crown of a standard or state halberd, and is, in the words of an expert, "a very fine object, quite a work of art." The specimen is unique, measures 15½ inches long, and weighs 5 lbs. 6½ ozs.

## (b) PALLAVAS

The other State before indicated as the possible source from which the coins in question may have issued, was the Pallava principality of Kánchí.

It is somewhat strange that a people which played no inconsiderable part in mediæval Dakhan history should have remained comparatively unknown until very recently. No mention of them is found in the vernacular historical legends, such as they are; they do not appear in the native lists of former dynasties, nor, unless for the incidental occurrence of one or two mythical names, was Colonel Mackenzie acquainted with them.[1] It was only in 1840 that they were brought into notice by the discovery of a copper deed,[2] in what has been called the Cave-character, recording the grant of a village by a Rája of Vengipúram, a place the site of which was unknown.

The plates having been found in the Kolár (Koláir) lake or swamp, inquiry was made in that part of the Musulipatam district, which led to the discovery of a group of villages near Ellore afterwards identified as the place in question. In the course of the quest three more copper *śásanams* of a similar description were met with, from which were obtained the names of certain princes ruling over the kingdom of Vengi, inhabited by a people of Pallava race. Further particulars derived from them were communicated to the "Indian Antiquary" by Professor Eggeling in 1874, giving an imperfect genealogical list, of what Dr. Burnell has designated "a yet nameless dynasty."[3] Additional light was thrown on their history by the inscriptions of the earlier Chalukya princes, so many of which have been edited by Mr. Fleet, and by two more of their own copper grants published by Mr. Foulkes,[4] all in the same periodical.

From these sources we learn that the Pallavas were a numerous and powerful race, inhabiting the middle and south Dakhan from a remote period. Little is known about them until towards the fourth century, about which time some Gujarát Rájputs of the Chalukya family began to seek a settlement further South. Their first attempts were met by a determined and at first a successful resistance on the part of the Pallavas. Eventually they effected a lodgement to the south of the Krishṇa, under Pulikesi I.

In the beginning of the seventh century, not content with their success on the table-land, the Chalukya leaders pushed their advances towards the East, and descended the ghâts under Kubja Vishṇu Vardhana, the younger brother of Pulikesi. There he overran the maritime

[1] Wilson, Catalogue Mackenzie's Coll. vol. i. pp. lviii, cxix-cxxiv. Calcutta, 1828.

[2] Mad. Journ. vol. xi. p. 302.

[3] Madras Journal Lit. and Science, vol. xi. p. 302 (1840); also vol. xiii. pp. 46, 52-53 (1844); Ind. Ant. vol. iii. p. 152 (1874); Burnell, South Ind. Palæog. pp. 13, 135, second edition (1878). All the copper plates have been edited by Mr. Fleet in the Ind. Ant. vol. v. pp. 50, 151, 176, and vol. ix. p. 101.

[4] Mad. Journ. vol. iv. N.S. pp. 78-9 (1858); Ind. Ant. vol. v. p. 73 (1876); vol. vi. pp. 78, 87; vol. vii. p. 219 (1878), and also vol. viii. pp. 167, 273.

province of Vengi, the seat of another Pallava principality, and established himself at Rájamahendri, which became the capital of the Eastern Chalukya dynasty. A third Pallava State then comes prominently into notice,[1] with which the Chalukya princes maintained a long desultory contest. Notwithstanding the reverses they sustained, the Pallavas did not despair, but struggled bravely against their Northern assailants, with occasional gleams of success, for nearly two centuries longer. They appear at times to have obtained assistance from their Southern neighbours, the "Choḷa and Paṇḍya kings." It is unfortunate that the little we hear of this chronic warfare is derived from one side only, and the Chalukyas, as might be expected, are not slow to magnify their own prowess.

The son, grandson, great-grandson, and great-great-grandson of Pulikesi, all claim to have defeated the Pallavas (the last three several times), and more than once to have taken the city of Kánchipúra itself.[2] But these vaunts are accompanied by the somewhat qualifying admissions of the conqueror that the vanquished Pallava king had been the destruction and humiliation of his family, and on a later occasion by the boast of Vinayaditya that he had conquered the enemy of his race.

This struggle was maintained from the seventh to the middle of the eighth century. After the middle of the eighth century we hear little of the Chalukyas, whose power suffered a collapse for more than a century and a half, the cause of which seems to have likewise affected the Pallavas. But after the Chalukya restoration to power, in an inscription of Kali Vikramá (Vikramáditya VI.), in the fifth year of his reign (1080 A.D.), we are told that "he overcame Balavarája of the Palavanya or Pala race, and sat on his throne."[3]

The paucity of contemporary records does not supply a full genealogical list of the dynasty, but from such as we have we obtain two or three lists, without, however, means of connecting several dynasties which may possibly have been altogether distinct. For, although all claim to belong to the Bháradwája *gôtra*, the earliest are said to be of the Sálankáyana race (or *kula*), while the latest are styled of the Panchum tribe. No date has been mentioned, nor has any coin been found with the epigraph of a name.

The best plan for the purpose of this paper will be to give the names as they stand in each grant, according to the following table:—

[1] When and how the Pallavas became possessed of Kánchí is unknown. It was primarily a constituent part of the ancient Kurumba-bhúmi, and is entered by F. W. Ellis in his "List of the kóṭṭams and nádus of Tondamandalam, as the second náḍu of the third or Icaṭṭu kóṭṭam" (Mirasí Right, Appendix, p. vi). Relics of the Jaina creed profe ssed by the Kurumbars can yet be seen. A large slab, with a life-size figure of a Jaina Tirthankara, might be seen lying by the wayside in the suburbs some years ago, and may be there still.

The allusion to the expulsion of the ancient inhabitants described as "persons offensive to religion," in the grant of an agraharam made by Nandi Varmá Pallavamalla, in honour of his successful general Udayachandra, seems to throw some light on the question. The removal of the obnoxious villagers had probably reference to their Jaina faith, and seems to show that the Pallavas had wrested this portion of the country from the Kurumbars before the conquest of Tondamandalam by the Choḷas.

Both the Choḷas and the Pallavas were worshippers of Siva, and it has been a noted shrine of the orthodox Hindus ever since.

[2] Indian Antiquary, vol. v. p. 73,; vol. vi. pp. 78, 87; vol. vii. p. 5; vol. viii. pp. 27, 28, 245; vol. ix. p. 129; vol. x. pp. 37, 134, 163, 165.

[3] J.R.A.S. vol. iv. p. 15.

The oldest of these is a *prákṛit* or *páli* composition, the characters of which are ancient and very rude.

| OLDEST GRANT. | SÁLANKÁYANA *kula*. | THREE GRANTS. | MR. FOULKES' GRANT. |
|---|---|---|---|
| Ind. Ant. vol. ix. p. 101, and vol. v. p. 175. | Ind. Ant. vol. v. p. 175. | Ind. Ant. vol. v. pp. 50–3. | Ind. Ant. vol. viii. p. 280. |
| I.[1] | II. | IV. V. VI. | VII. |
| Mahárája Vijaya Skanda Varmá. | Chanda Varmá.[2] | Skanda Varmá I. | Siṁha Vishṇu. |
| Vijaya Bhudda Varmá, the Yuvarája or Heir Apparent. | Vijaya Nandi Varmá. | Víra Varmá. | Mahendra Varmá I. |
| | | Skanda Varmá II. | Narasiṁha Varmá I. |
| | Ind. Ant. vol. ix. pp. 102-3. | | Mahendra Varmá II. |
| | | Sunha Varmá I. — Vishṇugópa Varmá. | Paraméśvara Varmá I. |
| | III. | Skanda Varmá III. — Sunha Varmá II. | Narasiṁha Varmá II. |
| | Attivarma, of the family of King Kandara. | Nandi Varmá.[3] | Paraméśvara Varmá II. |
| | | | Nandi Varmá, or Nandi Pota Varma.[4] |
| | | | Pallavamalla Nandi V. |

In the next we have the names of Chanda Varmá and Vijaya Nandi Varmá, who are stated to belong to the Sálankáyana *kula*. A third ancient grant is made by Rája Atti Varmá, of the family of King Kandara, of whom we have no mention in any other place, unless he is the person referred to in the inscribed rock at Ṣálván-kupam.[5]

The third column contains the genealogy as given in three copper deeds in vol. v. pp. 50–3, 154, and in vol. viii. p. 167.

The last has been edited by Mr. Foulkes, and differs only in containing two additional names.

The same gentleman has published a seventh[6] set of plates, the genealogy in which differs considerably from the previous documents, but purports to be issued likewise by the ruler of Káṇchí for the same lands, and while continuing to use the same *gótra*, states the family to belong to the Panchum race (or *kula*). The occasion of the grant was a reward

[1] This is the first of the Bháradvája *gótra*.

[2] Is he the same as Vijaya Varmá, the son of Skanda Varmá, in the grant at vol. viii. p. 171?

[3] The last two names in this grant are taken from Mr. Foulkes' grant in Ind. Ant. vol. viii. p. 167.

[4] Nandi Pota Vamá, about 740 A.D. (Ind. Ant. vol. viii. p. 24; and Fleet, p. 29). This gives us a date for the Kánchí king. Nandi P. V. was killed about 740 A.D., he was the eighth of the line; reckoning 15 years for a reign brings Siṁha Vishṇu to the beginning of the seventh century.

[5] Ind. Ant. vol. ix. pp. 102-3.

[6] The instrument itself relates to the same gift as the preceding, both having been subsequently confirmed by Rajendra Chola. Of the authenticity of this last we offer no observation, remembering how prone grantees have been found to strengthen their titles by spurious exhibits, and the possession of this Agraharam having been confirmed by the sovereign of a different dynasty.

to his dependent Udayachandra for his success in putting down certain feuds among Pallava chieftains fomented by foreign allies. Both deeds were confirmed by Ko Parakésari Varmá, the Tamil title of Rajendra Choḷa, who flourished in the eleventh century (1064–1113). Knowing as we do the date of Rajendra Choḷa, we are able to form some idea of the period during which the Kánchí Pallavas retained their power. Probably we shall not be far wrong in assuming that they were able to hold their own during the period of Raṭṭa ascendency in Kuntala, which lasted from the middle of the eighth till towards the latter part of the tenth century.

The preceding notices all refer to their more eastern localities, but they are found also to have flourished in the west of Kuntala. As early as the fifth century, Mrigésavarmá, a king of the Kadamba family, of Banawási, is called a "fire of destruction"[1] for the Pallavas, and his son Ravi Varmá is said to have driven[2] the Pallavas out of Palásiká, the modern Halsi. In a Maisur copper-plate grant of the eighth century, a Chéra or Koṇgu king makes a grant, at the request of a certain Rája of Nirgund,[3] for the endowment of a Jaina temple erected by his wife, the grand-daughter of the Pallavâdhirâjâ.

These examples, and more might be cited, show the extensive range of the Pallava race. Tradition carries them still further back, and ascribes to a king, called Trilóchana Pallava,[4] the frustration of the first attempts of the Chalukyas upon the Dakhan.

It is probable that the term Pallavas is the *prákṛit* form of Pahlava,[5] a name applied to a race of people often mentioned by Sanscrit writers, and generally rendered Persian, apparently on no very exact grounds.

What then has become of them? The Raṭṭas, the other predominating people of Kuntala, survive in the Mahásaṭṭas; but we can only suppose that the Pallavas, who held an equally important place among the early inhabitants of Kuntala, have been absorbed in the existing population. Some traces of them are still to be found in Drávida, where three castes claim to be connected with them, Veḷḷáḷas, Kaḷḷars, and Paḷḷis.

To the west of Tranquebar, near Mayavaram, a village called Pallavarayanpetta still exists.

Pallavarája is one of the thirty-two *gótras* of the true pure Tamil-speaking Veḷḷáḷas of Madura, Tanjore, and Arcot. It is borne by the Choḷa Veḷḷáḷas inhabiting the valley of the Kávari in Tanjore, who lay claim to the first rank. According to a Tamil MS., called the Dina Charai, they found their claim on the assertion that all their women are of royal

1 Ind. Ant. vol. vi. p. 25.

2 *Idem.* p. 30.

3 Ind. Ant. vol. ii. p. 161. Which of the Pallava chiefs is here alluded to is not clear, nor can we say precisely where Nirgund is. Mr. Rice mentions a principality of that name in Maisur, but there is a remarkable hill fort of the same name in the middle of the extensive plain east of Dhárwár, a noted stronghold, the owner of which joined in the rebellion of 1858, and murdered the Assistant Collector, Mr. Manson, for which he was executed and his estate confiscated.

4 Mad. Journ. xx. N.S. iv. 78, and Ind. Ant. vii. 243.

5 See Böhtlingk and Roth's Lexicon, *sub voce.* In the Vis. Pur. at p. 187 of vol. ii. *note* 6, Pahlava and Pallava are given as variants of Pahnavas, which occurs among a list of Northern tribes (p. 184, *note* 3). See, too, vol. iii. pp. 294–5, *note* 1, where they are associated not only with Northern races, but *inter alia* with Drávidas, Kirátas and others. See also Manu x. 44; Muir's Sanscrit Texts, vol. i. pp. 97, 177, 180 (1858), and vol. ii. p. 268 (1860). The officer of Rudra Dáma, in the Girnár inscription, who repaired the tank, was a Pahlava.

race, and all their men of sacerdotal descent. This saying has a curious bearing on the peculiar Turanian law of descent still prevailing in South Malabar, where property is conveyed through the mother, of noble or Nair descent, to her female offspring born to a Nambúrí Bráhman, as is even the case with the royal family now reigning in Travancore.

This practice lends colour to the supposed connection of the Veḷḷáḷas with the predatory classes mentioned in the proverb, and it is further remarkable that they hold the first place among the Tamil agriculturists, just as the Reḍḍis do among the Telugus, and the Kunbis among the martial Mahrattas, all pointing to a Turanian origin. Ellis, it may further be observed, refers to three sections of the Veḷḷáḷas, one of which he designated Tulava Vellálas, who had been brought from the Malabar Coast to repeople Tondainádu. The remaining two castes are, it is true,[1] held in inferior estimation, but there is a common proverb[2] to the effect that "The Kaḷḷan, Maravan, and the honourable Agumbadyan, rising slowly, slowly became by degrees the Veḷḷáḷan." Such an assumption would doubtless be scouted by the aristocratic Veḷḷáḷan of the present day, but it derives some support from the foregoing proverb

The above explanation, however, will only account for a very small portion of a people so widely distributed as the Pallavas. With regard to the Kaḷḷar, it is remarkable that the Tondiman Rája Bahádur of Pudukotah, the faithful ally of the British in the Carnatic Wars, and chief of the Kaḷḷar tribe, has the title of Pallava Rája, which he probably inherits from one of the many Pallava chieftains, of whom we have seen frequent mention, and one of whom may have been seated at the not distant site of Mamalipurum,[3] now known as the Seven Pagodas; in the immediate vicinity of which I found the ruined Portico of Sálvánkupam,[4] at which is the remarkable incised rock, with the name of Attirana Chanda Pallava[5] in two different characters, who may have been the Atirana of the Copper Deed[6] before mentioned.

Can it be that this tribe, which belongs to what have been called the predatory classes, represents a portion of the Pallavas? Their bold, indomitable, and martial habits accord well with the characteristics of that ancient people.

Until very recent times they exercised a formidable control over the peaceable inhabitants of the Carnatic, from whom they exacted payments for forbearance, under the name of *ménkával* fees, in return for which they placed one of their followers as guardian or

[1] Kallar and Maravar are the well-known predatory classes; the former being the synonym for thief. The Agumbadyan, though now a low class of artizans, are probably descended from the ancient landholders of the country; the word Agum being the Tamil for land, equivalent to Northern Bhoomia. According to native grammarians the root of the word signifies also, "the mind, the soul, the will," and the occupation of the caste is said to be "attendance in kings' palaces (see Rottler's Dict. p. 3) and pagodas." According to Mr. Nelson they are intimately connected with the Maravars and intermarry with them (Nelson's Madura, pp. 42-3). They are thus enumerated among the Royal guards of the Rája in the Kéraḷa Ullpatti.

[2] This is said to be quoted on public occasions in asserting caste privileges, or in disputes for the possession of land, as follows:—

கள்ளன் மறவன் கலந்த வகமுடையா
ன் மெள்ள மெள்ள வந்துவெள்ளாழன்

Kaḷḷan, Maravan, kalánda Agamudayan,
Meḷḷa meḷḷa, Vandu, Veḷḷáḷan.

[3] See Mr. Rice's paper on Mahávali dynasty in Ind. Ant. vol. x. p. 36.

[4] Sálvámkupam, literally, "Hamlet of the Saluvas" — name of a once numerous people, some of whom are still to be found in the South-East Ghâts (Vish. Pur. vol. ii. *note* 1, pp. 133-4).

[5] Mad. Journ. vol. xiii. 46, 50.

[6] Ind. Ant. vol. ix. p. 103.

watchman in each village, who was responsible for the protection of the place from plunder and robbery. Such a systematic levy of black-mail being incompatible with the existence of a settled Government, ceased on the establishment of the British power, when many of the chief *Ménkávalgárs* received pensions, payable during good behaviour. If this surmise be admissible, the similar tribes of the Maravars, Bedars, Ramuses, etc., may be included in the same category; all of whom still flourish under their petty chiefs, commonly called Polygars (*palaiyakárar*), some of whom were even petty princes, as the Rájas of Bednúr and Shorapur. The only other way in which they could be absorbed was by the rise of the Lingáyat sect in the twelfth century, which, levelling all distinctions of caste, united the bulk of the Ṣúdras of the Dakhan under the new faith, including even Pariahs, many of whom were principal supporters of Basava, the founder of the new creed. One of its leading sections bears the name of the Panchum Lingáyats, which, it will be remembered, is the name of the family (or *kula*) of the Kánchí Rája, the author of the seventh Pallava grant.

But the Lingáyats are noted for their peaceable and industrious habits.

Having considered these two powers, to which it was thought the coins might be assigned, the arguments in favour of the authorship of the Kurumbars rest, as before stated, on their higher knowledge of art, and the limited extent bordering their country in which the coins are found.

On the other hand, the seals of the two Pallava grants, published by Mr. Foulkes have the figure of a bull, the one recumbent, the other standing, like that borne on the coins, but no similar specimens have been found commensurate with the wide extent of the Pallava rule in other parts of the country. As stated above, many of the coins exhibit short and imperfect legends in the Cave character, which occasionally passes into a form peculiar to the south. None of these, which have been carefully analysed by Mr. Thomas, afford certain results.[1] One name only has a somewhat recognizable form resembling Kadamba, but the Kadambas never, as far as we krow, obtained a footing on the east coast.

[1] [Sir W. Elliot's facsimile legends, Nos. 82, 84, of plate x. vol. iii. of the Madras Journal, read clearly, in Devanágarí, कटम्प टक *Kaṭampa ṭaka*. There might be a doubt about the value of the second letter and its counterpart, the penultimate, which might subside into *ḍa* or *da*; but the compound म्प *mp* is indubitable. The coins themselves will be given, in autotype, in the subjoined Plates.—E.T.]

## PART II. SECTION i.

# ORIGIN OF METRICAL SYSTEM.

LONG before the appearance of the die-coinage introduced by the Andhras, the necessity felt in all early stages of civilized society for avoiding the inconvenience of barter led to the adoption in India, as elsewhere, of a metallic currency, the earliest known form of which is represented by the irregularly-shaped pieces of silver, stamped with rude symbols, which are found in all parts of the country.[1] At what time and by what people they were first employed is unknown, but they probably came into use gradually. They were regarded as prehistoric by the older Indian writers, and may therefore be presumed to have been found in circulation when the Aryans entered Hindustan.

They have been discovered among the ashes of the men who constructed the primitive[2] tombs known as the *páṇḍu kuḷis* (or kistvaens) of the South, and unearthed from the ruins of buried cities in excavating the head-waters of the Ganges Canal.[3]

In all parts, from the Sundarbans[4] of the Ganges to the frontiers of Affghánistán, they turn up from time to time.[5] Yet they have no recognized name in any of the Vernacular Dialects. They appear, however, to have been known to the earlier Sanscrit writers under the designation of *puṛána*, a term which itself signifies ancient.

Of this use of the word, Burnouf has collected many examples,[6] and the same term occurs in Manu,[7] who wrote some centuries B.C., where he defines the relative proportions of the several weights then in common use.[8]

[1] H. H. Wilson, Cat. Mackenzie, Coll. vol. ii. p. ccxxvii; Prinsep's Essays, vol. i. pp. 209-16; Journ. As. Soc. Bombay, vol. x. pp. xxi-iv.

[2] Letter from Mr. Garrow to Col. Mackenzie (1806) with coins of Augustus. Mad. Journ. of Lit. and Science, vol. xix. (N.S. p. 227).

[3] J.A.S.B, vol. iii. p. 44.

[4] Prinsep's Essays, vol. i. p. 210.

[5] E. C. Bayley, Num. Chron. 1873, p. 209; Cunningham, Arch. Rep. vol. vi. p. 198; also Bhilsa Tope—"throughout all India, from Nepál to Ceylon, and from Kandahár to the Delta of the Ganges"—p. 354.

[6] Introduction à l'Histoire de Buddhisme.

[7] Institutes, Haughton's Translation, chap. viii. *sloc.* 131-136.

[8] In the absence of a recognized native name for these pieces, numismatists have had recourse to sundry arbitrary terms, as *ch'hapas*, punch-coins, *saldkis*, dominos, not always very appropriate. The word *sildling*, adapted from the Anglo-Saxon *sld*=old, represents exactly the Sanscrit puráṇa, and might be adopted with advantage. A similar term occurs in that "pure well of English undefiled," the Authorized Version of the Bible, where the value of the Jewish vine is expressed in *silverlings*, which were probably uncoined pieces of silver of given value like those under consideration (Isaiah vii. 23).

It is by a preliminary investigation of the ancient weights of Southern India, that an insight may possibly be obtained into the origin of this very primitive description of money. Such an enquiry, owing to the changes arising from lapse of time, and still more from the wars and revolutions that have swept over the plains of India during thirty centuries, is not unattended with difficulty. But extant traces of the past may still be detected in places less exposed to external interference.

Such a favoured region is found in the South-Western extremity of the peninsula, where the province of Malabar, lying between the mountain barrier of the Sahyádri range, with the primeval forests that clothe their base on one side, and the sea on the other, occupies a narrow strip, which has been signally exempt from foreign rule.[1] Hence the people retain much of their aboriginal character, and have preserved institutions brought by the earlier colonists from their Northern home. These, abhorrent as some of them are to the great body of Hindus, still flourish unchanged, although no longer observed in their original seats. Such is the practice of polyandry,[2] with all the peculiar rights of succession and inheritance dependent on it, as well as the social observances to which it has given rise.

Not the less, however, has the silent influence of Aryan science and philosophy leavened the literature of the province, and hence the popular treatises on Arithmetic in other Southern dialects have been framed on the model of the "*Lilávati,*" the standard Sanscrit work on Mathematics; so that, while many of the weights retain their old vernacular names, they are arranged according to the formulæ and rules of Bháskarácharya (the author of the *Lilávati*), who is supposed to have lived about the eleventh or twelfth century A.D.[3] It cannot be supposed that native works on such a subject did not exist at an earlier period, but they have gradually become obsolete and fallen into disuse. We have been fortunate enough to meet with one such treatise, through the kindness of Dr. Gundert, who quotes it among the authorities used in his admirable Malayálim Dictionary.[4] It is entitled *Kaṇakku Sáram*, and is written in good Malayálim, with less than the usual infusion of Sanscrit; but the work has become extremely rare, and a perfect copy is seldom if ever to be met with. It differs materially from the *Gaṇita Sástram*, the popular treatise now in use, which contains a greater number of Sanscrit words and phrases, and is framed on a more scientific system, the rules being more exact, especially those relating to fractions and the higher numbers. Of the six books or chapters into which the *Kaṇakku Sáram* is divided, the

[1] Malabaria, quæ regio natura sua et situ ab hostili impetu et expugnatione semper tuta mansi., atque etiam, raro, nisi nunquam, uni imperio fuit subjecta, ob merces et fructus suos undecunque terraram expetitos ab exteris semper maxime frequentabatur, etc. Gildemeister, Scrip. Arab. p. 48 (1838).

[2] "A trait once widely prevalent in the Himálayas and Thibet. Even the civilized tribe of the Newars, who, by the way, have a recorded tradition uniting them with the Malabar Nairs—a name, they say, identical with Náyar or Newar, who were once polyandrists."—B. H. Hodgson's Essays, vol. ii. pp. 129-30, and 144; F. H. Ellis, Law Book of the Hindus, in Trans. Mad. Lit. Soc. 1827. 4to. p. 17; and Essay on Malayálim, Ind. Ant. vol. vii. p. 286.

[3] Weber, Hist. of Indian Literature.

[4] Of the author Nílakaṇṭha, or of his era, nothing is known, but his work must be of high antiquity. It consists of six books or chapters; the 1st treats of fractions, literally "what is below one"; second, of decimals, "what is above one"; third, *Idangali*, measures of capacity; fourth, *Kódam*, measures of length; fifth, *Kaḷanju*, of weights; sixth, *Kálam* of time.

fifth has the title of *kaḻanju*, and treats of the weights of gems, gold, pearls, etc., for ascertaining which it gives the following formula:—

| | | |
|---|---|---|
| A *nen-mani* (or grain of rice in the husk) is | = | 1 *visa túkkam*. |
| 4 *nel* (grains of rice in the husk) .......... | = | 1 *kunri* (or *rati*). |
| 2 *kunri* (or *ratis*) .......................... | = | 1 *mañjáḍi*. |
| 2 *mañjáḍi* .......................... | = | 1 *paṇatúkkam*. |
| 10 *paṇatúkkam* .......................... | = | 1 *kaḻanju*.[1] |

All of these, except the *paṇa*, are the names of well-known vegetable products, the first being the staple cereal of the province. The other three are the seeds of common trees or shrubs.

3. Deferring the further consideration of the second—the *kunri* or *rati*—for the present, the third, or *mañjáḍi*, claims the first notice, as being the earliest used as a measure of weight. It is the seed of the *Adenanthera pavonina*, a tree common in most parts of India and the Eastern Archipelago.

The native name has been derived from *mañju* "a boat," and *áḍi* "with which one plays," and is said to have been taken from the form of the beans; and from their common use by children as playthings, and by the women who string them for necklaces. They are of a bright scarlet colour, hard, durable, and tolerably uniform in size and weight. When ground, the meal is sometimes used as an article of food.[2]

As a weight it is specially employed by goldsmiths and jewellers, and is commonly reckoned about 4 grains, but in reality it is somewhat more, or about 4½ to 5 grains.[3]

Of a convenient size, and at all times available, they would offer a ready expedient for determining the required proportion of a piece of silver bullion; and taken in conjunction with the first series of simple numbers, the result would be 10×4½ or 5×10=45 or 50 grains, a weight which was afterwards identified with the *kaḻanju*. This appears to have been the first and simplest application of the *mañjáḍi*; but as business increased, when a more artificial system was introduced, and tables were framed, from imaginary infinitesimal units, regulated by sub-multiples of two, its value was reduced by one-half, and its place usurped by its representative the copper *pana*. From the modern tables of weights it has disap-

[1] In Ceylon the *kalanda* is said by Mr. Rhys Davids to be equal to the weight of 24 *mara* seeds, or equivalent to 86 grains and a fraction (Part i. p. 12).

[2] Rheede's Hortus Malabaricus, vol. vi. tab. xiv. p. 26. Semina vero haud ingrati saporis, preter quod a plebeis sive cocta, sive comminuta in farinam comedantur, magnum præstant usum auri fabris et gemmariis, quippe ob æqualitatem, granorum vice in ponderandis mercibus adhibentur, singula namque *masjilina*, liceat mihi ob linguæ ignorantiam ita exprimere, quatuor pendet grana, quibus utuntur auri fabri; qui quoque ex contusis hisce seminibus aquâ madefactis una cum borace gluten ad elegantiora cum nova, tum diffracta vasa conglutinanda conficiunt.

[3] A parcel of 50 *manjáḍi* beans, taken at random and weighed in delicate scales, gave an average of 4·13 grains. Three different parcels of ten each, selected by the eye for superior size, averaged 5·02 grains, and 5·03, a single bean taken as the heaviest of several by the scales = 5·306 grains.

peared altogether, and is now relegated to the exclusive use of the diamond merchant.[1] But its influence may still be detected in the gradations of the metric scale, the unit of which, as stated above, is the *visam* or sixteenth of anything, and hence is the foundation of the one-sixteenth ($\frac{1}{16}$) or *ána* system of computation prevalent throughout India to this day.[2]

4. The *kalanju* of 10 *manjádis*, which we take to be the other normal unit of weight, is the name of a prickly climbing species of Cæsalpinia,[3] very generally distributed both in the East and West Indies. The smooth, grey, hard, nearly spherical seeds are to the native youth what marbles are to our schoolboys. Strung like beads to form necklaces, they are worn as amulets by the women in Egypt, and floated by the waves to the west coast of Scotland, they are known as Molucca beans.[4] Besides serving for weights, they are valued highly for their therapeutic qualities.[5] The few seeds I possess seem to have been gathered before they were quite ripe. They weigh about 40 grs. each, one only reached 42 grs. Mature seeds would probably average from 45 to 50 grs.

It was on these two seminal units, the *manjádi* and *kalanju*, that the normal metrical system of the South appears to have been founded, smaller and more delicate weights not being required in the rude transactions of earlier times.

2. The *kunri* or *rati*, as has been observed, did not come into use till a later period.

Rhede, who carefully notes the economic uses of every plant included in the Hortus Malabaricus, does not allude to its employment as a weight at all.

It was probably introduced into the tables from the Lilávati as part of the more advanced system derived from Sanscrit treatises. It is unnecessary to dilate further in this place on its use as a measure of weight, because the subject has been so fully discussed by the

[1] These artificial *manjádi* weights are now carefully made of brass, in the form of an octahedron, the primitive crystal of the diamond. A set of them given to me by a Márwári friend, one of the first dealers in diamonds and precious stones in the South, yielded the following results when tested by a set of delicate scales and weights:

| | | Grs. | | |
|---|---|---|---|---|
| The 20 *manjádi* octahedron weighed | | 93· 2, | average | 4·660. |
| „ 10 | „ „ | 46· 4 | „ | 4·640. |
| „ 5 | „ „ | 23·35 | „ | 4·670. |
| „ 2 | „ „ | 9· 4 | „ | 4·7. |
| „ 1 | „ „ | 4· 8 | | — |

The fractional weights were flat triangular pieces; that for ½=2·4 grains; for ¼=1·2 grains.

The intermediate pieces have been lost.

[2] Thus, taking the *visam* or $\frac{1}{16}$ represented by a grain of paddy or rice-corn, at $\frac{3}{10}$ of a grain, we obtain—

| | | | |
|---|---|---|---|
| *manjádi* $\frac{1}{16}$ | = ·3 grains; | or, according to Gen. Cun. | 0·3585. |
| „ $\frac{1}{8}$ | = ·6 „ | „ „ | ·717. |
| „ $\frac{1}{4}$ | =1·2 „ | „ „ | 1·434. |
| „ $\frac{1}{2}$ | =2·4 „ | „ „ | 2·868. |
| „ 1 whole | =4·8 „ | „ „ | 5·736. |
| „ 10 | =48 „ | „ „ | 57·360. |
| | | | =1 *kalanju* or 1 *pagoda*. |

General Cunningham assigns a somewhat higher value to the rice-corn, which he makes =0·3585, which appears somewhat high, but the result obtained from the lower estimate, both for the *manjádi* and *kalanju* would allow for a somewhat higher average (Num. Chron. 1873, p. 197).

[3] Guilandina bonduc *vel* Bonducella, L.—Rheede, Hort. Mal. vol. ii. p. 35, pl. 22; Roxb. Fl. Ind. vol. ii. p. 357; As. Res. vol. xi. p. 159, 8vo. ed.

[4] Drury's Useful Plants, p. 244.

[5] The seeds are intensely bitter, and are prescribed with advantage in intermittent fevers. The native name is difficult to transliterate, owing to the peculiar cerebral letter in the second syllable. It may be written *kalanju*, or *karanju*, or *kazhanju*, according to the system followed by Gundert, Caldwell, or Ellis. Rheede has *kalutti* and *caretti* for the Malayálim names, and Gundert *kalanju* for the weight ("=2 silver or 10 gold fanams"), and *kalacci* or *kalacchi* for the tree, as also *kalanju-kol* = scales for weighing (Dict. 227). In Rottler's Tamil Dictionary the same word occurs under several forms, all derived from the root *kalal*=a weight (Dict. vol. i. p. 52). In Wilson's Glossary we find *karancha*, a weight=to 10 fanams (p. 263). In Bengali the name given to it is *nata*, whence the Hindi *nata-caranja*, and in Dakhini *gachaka*, probably from the Telugu *ga-chakdi*.

Editor in his introductory Essay;[1] but it affords an opportunity for stating some of the results obtained in some recent trials, which help to throw light on the original use of the *manjaḍi*.[2]

The inconvenience attending the use of seeds, no two of which were exactly equal, in process of time led to the substitution of metal equivalents, the first of which we may assume to have been the copper representative of the *manjáḍi*, under the name of *paṇa*. This, under the more familiar name of *fanam*, became the foundation of the Southern monetary system, and continued current down to modern times.

The origin of the word *paṇa* is not very clear. It is claimed as an original root both by Sanscrit and Dravidian grammarians, but in all likelihood it pertains more justly to the latter.[3] From what has been stated, it may be inferred that the metric system is based on the *manjáḍi* or *paṇa*, and its multiple the *kalanju*. It may therefore be reasonably inferred that the *eldling* or *purána* is simply a silver *kaḷanju*.

In all the countries with which we are best acquainted, the metal first used for monetary purposes was silver;[4] to which India (except in the case of the Andhras) forms no exception.

The proportion of bullion to be given as a medium of exchange was adjusted by weight.[5]

In course of time, to obviate constant recourse to the scales, the use of uniform pieces,

---

[1] Int. Num. Or., Ancient Indian Weights, pp. 10-13, 68-70; and Mr. Rhys Davids' article on Ceylon Coins in vol. i. p. 4, note 2.

[2] (*a*) One hundred seeds, taken at random—

| | Weight in Grains. | Average. |
|---|---|---|
| from a large parcel which had been in England for several years, carefully weighed in delicate scales, gave ..... ..... | 135· 9 | 1·3590 |
| (*b*) A parcel of (50), excluding the above ..... | 69· 2 | 1·384 |
| (*c*) „ (50) „ „ ..... | 67· 7 | 1·354 |
| Average hundred ..... | 136· 4 | 1·364 |
| (*d*) Ten selected by the eye for their larger size | 17· 30 | 1 ·730 |
| (*e*) Ten others „ „ „ | 17· 05 | 1 ·705 |
| (*f*) Ten others „ „ „ | 16· 50 | 1 ·650 |
| | 50· 85 | 1 ·695 |
| (*g*) The two heaviest in these three parcels *d*, *e*, *f* ..... ..... ..... ..... ..... ..... | 1·875<br>1·855 | |
| | 3·730 | 1 ·865 |

which may therefore be taken as the maximum.

At the present day the employment of the actual seeds for the purposes of weighing is confined to village goldsmiths and petty jewellers. Merchants dealing in precious stones employ standard artificial weights, neatly made of brass, like our apothecary and troy weights. They are called emerald weights, but are used for all kinds of gems, except the diamond. A set of these was likewise given to me by my Márwári friend. They retain the name of *ratis*, and consist of square pieces, the value of each being indicated by impressed dots. These tested by delicate scales yield the following results: proving the gem-*rati* to be double the normal seed-*rati*, and to be in fact an approximation to the *manjáḍi*.

| | Grs. | |
|---|---|---|
| The 50 *rati* piece with 5 dots = | 168·05 | or 3·361 |
| „ 20 „ 2 „ = | 67·40 | „ 3·370 |
| „ 10 „ 1 „ = | 33·75 | „ 3·375 |

Smaller pieces:

| | | |
|---|---|---|
| The 5 *rati* piece with 5 dots = | 16·80 | or 3·360 |
| „ 3 „ 3 „ = | 10·05 | „ 3·350 |
| „ 1 „ 1 „ = | 3·04 | „ 3·04 |

Smallest or fractional pieces:

| | |
|---|---|
| The ½ *rati* piece with 1 dot = | 1·65 |
| „ ¼ „ 2 „ = | ·82 |
| „ 1/16 „ | ·21 |

From the above it is seen that the *rati* of the dealer in precious stones is in reality a double *rati*, and differs from the *manjáḍi* of the diamond merchant in being about a grain lighter. From this it follows that the normal weight of the seminal *rati*, accepted by the people of the country best qualified to determine, is 1·68 gr. = to half the weight of the emerald *rati*.

[3] Dr. Caldwell includes *paṇa* in his list of words, "the common property of Sanscrit and the Dravidian tongues." The root *paṇ* = to make, to work, to produce, is undoubtedly a primitive Dravidian element, but *paṇam* = money, is deduced by Dravidian grammarians from the Sanscrit root *paṇ* = to do business, a subtle distinction. Comparative Grammar, p. 483.

[4] Gen. xxiii. 16; xliii. 21; Ex. xxx. 13; Job xxviii. 15; Jer. xxxii. 9, 10; Zech. xi. 12; Madden's Jewish Coinage, 1-8; Wilkinson's Ancient Egyptians, (First Series) vol. ii. p. 10, woodcut 78; vol. iii. pp. 237-9; Smith's Dictionary, Greek and Roman Antiq., *s.v.* Argentum Nummus. pp. 132, 808.

[5] The old Tamil name for scales is *vellickol*, hence the proverb, "veḷunáyi sandai ku ponal veḷḷikólal adi pattu varum," *i.e.* "the hungry (lit. empty) dog going to market will be beaten with the steelyard" (Rotth. Dict. vol. iv. p. 233). The veḷḷikol, however, was not a steelyard, probably so called, but scales dependent from a beam. The Egyptians, according to Wilkinson, were equally ignorant of the steelyard, using scales for weighing bullion, as represented in the paintings. Manners and Customs, vol. ii. p. 10 woodcut 78, and vol. iii. p. 222, woodcut 374.

certified by an authoritative mark, suggested itself. Such pieces taken from a bar or plate, trimmed and cut to the required standard weight, received the impress of a symbol, guaranteeing their acceptance. The oldest Indian examples of the *eldling* are of all shapes, oblong, angular, square, or nearly round, with punch-marks on one or both sides, the older signs often worn away by attrition; in almost all cases the earlier ones partially or wholly effaced by others subsequently super-impressed upon them.[1]

Other specimens, which are more circular, and thicker, with sharper attestations, are probably of later date. All weigh about 50 grains troy.

A parcel of forty-three very old-looking pieces, part of a large find in Nagar (Nugger or Bednore), a province of Maisur, weighed 2025·5 grains, giving an average of 47·1, but the heaviest was 50 grains, the lightest only 37·75.

Seventy-eight others, from all parts of the South, and of every variety of shape, weighed collectively 3720 grains, with an average of 47·69. Of these, twenty of the broadest, thinnest, most diversely-shaped, averaged 46·7; while five, quite round, thicker, and of smaller diameter, gave 49·5, and the heaviest specimen that could be found reached 54 grains.[2] The symbols on all these were much the same; exhibiting figures of the elephant, ox, dog,—of fish,—of foliage,—of the sun, stars, and of sundry nondescript types. Prinsep specifies and figures some from Colonel Stacy's collection, such as the human figure, the *swastika, chaitya*, tree and rail, which have not been detected in our specimens. No inscriptions or written characters have been met with, nor any mark to identify them with known dynasties or royal races.

The elephant was the type of the Chéra or Kongu dynasties, but it was also adopted by the Andhras, and on one of Col. Stacy's pieces it is represented with up-raised trunk (figure 26), as in the lead coins of that race.[3] The seal on the copper *sásana* of Vishṇu Gópa Varmá, one of the Pallava kings, has some resemblance to the dog-stamp, but much reliance cannot be placed on such rough workmanship.[4] A find in the Konkan displayed pieces, on which an animal, perhaps a lion, had been impressed in the centre, and above all the others. This was the ensign of the Kadamba kings; its introduction in this form may be connected with the rise of their power; it appears also to mark the transition period, like the more perfect gold coins of the same dynasty to be next noticed.

By whatever name the *eldling* was known in other parts of India, it probably in the

[1] Frontispiece plate, figures 4, 5; Mad. Journ. Lit. and Science, vol. iii. N.S. pp. 227-9. and plates vii, viii, fig. 13, 18, 22, 27, 25; Prinsep's Essays, Thomas's ed. pp. 74, 209-211.

[2] This inequality of weight is easily accounted for by the rude scales and careless manipulation witnessed at the present day, without invalidating the general average of 50 grains.

The tiny scales of the village *sónar* or modern goldsmith, with his array of red (*raktika*) and black (*krishnala*) *rati* seeds, flanked by a few copper *sháhi paisa*, show small promise of accuracy; while the wicker scales of the banya or bazaar dealer, dangling from the ends of a rod suspended by a rope from a beam in the roof, with sets of rude brass and iron weights, supplemented by water-rolled pebbles, inspire his customers with so little confidence that they often insist on shifting the article on to the other scale before closing the bargain (Jervis, Weights and Measures of Konkani, pp. 39-42; Heyne, Tracts on India, pp. 77 and 81). When Mr. Broun applied to the Travancore Dewan for specimens of the weights in use to enable him to frame a standard, the reply was that "the same nominal measure being different at different times in the same place, and continually changing," the Sirkar could not furnish him with examples.

[3] Prinsep's Essays, vol. i. p. 210, plate xx. fig. 25, 26, 27, 29; Mad. Journ. vol. iii. N.S. plates vii. viii. figs. 8, 11, 16, 18, 20, 21, 26. Prinsep thought he detected alphabetic characters on a single specimen (30), but it scarcely belongs to the series, and resembles a partly die-struck coin, p. 210.

[4] Indian Ant. vol. v. p. 50.

South may have taken the designation of the weight *kalanju*, which it represented; for the base of the outer wall of the great temples at Tanjore, Kánchí (Conjeveram) and other places is covered with inscriptions, recording gifts of land, cows, money for lamps, meat-offerings and other pious purposes; the latter generally specified simply in *kalanjus*, or in *kalanjus* of gold, which may refer either to weights or coins, but more probably the former.

Before quitting the subject of the silver *eldlings*, it may be asked where the supply of that metal was obtained to meet the circulation of so great an extent of country. Gold, iron, and copper were found in many parts of India, but no silver so far as I know. The only lead and silver mines specified by Medlicott and Blanford are those of Burma.[1]

The silver for the *eldlings* must therefore have been imported from abroad, and there is reason to believe that a considerable commerce was carried on by the people of the Coromandel and Malabar coasts with foreign countries at a very early period. Traces of the trading stations on the East coast have already been adverted to (p. 35).

Several coins, assigned provisionally to the Kurumbars (?) or Pallavas (?), bear the figure of a ship, and some of the symbols on the *eldlings* themselves seem intended for marine animals.

The oldest specimens of gold punch coins hitherto discovered (and to be noticed hereafter) were found imbedded in the sand of the island of Ramree, the result of some ancient wreck. The evil reputation of the pirates on the west coast, according to Ptolemy, testifies to the skill and daring of a sea-faring race.[2] Nor does the record of their naval habits rest on foreign evidence alone. A curious poem,[3] discovered by Dr. Gundert, "certainly the oldest specimen of Malayálim composition he had seen," turns entirely on maritime adventure, and "is replete with details of trade and ship-building."

*Kalanjus* continue to be mentioned in inscriptions till the seventh and eighth centuries, and perhaps later, but probably as weights only, for the pagoda[4] is only known in Tamil under the name of *varágan*, which, as derived from the Chalukya dynasty, could not have been established before the fifth or sixth century. Before that they were probably *suvarnas* or *nishkas*.[5] Later the Canarese name seems to have been *gadhyánam*, a term likewise used in Telugu.

[1] Manual of the Geology of India, part ii. p. 708. Small quantities have also been met with, associated with lead, in Kulu and Mánbhum, and at Deogurh in the Sontal parganá. Piddington found some copper ore containing silver in the proportion of 50 oz. to the ton, but the ore was very irregularly disseminated, and in very small quantities through the rock, and some samples contained no silver at all (Blanford, Journ. Soc. of Arts, 11th April, 1873, p. 387).

[2] Βαναδυσαι [Pal.] Βανανδσαι
Τῶν δὲ ἀνδρῶν ΠΕΙΡΑΤΩΝ μεσόγαιοι
Πόλεις αἴδε.
Geogr. viii. i. p. 205 [or MS. 174].

And on a previous page (MS. 168) he had noted between the gulf of Broach (Barygaza) and Limyrice = the coast about Honáwar (Balipatna) and Mangalore (Mandagara) as being that of the Pirates τῶν ἀνδρῶν Πειρατῶν.

[3] Mad. Journ. vol. xiii. part ii. p. 11.

[4] The word pagoda is of European origin, and unknown to every native dialect. It has superseded all the other designations in English, and is applied equally to the gold coins and a Hindu temple. At Madras, where it originated, it is supposed to be of Portuguese origin, and to have arisen from the first navigators and merchants being told in their reply to their enquiry what was the building with the lofty *góparam*, or Propylon, or whose was the image on the coin, that they were those of the goddess (Bagavadi), the tutelary deity of Madras. Such at least is the tradition (Moor's Hindu Pantheon).

Every township has its Grama Devi or Village Goddess, being some form of Kali or Durgi, to whom an annual bloody sacrifice is offered. At Madras she is worshipped under the designation of Yagamma or Yagáttál (Journ. Eth. Soc. vol. i. N.S. 1868, p. 96).

[5] See Burnouf *ante*, and Kadamba grant of Vishnuchitta, Bom. Journ. vol. ix. p. 286, vol x. p. liii.

The sway of that powerful family was at first confined to the Karnataka and Northern districts of the Dakhan, and some time must be allowed for its extension to its southern limits under the later sovereigns, after the restoration of the dynasty in the tenth century in the person of Tailapa Déva.

As in the Malabar, so in Tinnevelly, these primitive weights still retain their hold on popular usage,[1] and the names may also be traced in old Tamil writings, although the things themselves have now been displaced by more modern innovations.[2]

In the Telugu treatises the normal system disappears altogether, and gives place to the *ána* or sixteenth mode of reckoning. And the same may be said of Canarese.

[1] The following is a tabular statement of the Tinnevelly weights:

| | |
|---|---|
| 4 *pakka pagaru* (seed of Phaseolus radiatus, L.) | = 1 *kunri, mittu*, or *rati.* |
| 2 *kunri* | = 1 *manjáḍi.* |
| 20 *manjáḍi* | = 1 *kaḷanju.* |

This makes the *kaḷanju* between 60 and 70 grains.

[2] An old Tamil palm-leaf MS. has the following table:—

| | |
|---|---|
| 2 *pilaru* (or split peas = half *ratis*) | 1 *kunri* or *rati.* |
| 2 *kunri* | 1 *manjáḍi.* |
| 5 *manjáḍi* | 1 *kal.* |
| 4 *kal* | 1 *kaḷanju.* |
| 2 *kaḷanju* | 1 *kásu.* |
| 4 *kásu* | 1 *pala* (vulgo *poliam*). |
| 100 *palas* | 1 *tulá* or *tulám.* |

Here the *manjáḍi* retains its original form of five or six grains, but the quarter *kaḷanju* is raised to 25 or 30 grains; and, consequently, the *kaḷanju* itself is raised to 100 or 120 grains. The *kásu*, which is the smallest of copper coins, and serves the same purpose as the Bengal *kauṛi* (*cowrie*), here becomes a measure of large capacity as a constituent of the *pala* and the *tulám* still in use for heavy articles, and equivalent to nine or ten pounds. The above formula seems to be an attempt to reconcile the primitive standard of the South with that introduced from the North, as it is found in the Amara, thus:—

| | |
|---|---|
| 5 *gunja* | = 1 *adya-macha.* |
| 16 *adya-m* | = 1 *karsha* or *aksha.* |
| 4 *karsha* | = 1 *pala.* |
| 100 *pala* | = 1 *tula.* |

## PART II. SECTION ii.

# EARLIEST INDIGENOUS COINS.

### (*a*) GOLD. (*b*) SILVER. (*c*) COPPER.

### (*a*) GOLD COINAGE.

IT is a somewhat difficult matter to trace the origin and progress of the gold coinage, and its relation to the metrical system just described, owing to the rarer occurrence of examples; for although hoards are often discovered, they at once find their way into the crucible to be converted into ornaments.

The oldest specimens I have seen are spherules quite plain and smooth, save for a single very minute punch-mark too small to be identified—by the impress of which they have been slightly flattened.[1] They weigh about 52 grains; evidently derived from the *kalanju*, their original name being *pon*, which simply means gold in Tamil, becoming *hon* in Canarese, and the origin of the Mahommedan *hún*. They appear to have been in use for a great length of time, and probably constituted a considerable portion of the vast treasures transported to Delhi by the armies of Ala-ud-din and his successor in the fourteenth century.[2] These, besides what were recoined in the royal mint, were distributed with such a lavish hand among the nobles and followers of the Court, as related by their own historians, that examples were still to be seen at Delhi long afterwards. For Tavernier, who visited India in the seventeenth century, has figured this[3] and some other early types of Southern coins, under the title of *pagods*, "which are current in the territories of the king of

[1] The name given to these coins in the old Canarese dialect is *gulige*, meaning a globule or little ball, whence the form *gu* with a numeral is employed in old accounts as the sign for expressing pagodas.

Several of these were procured in the Sunda pargana in 1828, and were sent to Dhárwar, whence some were transmitted to the Madras Central Museum.

[2] Briggs's Ferishta, vol. i. pp. 374-5; Elphinstone's India, vol. ii. p. 47; Zia-ud-din Barni in Sir H. Elliot's Historians of India, vol. iii. pp. 203-4; Thomas's Pathán Kings of Dehli, pp. 144, 157, 169, etc.

[3] See plate, fig. 1, edition of 1680. London, published by Edward Everard.

Golconda, the king of Visapour, the great Rája of Carnatica, the Rája of Velouche (Vellore?) and at the Diamond mines."[1]

A unique specimen of this primitive form, with a deep punch-mark, but of a later date, because stamped on the reverse, was obtained by Mr. Gibbs from the Western provinces of the Bombay Presidency during the famine of 1878–9. It weighs 65½ grains, and has a single punch-mark of large size, covering nearly the whole of the obverse, giving it a cup shape. The punch-mark represents an animal, apparently a monkey (Hanuman?). The convex reverse has also an animal in relief, which seems to be a lion looking backwards (?)—the symbol of the Kadamba dynasty.

Of an earlier date than this, and apparently the second step in advance from the primitive form, is that of very thin almost circular pieces, nearly an inch and a half in diameter, weighing about 66 grains, noticed on p. 51. The very few examples that have been met with, all of which were found beyond the limits of India proper, are recognized by the figure of a boar in the centre, as well as by the legend, to belong to the Chalukya dynasty. The letters, which are few in number, are large and rude, have been impressed singly round the periphery by means of separate punches, and correspond with characters of the fifth or sixth century.

These were succeeded by flat, round, thicker pieces of superior workmanship, which have received the name of *padma-ṭankas*, from having what is called a lotus in the centre, a favourite emblem amongst the Jainas, who were then the most influential sect in the South, and were distinguished for their skill in elegant art. The central figure is surrounded by punch-marks, generally four in number, struck afterwards. This form, as will be noticed, was imitated by the Chalukyas in supersession of the thin plates above described, the figure of the boar being substituted for that of the lotus. All these were of heavier weight than the *pon* or *hún*, which, under the name of *varaha* or pagoda, afterwards became general. The normal weight, as in the oldest pieces first mentioned, was from fifty to fifty-two grains, whereas these are from fifty-five to sixty-five, or even seventy grains. The reason of this I am unable to explain, unless it be owing to the ruder and less accurate processes of earlier times. The gradual improvement exhibited in the later pieces is probably due, as above observed, to the skill of the Jaiṇas.

The small number of specimens extant do not allow us to trace the steps by which the use of the punch gradually gave way to the exclusive employment of a matrix or die. The die at first was of the simplest form, and appears to have been a reversal of the superior action of the punch by striking the gold plate upon the single symbol placed below, and then adding the additional symbols by the old-fashioned process around the central device,

[1] To this he appends representations of eight of these *pagods*, four of half *pagods*, "and five of smaller pieces of gold called *fanos* (fanams), which are of different value. There are some, whereof six go to a crown; others from ten to fifteen, and some are very base metal. This is the money that passes all along the coast of Coromandel, from Cape Comorin as far as Bengala, and they have very little other than that, besides the *pecha* (paisa) of copper and the shells (cowries) which pass for small money."—Tavernier's Six Voyages, part ii. pp. 4-5.

leaving the other side or reverse plain, except where it shows the grain of the anvil or basis on which it rested. The force of the blows has in many instances given the upper side a concave surface. This, although accidental, appears to have led to the use of cup-shaped dies at a later period, as exhibited in the *Ráma-ṭanka* medals.

The superior execution of the *padma-ṭankas* ruled for a considerable time with many variations, until the adoption of the double die led to the final and complete disuse of the punch.

The earliest design on the reverses is that of an elegant floral or arabesque pattern, whence perhaps the name of *p'húlihún* = flowery pagoda, was derived. It appears to have been very generally adopted, for it is found on the Chalukya, Chéra, etc., coins. The oldest example of this device with which I am acquainted is that figured in the Madras Journal, vol. iii. N.S. pl. viii. fig. 30, from an example in the Madras Government Museum.

The object on the obverse appears to be a seat or couch on which is a small globular body, and above it three others placed horizontally, the whole within what may be termed some kind of edifice.

The origin and authorship of this coin we have been quite unable to discover, but it and some others of a similar character call for fuller notice.

The first to be mentioned, because probably the oldest, the reverse being plain, are the silver coins found at Sultánpúr, near Wai, in the Sátárá district, which Dr. Codrington has so well described in the Bombay Journal, vol. xii. p. 400. Out of the fifty-two pieces found, fifty bore on the obverse a curious device, which may be described as three bosses or elevations, the biggest surrounded by a larger circle from which pass double lines connecting it with the smaller ones. They are of three sizes, which appear to be whole, half and quarter pieces, weighing respectively from 99 to 105 grains, from 45 to 58 grains, and from 21 to 23 grains, in which we may trace an approximation to the double, single, and half *kaḷanju*.

Another of the symbols is likened by Dr. Codrington to one of the figures selected from punch coins published by Mr. Thomas in Prinsep's Essays,[1] and repeated by him in this work (Vol. I. p. 62).

The image on the third is indistinct, but has been compared to a quatrefoil. The latter weigh from 108 to 110 grains respectively.

In 1877 three gold pieces were found near Ahmadnagar, which appear to belong to this same class. Dr. Codrington was good enough to send me casts taken from wax impressions of them, but they are too indistinct for accurate description. Traces of figures similar to those on the silver pieces can be detected. The reverse is plain, showing only the marks of the base on which it was struck. Their weight was not stated.

Next we have a coin which is only known from the figure (2) published by Tavernier in his list of *pagods* before mentioned. It is a gold piece with four transverse horizontal bars, two and two, in contact with each other, and between the pairs a considerable space in which

[1] Vol. i. p. 211.

are four smaller vertical bars curved at the bottom, and some indistinct marks above and below the transverse bars. The reverse is not figured, and may therefore be considered to have been plain.

The last to be noticed is a gold pagoda, with perfect obverse and reverse, specimens of which, still extant, are by no means very rare, and may probably be of later date. It has been figured by Marsden.[1] The curious figure on the obverse may be described as a heart-shaped symbol, from the upper lobes of which two pointed lines rise (often truncated by the margin), and between them a dot; sometimes to the left of these are another dot and a curved line. The figure on the reverse resembles a flat dish in which are two rounded forms like balls. Marsden calls the piece a "Hún of Vijayapura, Bijapúr, or Visiapoor," and states, "it exhibits emblems, the signification of which is entirely unknown." This he seems to have done on the authority of Tavernier, who represents it in the plate before mentioned, as figs. 3 and 4, under the designation of the "king of Vasapoor's *pagod*." He hesitates, however, rightly, to assign it to the Adil-Sháhi dynasty, which dates only from the end of the fifteenth century (1489 A.D.), and conjectures it to have been struck by some Hindu prince who reigned there at an earlier period; a suggestion which received support from the appearance of Persian characters on two specimens in Dr. Codrington's possession, one of which has the letter *(ain)* ع, and the other *(sin)* س impressed on the heart-shaped symbol. I conjecture, therefore, that Yussuf Adil Sháh, finding these pieces in circulation in a part of his newly-conquered territory, continued their issue, with the simple addition of the letters above mentioned, until he could establish an orthodox Moslem type of his own.

The Madras Museum possesses one with apparently some indistinct marks in the centre, and there is a similar one in the British Museum.

It is not easy to discover what is typified by the remarkable symbols on the several pieces just mentioned. They form a class altogether singular, and differing from any other description of money I have ever seen, but as they undoubtedly belong to the Western side of India, where the Jaina faith has so long flourished, they may not improbably be connected with that remarkable people.

Gradually the gold coinage came to exhibit more definite devices, with the legends in Háḷa-kannaḍa (or old Canarese) and Nágari characters. The coins themselves became narrower and thicker, but without any alteration of the standard weight, and this continued to be the prevailing character down to 1833—thus more nearly corresponding with the original simple type first mentioned. They were also coined in halves under various names, as *pratápa, máda,* etc., having the same device as the full-sized piece. This is likewise repeated on the gold fanams of $\frac{1}{10}$ pagoda of the same period. Other fanams of later date have a character of their own, and cannot be assigned to any particular mint. They are of the standard weight of five grains, and will be more fully noticed in connection with the Dravidian coinage.

[1] Edition of 1823, pl. xlviii. fig mlxxvii.

## (b) SILVER.

From the extensive range of the silver *eldling* as the prevailing medium of exchange, we might naturally look for an abundant succession of silver die-coins when the former passed out of use. But such is not the case. Antique die-struck pieces of silver are rarely to be met with. The absence of all mention of silver money is conspicuous in the narratives of the plunder of the Dakhan. Ferishta indeed expressly states that in A.D. 1310-11, Malik Káfur, on his return to Delhi, presented his sovereign Alá-ud-din with the plunder he had collected,[1] including 96,000 maunds of gold alone,[2] adding: "It is remarkable that silver is not mentioned as having been taken during this expedition to the Carnatic, and there is reason to conclude that silver was not used as a coin in that country at all in those days. No person wore bracelets, chains, or rings of any other metal than gold; while all the plate in the houses of the great and in the temples was of beaten gold." In fact, the currency continued to be mainly of gold until the Mahommedans came to be permanently established in the South. Their preference for the Rupee led to the introduction of a silver currency, without, however, displacing the gold previously in circulation.

Nevertheless, it would be rash to conclude from such negative evidence that silver was never coined in early times, for I have five specimens of Choḷa coins, of the Rája Rája type, struck in the eleventh century, which, as well as the pieces found at Sultánpúr (page 55), are undoubtedly silver. It is also probable that the Kurumbar coins, alluded to at page 36, although I was unable to test them, are of the same metal. Early Choḷa coins have also been found of impure silver, and the Mackenzie Catalogue contains a few items, the description of which is too vague to allow of their identification.[3] In addition to these instances, I may add that I possess a few small pieces, found in Malabar, which appear to be those mentioned by Dr. Dellon as current in the seventeenth century, on the Western coast under the name of *târé*. Thus, describing the daily wages of labour, he says: "To every one of these natives you pay 8 *târés* per diem, which amounts to half a fanam. The fanam is a small piece of gold worth 16 *târés*, and the *târé* is a small silver coin worth a halfpenny. Each native has not above 4 *târés* a day when he keeps guard in a house" (*i.e.* home or domestic labour), "but when he travels he has double pay." My five specimens weigh 1 grain and $\frac{7}{10}$ (1·7) each, and have an erect formed figure on the

[1] Briggs's Ferishta, vol. i. p. 375.

[2] The diversity of the maund throughout India makes it difficult to estimate the value of this plunder; but taking the maund at 30, a medium between the Dakhani maund of 25 lbs. and the Ain-Akbari of 34½ lbs., we get the sum of £2,880,000, or nearly three millions sterling; and this, be it remembered, was the spoil of only one of the four expeditions conducted by the same leader.

[3] "No. 11. Ancient Hindu coins; two found, with the figure of Hanumán." (? Ceylon Rája Rája type, see above). "No. 12. Ditto, ditto; three found—uncertain." "No. 13. Nrisimha Deva's half rupees; four found." "No. 20. Old half rupees Bijanagar; four found; Rajaram's stamp in the Nágari character." Cat. vol. ii. App. pp. ccxxvii–viii.

obverse, with the anomalous symbol of the gold fanams, to be noticed afterwards, on the reverse. They have long ceased to be current, and the very name *târé* is scarcely known to the present inhabitants, but may be recognized in the Malayálim and Canarese *tàram* "A copper (??) coin half a pice, or $\frac{1}{3}$ fanam" (Gundt. Mal. Dict. p. 445).[1] Another small silver piece, received with the former, weighs 2 grains and $\frac{7}{10}$, and has a rude standing figure on the obverse, with the hexagonal diagram, formed by two triangles interlaced, on the reverse. I have also seen a few others in the Dakhan, of no great antiquity, weighing from three to three and a half grains.

The substitution of silver money increased with the intercourse of European traders. Single and double fanams were coined at the different factories of the English, French, and Danish settlements; the French distinguished by the *fleur-de-lis*, and afterwards by a cock; the Danish by the cipher of King Christian. The same practice was adopted in Maisur after the fall of Seringapatam, and the Travancore State issues large numbers of silver *chakrams* to the present day.

In the English factory at Madras, in 1811, a silver pagoda coin was introduced about the size of a half-crown, having a rude representation of a goddess on the obverse, and the gate-tower, or *góparam* of a temple, on the reverse, with the monetary designation of the piece in English, Tamil, and Telugu characters.[2] At the same time the authorities issued a large supply of single and double, half and quarter rupees, and silver fanams of an improved form, in pieces of one, two, three, four, five fanams; the silver rupee of 180 grains being convertible at the rate of 350 Rs. for 100 pagodas of account.

## (*c*) COPPER.

The oldest form of a copper coin that has been observed is a round ingot or spherule, somewhat depressed by the impact of an obscure sign above, with an occasional mark of the anvil or support beneath. The few before me weigh from 16 to 59 and 61 grains, and still smaller pieces from grs. $2\frac{8}{10}$ to 4, and $7\frac{8}{10}$, having apparently some reference to the double silver *târé*, mentioned in the preceding section.[3] Flat, square, and perfectly smooth pieces also occur, two weighing $10\frac{1}{2}$ and $34\frac{1}{2}$ grains. These examples[4] are too limited in number to authorize us to pronounce on the relation they bear either to the unit of the system, or to each other; but they appear to exhibit an affinity to the *kaḷanju*.

[1] Madras Journal, vol. xvii. o.s. vol. I. N.S. 1856, pp. 49-50. Claude Dellon, a French physician, sailed from Port Louis in 1668, and after visiting the islands of Bourbon, Madagascar, and the Malabar coast, settled at Daman, where he practised several years. He published the Relation d'un Voyage fait aux Indes Orientales in 1685, and a translation in English, by T. Crull, appeared in London in 1698.

[2] See note 4, p. 51 *ante*.

[3] I regret that I did not pay more attention to these when I had the opportunity, for though not uncommon they are unattractive to the collector.

[4] See also pl. vii. vol. iii. N.S. Madras Journal, figs. 2, 3, and $5\frac{1}{2}$.

The smallest denomination of the copper currency was the *kásu*, a true Dravidian word, common to the Tamil, Telugu, Canarese, and Malayálim dialects. Although latterly it was used chiefly as a term of account, it has also the general significance of money, wealth, and likewise of coin, as *pon-kásu* = gold coin, *vella-kásu* = silver coin, *semba-* (or red) *kásu* = copper coin; and as well as of particular coins, *e.g. anai-* (or elephant) *kásu* applied to the pagoda of the Chéra or Koṅgu dynasty, stamped with the figure of that animal; *sanar-kásu*, the Venetian ducat or Sequin,[1] the large numbers of which on the Malabar coast testify to the once extensive commerce with Italy by way of the Red Sea. The *kásu* represents the cowrie of Bengal, eighty of which make a *paṇ*, and is in fact a copper cowrie; eighty *kás* in like manner constituting a *fanam* or *paṇa*.[2] The *kásu* has been identified by Mr. Ellis with the Sanscrit *karsha*, and they are probably both derived from the same original source; for according to the law-books "a *karsha* or eighty *ratis* (*raktikas*) of copper is called a *paṇa* or *karsha paṇa*." Afterwards it came to be restricted to "a weight of gold or silver equal to 180 grains troy,"[3] and it is in this view it is to be understood in the Andhra inscriptions at Nasik. But that it was originally a small copper coin seems clear, for in the legend of Purna quoted by Burnouf in the Introduction to the History of Indian Buddhism, Vásavadattá, in the passage where the silver money is quoted in *puránas* and the gold in *suvarnas*, speaks of the *karsha paṇa* as of the smallest value; as if, according to Burnouf, it responded to the expression, "Not worth a sou," just as the people at Madras now use the exactly similar saying, "Not worth a *cash*."

In addition to the changes in value attaching to the same names from lapse of time, local usage, and their reference as measures of weight to different metals, they also come to have a special meaning as terms of account. Until the introduction of the Rupee Standard, the public accounts of the Madras Presidency were kept in pagodas. According to this formula,

80 cash ........ = 1 fanam. 42 fanams ....... = 1 star pagoda.

This was founded on the exchange and relative value of the cash to the silver fanam, according to which twelve and a half of the latter went to the rupee, and three and a half rupees to the pagoda, giving forty-two fanams for the latter. The rate of exchange for the pagoda varied in the bazaar from thirty-five to forty-five silver fanams, native merchants adopting the larger or forty-five fanams in their accounts. Besides the earlier silver coinage of the East India Company before 1837, they issued copper pieces made at Birmingham so early as the end of

[1] So called from the figure of the Doge standing in front of St. Mark's Cross, in which the native imagination sees the *sánár* or toddy drawer preparing to climb the palmyra-tree.

[2] The use of the cowrie shell as a medium of exchange has long been known in Bengal; but that they were well known in Drávidadésam is proved by their Tamil name *kavaḍi* (cowrie?). The popular name of cowrie has been derived from the Persian word *khurmohra* خرموهر = ass or mule trappings, which are ornamented with strings of these shells. But more probably it is the Tamil name *kuwri* for the *abrus* or *rati* plant, and is still used in Tinnevelly, as we see it in the table of weights in Note 1, p. 52. The Arabic name, according to Ibn Batuta, who makes mention of their export from the Maldives, is *wudá* (وَدَع) whence they still come to Bengal in large quantities, as proved by their fluctuating value in the market. In 1740 a rupee in Bengal exchanged for 2,400 cowries; in 1840 for 6,500.—Sir H. Elliot, Supp. Glossary, p. 373, and Vol. I. Part. I. I.N.O. p. 38.

[3] Colebrooke's Misc. Essays, vol. i. p. 530; Wilson's Sans. Dict. p. 199; Wilson's Glossary, pp. 265, 267, and pp. 17–22, etc.; Vol. I. Part I. of the I.N.O.

last century in the form of one, five, ten, and twenty cash pieces, the last weighing 180 grains.[1] Assuming the *karsha paṇa* of copper to be of the same weight as that stated above, on the authority of the lexicographers, to be that of the *karsha paṇa* of gold and silver or 180 grains, this twenty-cash piece would be its representative in copper.[2]

The conclusion to be drawn from the foregoing details is that the monetary system of India (certainly of Southern India) is of indigenous origin, based on rude seminal and testaceous exponents of value, which have been exchanged for definite metallic counters, regulated by artificial skill, their original names, and the numerous changes and variations in which exhibit a certain affinity, indicative of their common origin; but, as Prinsep observes, "the discrepancies are common throughout, the simple word being all that can be identified as having survived the changes of system."

An endless variety of copper coins, not falling under any of the foregoing descriptions, is now met with in the bazaar throughout India, derived from the right assumed by every petty Rája and local chief to issue money in his own territory.

The process of deterioration had made some progress in the latter days of the Vijayanagar dynasty, for when Cæsar Frederick visited Vijayanagar in the year 1567, only three years after the battle of Talikota, he states that in travelling thence to Ankola on his way back to Goa during the Monsoon he suffered much inconvenience from the rain. "Another trouble we had," he continues, "as bad as this was, that when as wee came into a new governour's countrey, as every day we did, although they were all tributary to the King of Bezeneger, yet every one of them stamped a several coin of copper, so that the money that we tooke this day would not serve the next."[3]

The country, therefore, was probably in a state of anarchy and confusion; but the change of the ruling power was too recent to give rise to such a diversity of coins, if the practice had not existed for some time previously. Such a licence in a country which has undergone so many revolutions, and where the same inducement to convert the copper to other purposes, as in the case of the precious metals, does not exist, has left an endless variety of form and device belonging to every age. These it would answer no useful purpose to attempt to classify and describe.

One denomination, however, has a larger circulation, especially in the Dakhan, under the name of *sháhi paisa*. They are irregular-shaped pieces of thick copper, weighing about 150 grains.[4] The oldest are quite smooth, but others, more recent, coined in the Nizam's dominions, have occasionally two or three Persian letters. In the English territory they are being gradually superseded by the issues of the regular mint, but are still numerous in the Haidarábád country.

[1] Prinsep's Useful Tables, p. 52.

[2] In the shell or cowrie system the *kahan* of sixteen *paṇa* seems to have taken the place of the *karshapaṇa*; at least Wilson in the Glossary gives it as a synonym of *kahan*. *Vide* Gloss. p. 248.

[3] Hakluyt Col., vol. ii. pp. 348–9.

[4] One hundred pieces selected gave an average of 141·54 grs.; several being above 150 grs., some less. This is less than the weight of the piece which Heyne (Tracts on India, p. 81) recommends, under the name of the Masulipatam *dub*, to be adopted as the standard weight of the country. He states it weighs nearly half an ounce.

## PART II. SECTION iii.

## SOUTH-WESTERN COINS.

ANCIENTLY the country at the extreme south of the peninsula (Dravida-désam) consisted of three leading States, one or other of which was generally in the ascendant. Such appears to have been the position of Chéra before the fourth century, when its dominions comprehended that part of the Western coast known as Kéraḷa, extending from Cape Comorin as far north as Gokernam and Goa; but which in its more restricted sense was confined to the country south of the Chandragiri river, including the districts of Kuva and Mushika, which, although often enumerated among the seven Konkans, are likewise also considered as subordinate divisions of Kéraḷa proper. See Introduction, p. 3, *note* 2.

The population of this tract is very remarkable, consisting chiefly of two leading classes: A tribe of Turanian[1] warriors,—the Nairs, who are supposed to have been led from the Himálayas by the mythical hero Parasu Ráma, and a tribe of Bráhmans called Nambúrís, exercising a predominating influence, which they still retain, over the fortunes of the province.

Parasu Ráma is represented among the *Avatárs* of Vishnu as a warrior wielding a battle-axe, still recognizable perhaps in the national weapon, or *Ayudha-katti*, of his followers the Nairs. Under the Chéra kings Kéraḷa was administered by Viceroys, who had the title of Perumál, or Cherumán Perumál, deputed from the capital of Dalavanpura (Talkáḍ), and residing at Kodungalúr or Cranganore. According to the *Kérala Ulpatti* they appear to have been assisted, and perhaps in some degree controlled, by the Nambúrís and the Nair chieftains, until the middle or end of the fourth century. About this time the two latter threw off the Chera yoke, proclaimed their independence, and partitioned the territory amongst themselves. This, according to F. W. Ellis, whose accuracy is well known, occurred in the year 389 A.D., and being supported by other testimony, may be accepted with confidence.[2]

None of these obtained a paramount influence, nor have we any account of a dynastic power that has left its mark on the early coinage of the province. But according to the

[1] Mr. Brian Hodgson informs me that the Néwars of Nepál retain the tradition of the Náyars, or more commonly Nairs, having migrated from their clan, and claim kindred with them.

[2] Trans. Mad. Lit. Soc. p. 19, 4to., London, 1818.

somewhat vague traditions which have reached us, the country seems to have been divided into seventeen or eighteen districts (or *nádus*),[1] the heads of which were either Bráhmans, as the Nambúrí chief of Tirumánachéri, or Kshatriyas, of whom five, called *Kóvil* Rájas (from *kóvil* a palace), are noted, viz.

1. Ayarúr (or Ayatúr kóvil) ... } Near Chéttuva.
2. Shárkara ... ... ... }
3. Cury or Parappur, near Beypúr. Its prince is called the Veypúr Rája.
4. Padinnattedam (Western Palace). The dynasty of Kodungalur, now Cranganore or Mangáttu.
5. Mádattinkil, also Mádattal (Lower Palace). Probably the dynasty of Karunágapalli. Title now assumed by the Rája of Cochin;

and an inferior class usually called *Sámantas*,[2] of whom eight are specified, viz. Kólattiri, Travancore, Calicut, Valluva, Kurumba, Nedungádu, Ona, and Vimbala.

In course of time all the above-mentioned merged into four independent States, which became the ruling powers in the land, two in the South and two in the North. They were called *Swarúpas*, and the Rájas of three of them were further distinguished as *Sámanta*,[2] a term now restricted to the offspring of a Nair princess and a Nambúrí father.

The first, Vénádu, now Travancore, comprises the two most southerly konkans, Kuva and Mushika, and a part of Kérala proper. It is still an independent kingdom of considerable extent, having been enlarged by conquest in the last century. The other, Perimpadappu, now Cochin, is also independent, but smaller, and is included in Kérala proper. It had been considerably reduced by the encroachment of the Zamorin, when the Portuguese came to its aid and restored its power. The Rája also takes the title of Mádattinkil or Mádattal, which belonged to one of the five Kshatriya chiefs, whom he probably represents.

The rest of Kérala, to its northern boundary the Chandragiri river, was, in the main, divided between the two northern states, Nediyirippu or Neduvirippu, now Calicut, and Koláttiri. The chiefs of the former were distinguished for their military prowess. The first, one of the *Sámantas*, called Sámudri, whence the Portuguese term of Zamorin, is said to have been invested with a sword by the last Chérumán, who at the same time presented a shield to the head of the Arngottu family in Waluvanádu, and enjoined them to live in peace, an injunction the Zamorin soon forgot. This chief is also called Támútiri, with the proud addition of Kunn-ala-kónátiri=Lord of the hills and waves. He built the city of Calicut, and encouraged the resort of Arab merchants, whereby he shared

[1] In local parlance all these eighteen divisions are now comprehended under the general terms of *náds*, *kóvils*, and *edams*.

[2] Gund. Mal. Dict. p. 1052, s.v. *Sámandán*. The word has two meanings; the first applicable to chiefs in general, as where it first occurs above; the second as will be found in the next paragraph, to the issue of a particular marriage.

in the profits of the western commerce, and succeeded in humbling Cochin, until the arrival of the Portuguese diverted the course of trade from Calicut to Goa and Cochin. The other, Kólaṭṭiri, was better known under its Portuguese form of Cólastri, a name sometimes erroneously confounded with the eastern district of Kálastri. The chief of this state is generally termed by Portuguese writers King of Cannanore, from whom they received permission to construct a fort and establish a factory. It was taken by the Dutch 1664 A.D., and later passed into the hands of the British. In the town of Cannanore a merchant's family rose to eminence about three hundred years ago, and acquired considerable power, which they still retain. They bear the title of Ali Rájas, the head of which, according to the female law of inheritance adopted by the sect, is styled the Bibi of Cannanore. All of these probably exercised the right of coining money in their own name, and the Rájas of Travancore and Cochin continue to do so, but I have not met with any early productions of their mints.

The commerce of the West introduced large quantities of Venetian sequins before mentioned as *sánár-kásus.* From their long-continued currency they came to be considered by the people as of native origin, and have still a limited circulation. The remaining portion of Kéraḷa from the Chandragiri river, which is also the boundary of the Tulu and Malayálim dialects northward, was not appropriated by the chiefs who expelled the Perumál, but was probably held by similar petty landholders. Ultimately it fell under the dominion of the Kadamba dynasty.

## PART II. SECTION iv.

# DYNASTIES AND COINS OF KUNTALA.

### 1. KADAMBA DYNASTY.

THE Kadamba kingdom is the earliest of which we have any reliable knowledge in South-western Kuntala. It arose, probably, about the fourth or fifth century in the Forest of Sunda, and comprehended likewise the greater part of Tuluva below the Ghâts, and the North-western portion of Maisur. Its capital was the city of Banawási (in the district of Sunda, Sudha or Soda), which appears to have been a place of importance at a very early period, as it is mentioned by Ptolemy.

The population of Sunda consists mainly of two classes, one a peculiar sect of Bráhmans called Haigas, the other, a class corresponding to the military tribes of the table-land, and known by the name of Haḷepáiks, but now engaged in extracting the *táṛi* (toddy) juice from palm trees. The former, unlike the generality of the twice-born castes, are agriculturists. They dwell apart, engaged in the cultivation of the cardamom, the betel-vine, and areca-palm, in secluded spots called *káns*, rarely invaded by the axe, and into which the rays of the sun with difficulty penetrate. Their account of themselves is that they were brought from a place called Ahi Chhatra[1] (in Rohilkhand) by a prince named Mayúra Varmá. But this statement requires confirmation. It was probably devised by the Haigas themselves to give importance to their sect. They use the Canarese language, and are votaries of Siva, belonging to the *Smárta* sect. Who this Mayúra Varmá was we have no certain knowledge; but the general voice of the country recognizes him as the founder of the Kadamba family. Other traditions declare that the first of the race was born under a kadamba-tree[2] from a divine personage, who, under the names of the three-eyed and four-armed Mayúra or Jayanta of Trilóchana, of Trinetra, which are all epithets of Śiva, is associated with the worship of that deity. But Mayúrá was a Jaina,[3] as were also his successors, and the

[1] Cun. Anc. Geo. p. 360.

[2] Kadamba is the Malayâlim name of a well-known tree—the Nauclea Kadamba. Gundert in his Malayâlim Dictionary (p. 192) gives this signification, but adds two others which are not admissible. Mr. Rice states the name is that of a species of palm from which toddy is extracted. Of this there is no sufficient proof. The word is not in Rheede (Hort. Mal.), who gives the figure of another species, Nauclea Purpurea, with a different native name.

[3] Buchanan's Journeys, vol. iii. p. 213.

of the people long professed the same faith, which still survives in many places. It is easy to imagine that an alien tribe like the Haigas should desire to associate their arrival with a name so honoured as that of the founder of the celebrated dynasty. But it is not likely that he led their migration. The arrival of the Haigas probably took place before his time; this, owing to the early relations of Kéraḷa with Northern India, may well have been the case. We must therefore be content to accept the simple belief that Mayúra was the first of his family, and that he and his successors raised the kingdom to a degree of power and importance that enabled it to oppose the advancing progress of the Chalukyas at a later date, on something like equal terms. This we learn from the Aihoḷe inscription of Kírtivarmá Chalukya I., and of his brother Mangalísa at Bádámi. The first states that that powerful king was the "night of death to the Naḷas, the Mauryas, and the Kadambas," and again, that "straightway the Kadamba-tree, which was the confederacy of the mighty Kadambas, was broken to pieces by him."[1] A further confirmation, Mr. Fleet observes, is found in the inscription at Áḍúr near Hángal,[2] in the heart of the Kadamba territory, by the Chalukya king conferring a grant of land on a Jaina temple near that town.

But the subjugation of their country does not seem to have then been complete, for in the minority which followed Kírttivarmá's death, Mangalísa, who seems to have been equally powerful by sea as by land, is represented as laying siege to Banawási itself, supported by his ships on the western coast, after having worsted a hostile fleet, perhaps the allies of the Kadamba king. These events must have occurred about the middle of the sixth century, after which it is doubtful whether the Kadambas continued to be an independent power; for about this time three minor Kadamba States are found to be existing at Banawási, Goa, and Halsi, exchanging their sovereign title for that of Mahámanḍalésvara.[3] In this subordinate capacity they are mentioned on several occasions acting as faithful and loyal feudatories of the Chalukya kings, and this will account for the somewhat strange assumption by the Halsi branch of the Chalukya style and titles (Mánavyasa-*gótra*, Háríti-*putra*, meditating on the seven mothers of the sage Mahásénа) which can hardly have been accidental, and is more likely to have been a mark of favour and condescension conferred by a superior.

In the eleventh century Káli Vicrama (Vicramáditya VI.), who had been viceroy, under his father, of Banawási, received material assistance from Jayakési, the feudatory Kadamba chief of Goa, to whom he had given his daughter in marriage, in quelling the rebellion of his younger brother. These events indicate the subordinate position into which this

[1] Ind. Ant. vol. viii. p. 243.

[2] Ind. Ant. vol. xi. p. 68.

[3] In the copper deeds translated by Mr. Fleet the grantors have no royal titles, but are styled simply Rája and Mahá Rája, a conventional form in general use. The same may also be observed in another Kadamba *śásana*, that of Gangapemmanáḍi-Bhuvanaikavira-Udayádityadéva (A.D. 1075), at Baḷḷigáve in Maisur (Ind. Ant. vol. iv. p. 208-10), who in the face of his declared fealty to his sovereign Bhuvanaikamalla Chalukya, not only omits the style of a subject (Mahámanḍalésvara), but assumes some of the titles of an independent sovereign; and further, uses the epithet of Bhuvanaikavíra, a near approximation to the title of his royal master. The subordinate title is found in most of the other Kadamba inscriptions at Bankápúr, Hánagal, Baḷḷigáve, etc., all of which refer to Mayúra Varmá as their founder.

great family had declined, although it still continued to flourish long after the loss of its sovereign power.

The palmy days of Kadamba independence were probably during the fifth and sixth centuries, of which unhappily we have no record; but we may assume it to have been a period of prosperity and advance, favourable to that growth in art and civilization, for which the Jainas were conspicuous. It is to this period that I ascribe the origin of the *padma-ṭankas* mentioned in a previous section. We have nothing of an earlier date of which we can speak with any confidence, unless it be a hoard of eldlings found in the Konkan with the figure of a lion (?) superimposed on the earlier punch-marks. The symbols on the best known *padma-ṭankas* are, what is called a lotus (*padma*) in the centre, round which are four punch-marks, two resembling letters supposed to represent the word Śri, opposite each other. On the third a *ṣaṅkha* shell (Turbinella rapa), and opposite it a weapon, frequently a bow, the emblem of the Chéra dynasty. There is nothing to show by what particular ruler they were issued. They can only be assumed to have belonged to a Jaina dynasty, which the Kadambas are known to have been. Other coins of the same type can with more certainty be referred to the Kadambas as being impressed with the figure of a lion looking backwards, which is the undoubted cognizance of the race. Another of their insignia was the monkey god Hanumán,[1] and both these, it will be remembered, are exhibited by Mr. Gibbs' spheroidal piece before mentioned. Next, by an easy transition, we find the *padma* or lotus surrounded by four punch-struck lions, with floral reverse, and then the central symbol superseded by a *swastika*, with the same accompaniments, and that again by a lion with four smaller symbols interposed between the smaller lions, making eight in all, the reverse being plain.[2]

The next step in the Kadamba coinage is the introduction of the die, as exhibited in the discovery of a deposit at Hewli,[3] in which the lion fills the whole obverse with a floral device on the reverse, surrounded by what have been called Telugu letters, but which appear to be ornamental signs (?).[4] After this the Kadamba coins assume a more modern aspect. Gold pieces of the twelfth century with the names of Jayakési and Sivachitta are described but not figured in Bombay Journal, vol. x. Proceedings, pp. xxiv, liii, and the Bombay Asiatic Society is supposed to possess specimens of them. According to inscriptions of the same date they are called *nishkas*,[5] a term not before met with as applied to any specific coin.

Allusion was made in the previous section to the rude coins of the Chalukyas. These examples are very curious and deserve fuller notice. Not only were they not discovered in the Chaluyka territory, but they have not hitherto been found within the limits of India proper. The only authentic instances of their occurrence have been on the shore of

[1] Bomb. Journ. vol. vi. p. lxvi, and vol. ix. p. 230; also Ind. Ant. vol. vi. p. 22, vol. x. pp. 250, 254.
[2] Gleanings, pl. ix. figs. 34, 35, 36; Mad. Jour. iii. N.S.
[3] Bomb. Journ. vol. ii. p. 63, pl. xii.; Gleanings, p. 235, pl. ix. fig. 37.
[4] Most of the preceding are described on the faith of others, a few only being found in my own collection.
[5] See Int. Num. Or. Vol. I. Part I. pp. 13, 15, etc.

the island of Ramri,[1] though others have been brought from the kingdom of Siam. Yet of their origin there can be no question, for they bear the undoubted impress of the Chalukya boar, as well as the name Chalukya, in large, rude Háḷa-kannuḍa characters of the fifth or sixth century, each one impressed by a separate punch. Their occurrence in such distant localities may be explained by the description given of the exploits of Maṇgalíśa Chalukya, during a reign which lasted from A.D. 567–610, among which was the final overthrow of the Kadamba independence. He is also stated to have carried on expeditions by sea,[2] and to have especially achieved the conquest of Revatidvípa, a place Mr. Wathen, following Colonel Wilford, suggests may have been Sumatra. Prof. Wilson is of opinion that it may have been an island off the coast of Malabar. But we know of no such place, and the discovery of the coins on the coast of Aracan and in Siam, is in favour of a more distant locality. If the above surmise is correct, we may suppose them to have been coined by Maṇgalíśa or some one of his predecessors before the siege of Banawási, when the conqueror, struck by the beauty of the *padma-ṭankas*, adopted them as a model, in substitution of the ruder type which formerly prevailed in the Chalukya mint. The exact copy of the Kadamba type in two of the earliest Chalukya coins I possess, in which the figure of a boar is simply substituted for the lotus, while all the other characters are retained, seems to establish the correctness of this explanation. The genealogies of these later Kadamba chiefs are now pretty well known, but of the royal successors of Mayúra Varmá we have no reliable list; that in the inscription on stone at Kargudari, professing to deduce the names from Mayúra Varmá, being evidently imperfect on the face of it, while the Halsi line, as taken from Mr. Fleet's copper plates, does not correspond with any of the others.

[1] J.A.S. Beng. vol. xv. p. 240, pl. iii. fig. 6.

[2] In the abstract of the copper-plate inscription found at Miraj (J.R.A.S. vol. ii. p. 382; vol. v. p. 345) Mr. Wathen observes, "A singular circumstance is mentioned respecting a certain Rája of this dynasty having sent an army in ships across the sea, and having conquered an island called Revantidvípá. A very great intercourse prevailed, from the most ancient times, between the Coromandel coast and the eastern or Malay islands, into which the Hindú religion was introduced, together with the Sanskrit language. It therefore seems very probable that this alludes to some conquest made over Sumatra, Java, or some one of those islands." The fact is further confirmed by the inscription on stone in the Méguṭi temple at Aihoḷe (Ind. Ant. vol. viii. p. 243, and vol. v. pp. 71, 72), translated by Mr. Fleet, where we find the following mention of Maṇgalíśa, "And again, when he wished quickly to capture Révatídvípa, straightway his mighty army—which abounded in splendid banners, and which had beset the ramparts—being reflected in the water of the ocean, was as if it were the army of Varuna that had come at his command."

The following are these genealogical lists such as we have them:—First, that at Kargudari, Journal Royal Asiatic Society, vol. iv. p. 35, also Ind. Ant. vol. x. p. 249.

Mayúra Varmá
|
Krishṇa Varmá
|
Nága Varmá I.
|
Vishṇu Varmá
|
Mriga Varmá
|
Sataya Varmá
|
Vijaya Varmá
|
Jaya Varmá I.
|
Nága Varmá II.
|
S'ánti Varmá
|
Kírtti Varmá
|
Áditya Varmá
|
Chaṭṭaya, Chaṭṭa, Chaṭṭuga
|
Jaya Varmá II. or Jayasiṁha

- Mávuli.
- Taila I. or Tailapa I.
  - Kírtti Varmá II. Kirttedéva I. or Tailana Singa (1068 and 1077 A.D.)
- S'ánti Varmá II. S'ánta or S'ántaya (1088 A.D.)
  - Taila II. or Tailapa II. (1099 and 1150 A.D.)
    - Tailama
      - Kirttedéva II.
      - Kámadéva or Tailamana Aṅkakára (1181 and 1196 A.D.)
- Choki or Joki
- Vikramá or Vikramáṅka

In this inscription Mahámaṇḍalésvara Tailapa II. bears date, thirty-third year of the king=A.D. 1108–9. Now as he is only the sixteenth in the above list from Mayúra Varmá, and allowing fifteen years to each, it carries us back to 860 A.D., which manifestly cannot refer to Mayúra the founder. And even supposing the list to represent generations, which is hardly admissible, the usual calculation of three to a century would take us back to the middle of the sixth century, still leaving us short of the probable era of the first Kadamba.

2. That obtained from the Halsi copper-plates, Ind. Ant. vol. vi. p. 22.

- Kákustha, or Kákustha Varmá.
  - Sánti Varmá, or Sántivara Varmá
    - Mrigésa, Mrigés'vara, Mrigé's'a Varmá, or Mrigésavara Varmá
      - Ravi Varmá.
        - Hari Varmá.
      - Bhánu Varmá.
      - S'ivaratha.
    - (not named)
  - (not named)

The Halsi plates give these names, but have no date. Mrigeśa claims to be residing at Vaijayantí (Banawási), and his son Ravivarmá's allusion to the recovery of Palásiká or Halsi apparently from Chandadanda, the Pallava lord of Kánchí, may assist in fixing his date.

3. That of the Goa branch as deduced by Mr. Fleet from inscriptions on stone. See Journal Bombay Branch Royal Asiatic Society, vol. ix. pp. 229–249, and pp. 262–313; also Bombay Journal Proceedings, vol. x. pp. xxiv–liii.

- Guhalla
  - Shasthadéva I.
    - Chatta, Chattala, Chattaya (1007 A.D.).
      - Jayakesi I. (1052 A.D.)
        - Vijayádityá I.
          - Jayakesi II. (1125 A.D.)
            - Permádi, or Sivachitta (1147-1175 A.D.)
            - Vijayáditya II. or Vishnuchitta (1147 to 1171 A.D.)
              - Jayakesi III. (1175 and 1188 A.D.)
                - Tribhuvanamalla.[1]
                  - Shasthadéva II. (1246-1250 A.D)
                  - A daughter married to Káma déva or Kávana.

[1] These three last names *fide* Fleet.

## 2. CHALUKYA EMPIRE.

### WESTERN CHALUKYA DYNASTY.

The similarity found to exist between the *padma-ṭankas* of Banawási and the early, though not the earliest, Chalukya coins, bring us to the consideration of the influence exercised by the latter dynasty on the coinage of Southern India, an influence neither inconsiderable nor transient, for it still exists, and has descended to the present time.

But first we will say a few words regarding such of their coins as have come down to us. These have been figured in my Gleanings, figures 1 to 5 inclusive (Mad. Jour. iv. N.S.). Figures 1 and 2 are those already noticed for their similarity to the *padma-ṭankas*. It needs but a glance to see how exact the imitation has been—an imitation by which they superseded the older and ruder specimens described in the Kadamba section. No. 3, copied from Moor's Hindu Pantheon, pl. 104, fig. 13, was found in Tipú Sulṭán's repository at the taking of Seringapatam. The obverse represents a well-formed boar, on the reverse is the floral design only found on older coins. The two next are of ruder workmanship, and show considerable deterioration from the preceding examples, so much so, that I hesitated whether to assign them rather to the Vijayanagar era. The boar on the coins of the latter, of which a considerable number in copper have been obtained, as also the seals on some of their *śásanams*, have the addition of a sword in front of or over the back of the animal, and the absence of this characteristic on the two coins above mentioned inclines me to leave them among the Chalukya relics. From the extensive circulation of the Chalukya money bearing the figure of this animal, and its adoption by the succeeding dynasty of Vijayanagar, the name of the pieces in most of the vernacular dialects has come to be that of *varaha* or boar piece, even when the figure of the animal gave place to that of a deity, or some other symbol, as happened after the change in the Vijayanagar dynasty from the Kuruba to the Narsinga line.

The influence above adverted to, as still perceptible on the gold currency of the present day, is explained by the wide extent and long duration of the Chalukya power. Their history, though still by no means exhausted, has been so largely worked out by Mr. Fleet and others, that it is only necessary here to give a list of the two leading families, with a few of the most prominent incidents in their history, to assist in the identification of the coins.[1] Both lines descend from the same common ancestor—that Pulikési who first effected a permanent lodgement in the Dakhan. Their inscriptions contain the following high-sounding titles, viz.:—Chalukya *kula* (tribe); Mánavyasa *gótra* (lineage); Háríti *putra* (descended from); deriving the white umbrella and other ensigns of royalty from Kauśiki; preserved by the

[1] That they were a northern family cannot be doubted, and that they were previously settled in Gujarát is also certain, as proved by the Kaira plates published by Professor Dowson (J.R.A.S. vol. i. N.S. p. 247). Although unsupported by any proof, the romantic legend of the poet Chand, in which he describes the inauguration of the four *agni-kula* families on Mount Abu, who became the progenitors of the warlike rulers—the Choháns, the Pramáras, the Pariháras, and the Chalukyas—is invested with a certain show of probability as indicating that the Bráhmans had recourse to the aid of the aboriginal mountaineers when their differences with their Kshatriya compatriots became irreconcilable. See Col. Tod's graphic description in the Annals of Rájasthán, vol. i., also Jour. Eth. Soc. London, 1869, vol. i. N.S. p. 126.

seven mothers; worshipping Svámi Mahásêṇa; who acquired the insignia of the peacock's tail (*mayúra pinch'ha*) and the spear (*kunṭá*) through the excellent favour of Kárttikêya; the (*varaha lánchana*) boar seal from the favour of Bhagávan Náráyaṇa. The other ensigns of royalty above referred to are the conch shell (*sankha*); the noubat (*pancha mahásabda*); the banner of the sharp sword (*páli*[1]), and the *pratidakká* (sort of drum); the sign or standard (?) (*pada*) of the Gaṇgá and the Yamuná; the throne (*sinhásana*); and the golden sceptre (*kanaka danḍam*).[2] Several of these symbols appear on the seals attached to their copper deeds, and might perhaps occur on their coins.

The earliest record of this family that has yet been found is in the Kaira copper-plates above mentioned, which record a grant made by Śrí Vijaya Rája Sarvva, son of Buddha Varmá Rája, and grandson of Jaya Simha, in A.D. 472, who must have lived, at least, thirty or forty years earlier. They were then a powerful family in Gujarat, with a mythical tradition of having previously reigned in Oudh, and distinguished by most of the same titles (Mánavaya-*gótra*, Háriti-*putra*, etc.), which appear in their later grants. No reliable mention of their settlement in Kuntala is found until, after some unsuccessful attempts, Pulikési I. crossed the Narbadá and took Vátápi (or Bádámi). These events probably occurred at the end of the fifth or beginning of the sixth century of our era, because Pulikési I. was the son of Raṇarága, Buddha Varmá's brother, and his cousin Vijaya's grant is dated A.D. 472. The legend published in the Madras Journal,[3] on the faith of a copper-plate inscription of Rája-rája II., the Choḷa-Chalukya, of the eastern Chalukya branch, dated Saka 944, which ascribes the first invasion of Kuntala to an earlier Chalukya prince, has been critically examined and refuted by Mr. Fleet.[4] A similar legend, evidently based on the same tale, was found by Col. Mackenzie in the annals of the Kákatiya family of Woraṇgal, a notice of which is given in the introduction to the catalogue by Prof. Wilson,[5] affording another instance of the tendency of history to repeat itself. Pulikesi I. may therefore be considered to be the true founder of the Dakhan family, and to have established his capital at Vatapi, identified by Mr. Fleet as Bádámi. Of his two grandsons, Pulikési II., surnamed Satyasraya, continued the line, hence distinguished as the Western, on the table-land, while his younger brother Kubja Vishṇuvardhana I., founded the eastern branch (of which a more particular notice will be given afterwards), below the Gháts at Rájamahendri in the province of Vengi, in the seventh century. The fortunes of the western house suffered a temporary obscuration, the date of which has not been accurately ascertained, but it must have been subsequent to Kírttivarmá II., for a grant by him is still extant,[6] bearing the date of A.D. 758.

No record remains of the exact time or of the circumstances which reversed the hitherto successful career of the Chalukya house; but two historical events which occurred about this

[1] Ind. Ant. vol. vii. pp. 111, 245.

[2] Grant of Vijayarája, Ind. Ant. vol. vii. p. 245.
" Pulikési " " vii. 214.
" Vikramáditya VI " " viii. 12.
Kaira Plates, J.R.A.S., i. N.S. p. 270. The meaning of the terms *páḷi* and *pada* is not clear. I give them as rendered by Mr. Fleet.

[3] Vol. iv. N.S. p. 78.

[4] Ind. Ant. vol. vii. p. 244.

[5] Vol. i. p. cxxvii.

[6] Ind. Ant vol. viii. p. 23.

time may have contributed to bring about that result. In the *Rájatarangiṇi* there is an account of the military expedition of the Kashmirian king Lalitáditya,[1] who with his victorious army is there said to have swept over the whole of Southern India, and returned to his capital content with this proof of his prowess. I at one time thought that this event might have shaken the throne of the Chalukyas. But plausible as this explanation appears to be, it cannot be accepted as certain, being unsupported by concurrent testimony. It rests on the single authority of Kalhana paṇḍit, author of the *Tarangiṇi*, and is by some, among whom I may include Dr. Bühler, who has paid considerable attention to this epoch, supposed to be altogether legendary. There is, however, abundant evidence to show that the prostration of the Chalukya empire was due to the rise of the Raṭṭa state of Mányakhéṭa, which maintained its superiority under a succession of warlike princes[2] for nearly two centuries, from the middle of the eighth to the middle of the tenth. The military prowess of one of these, Govinda III., rivalled the exploits of Lalitáditya. Between the years 785 and 810 A.D. he carried his victorious arms from the Tungabhadrá to the Vinḍhya mountains. Powerful as the Raṭṭas were, they were unable to retain their hold of these conquests, and were humbled and driven back to their old limits. The circumstances under which this took place are equally obscure. We only know that Tailapa II. is mentioned in several inscriptions as having defeated Karkara the last Raṭṭa king, and recovered the throne of his ancestors in A.D. 973. He reigned twenty-four years and transmitted the throne to twelve of his successors, who ruled with more or less splendour at their capital of Kalyáṇa until the succession of Taila III. (A.D. 1150). About this time his chief military officer (*danda-náyaka*), named Bijjala, of the Kalachuri family, set aside his master, usurped the throne, and, with his two sons, exercised the rights of sovereignty over a portion of the country.

The falling fortunes of the Chalukya house encouraged attacks from other quarters, and the invasions of the Yádavas on the west, and the Kákatiyas on the east, helped to precipitate their downfall. A show of independence was maintained by the feeble efforts of one or two of Taila's successors, until about 1189 A.D. the remnant of their dominions fell under the sway of the Yadavas.

The influence of their characteristic symbol, the boar, survives to the present time, not only in the vernacular name of the pagoda, but in the social habits of the people, who in some places employ weights and measures certified by the figure of a boar marked upon them, and use stamps or seals, similarly authorized, for marking the heaps of grain where the revenue is collected in kind, on the *metayer* system (Madras Journal, vol. iv. N.S. pp. 98–99).

The succession of the princes of this, undoubtedly the most important, dynasty of the Dakhan, is shown in the Genealogy appended on the following page.

[1] The exact date of Lalitáditya has been determined by Gen. Cunningham and Dr. Bühler, who have shown his reign to have lasted thirty-six years seven months and eleven days, or from 725 to 762 A.D. Now, as Kirttivarmá's grant, above referred to, was conferred in Maisur, it is quite possible that if Lalitáditya's success has any foundation in fact, it might have forced the Chalukya prince to retire to the extreme south of his dominions, and so have prepared the way for the success of other enemies.

[2] Dantidurga, or Dantivarma II., 725–755 A.D.; Kṛishṇa, 755 A.D.; Dhruva, 770 A.D.; Govinda III., 785–810 A.D.

# WESTERN CHALUKYA GENEALOGY.

- Jayasimha I.
  - Buddhavarmá
    - Vijayarája, or Vijayavarmá (472 A.D.)
  - Ranarága
    - Polekési I. or Pulikési I. (489 A.D.?)
      - Kírttivarmá I. (567 A.D.)
        - Pulikési II. or Satyáśayra I. (610-634 A.D.)
          - Ádityavarma.
          - Chandráditya.
          - Vikramáditya I. (670-680-1 A.D.)
            - Vinayáditya (680-1-696 A.D.)
              - Vijayáditya (696-733 A.D.)
                - (733-747 A.D.) Vikramádityá II.
                  - Kírttivarmá II. (747-757 A.D.)
                - Bhima I.
                  - Kírttivarmá II.
                    - Taila I.
                      - Vikramáditya III.
                        - Bhimá II.
                          - Ayyana I.
                            - Vikramáditya IV.
                              - Taila II. or Áhavamalla I. (973-997 A.D.)
                                - Satyáśraya II. (997-1008 A.D.)
                                - Dasavarmá.
                                  - Vikramáditya V. or Tribhuvanamalla I. (1008-1018 A.D.)
                                  - Ayyana II.
                                  - Akkadevi (1022-1047 A.D.)
                                  - Jayasimha III. or Jagadekamalla I. (1018-1042 A.D.)
                                    - Someśvara I., Trailokyamalla I. or Áhavamalla II. (1042-1068 A.D.)
                                      - Someśvara II. or Bhuvanaikamalla (1068-1075 A.D.)
                                      - Vikramáditya VI. or Tribhuvanamalla II. (1075-1126 A.D.)
                                        - Jayakarna
                                        - Someśvara III. or Bhulokamalla (1126-1138 A.D.)
                                          - Jagadekamálla II. (1138-1150 A.D.)
                                          - Taila III. or Trailokyamalla III. (1150-1159 A.D.)
                                            - Someśvara IV., Vira-Someśvara, or Tribhuvanamalla III. (1182-1189 A.D.)
                                        - Mailaladévi. (Married to Jayakési II. of the Kadambas of Goa.)
                                      - Jayasimha IV. or Trailokyamalla II. (1079-1081 A.D.)
          - Amberá.
        - Vishnuvardhana I. and his descendants of the Eastern Branch.
        - Jayasimha II.
      - Mangaliśa, Mangaliśvara, or Mangalarája (567-610 A.D.)
        - Satyáśraya-Indravarmá (? 610 A.D.)

## 3. RAṬṬA OR RA'SHṬRAKU'ṬA DYNASTY OF MA'NYAKHE'ṬA.

This seems to be the proper place to notice the dynasties just mentioned (the Kalachuris and the Yádavas) that arose upon the ruins of the Chalukya state, and to trace their influence on the coinage of the country. But first, I will return to the Raṭṭas, whose temporary occupation of Kuntala has been already adverted to.

In common with several other dynasties, they claim to be of Yádava descent, and to be lords of the city of Lattalura.[1] As we have before seen, they formed, with the Pallavas, one of the most important sections of the earlier inhabitants of the Dakhan, and, like them, offered a strenuous resistance to the settlement of the Chalukyas. Their range extended from Elura, in the north, to the Krishṇa in the south, embracing the whole of Western Kuntala. The first seat of their power appears to have been at Elura, where an inscription of Dantidurga is still extant,[2] and where his uncle Krishṇa constructed a magnificent temple on the hill at Elapura, another form, according to Prof. Bhandarkar, of Elura.[3] A succession of warlike princes greatly extended their dominions, till Amoghavarsha, after the battle of Vingavali, in the ninth century, established himself at Mányakhéṭa (now Málkhéḍ), considerably further south, in the centre of the Nizam's dominions, which thenceforward became the capital.

We have little doubt that they are represented by the modern Mahraṭṭa (Maha-Raṭṭa) nation, and must have occupied a space extending much beyond the limits of the present Maháráshtra. If their identification with the Reḍḍis of Eastern Telingana, as proposed by some commentators, be accepted, the conclusiveness of which however is doubtful, they will be found to occupy a much larger area than that at first supposed. For a considerable Reḍḍi principality was established on the fall of Worangal at Kondaviḍ,[4] and still later, the powerful Zamindars of Venkatagiri[5] are found to be descendants of the same stock.

As appears by their inscriptions, Raṭṭa chieftains were long settled at Saundatti, Parasgad, Belgaum, and other places in the Southern Mahraṭṭa country. Their name is sometimes found perpetuated in that of places, as Raṭṭihaḷḷi, a *táluk* south of Dharwaṛ; and, in the

[1] No city of the name has been found, but it occurred to me, on first reading the name, that it might have come from Lat-E'lurâ, a forced reading it is true. But seeing that the Ráshṭrakúṭa princes were rulers of Láta, and that E'lur was the first capital of the family, the surmise seemed not without a show of probability.

The province of Láta lay to the south of Gujarát. How far it extended in that direction is not clear, but probably it reached to the confines of Kuntala and the Konkan, and formed part of the Ráshṭrakúṭa dominions, whence they derived the title of Látesvara. Lassen considers it to be the Latiké or Lariké of Ptolemy.

[2] Arch. Survey Western India, by Burgess and Bhagvánlál Indraji, 1881, No. 10, p. 95.

[3] Ind. Ant. vol. xii. p. 229.

[4] Mackenzie, Cat. vol. i. p. cxxxiv.

[5] Taylor's Or. MSS. vol. iii. p. 476; also Madr. Jour. vol. vii. p. 372.

Koṅgudésa Charitra, the first prince of the Chéra dynasty in the far south is said to be of the "Reṭṭi" *kula.*[1] He and his seven successors are named in the Maisur inscriptions, p. xli.

The Ráshṭrakúṭas have been distinguished from the Raṭṭas as a northern or Rájpút race, we doubt if on sufficient grounds. The probability is that the Raṭṭas flourished under rulers of their own in Western, as the Pallavas did in Eastern, Kuntala, and that their power was broken by the earlier invasions of the Chalukyas, who, under Jayasinha, overcame Indra the son of Krishṇa (names occurring again in their later genealogies), their then chief, and although we have no specific mention of them subsequent to this event, they were probably reduced to subjection as the Chalukya conquest proceeded. The desire to magnify their origin may have led to the substitution of the Sanskrit term Maha Ráshtra for the simpler form of Raṭṭa, both which designations[2] are found as synonyms in the Saundatti inscriptions, and in an inscription obtained by me at Śirúr, near Dhárwáṛ, Amoghavarsha-Nṛipatunga is distinctly said to be "born in the lineage of the Raṭṭas." (I. A. vol. xii. p. 220). Dr. Burnell more distinctly refers to the Sanskritizing tendency of official scribes, when recording grants in that language, giving, among other illustrations, that of "Ráshtra from Raṭṭa=Reḍḍi."[3] A further point of similarity is found in the habits and pursuits of the two races; the Mahraṭṭa Kunbi and the Telugu Reḍḍi being equally conspicuous for their agricultural industry and skill.[4] For the genealogy of this family we are indebted chiefly to the researches of Dr. Bühler supplemented by those of Mr. Fleet.

[1] J.R.A.S. vol. viii. p. 2; also Madr. Jour. vol. xiv. p. 4.

[2] See inscription at Bail Hongal in Ind. Ant. vol. iv. pp. 115–16 and 279–80.

[3] S. Ind. Palæog. 2nd. ed Introd. p. x.

[4] The equivalent term for "Reṭṭi or Reḍḍy" in the Tamil dialect according to Rev. Wm. Taylor is "Veḷḷáḷa," the most esteemed of Tamil agriculturists.—Madr. Journal, vol. xiv. p. 4, *note*.

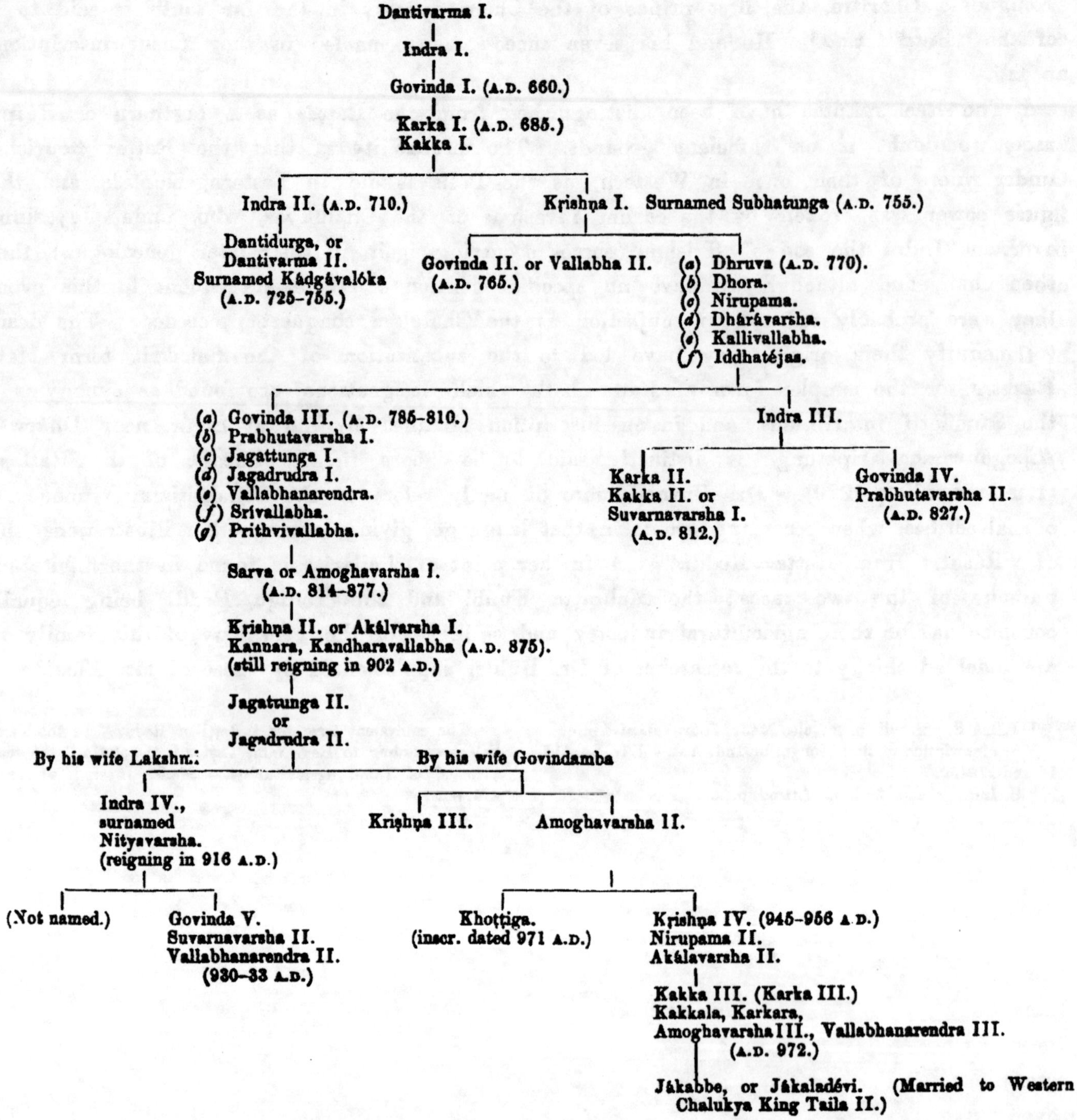


The inscriptions from which the above genealogical list has been prepared [1] show that seventeen or eighteen princes (for there is some confusion as to the succession of the later names) ruled in the land,[2] occupying a period of 312 years, and giving an average of 18·6 per reign. Some of these must have been much within that proportion; for the inscription at Śirúr, before mentioned, is dated in the fifty-second year of Amoghavarsha I.[3]

[1] Ind. Ant. vols. xi., xii.

[2] Ind. Ant. vol. xii. p. 255.

[3] Ind. Ant. vol. xii p. 216.

None of the coins of this State have come under my notice. Bhau Daji[1] has figured certain silver coins found in the Nasik district, which General Cunningham[2] ascribes to a Krishṇa Rája of the fourth century. But the epigraph has been very imperfectly read. The execution is superior to that of any Dakhani coin of that age with which I am acquainted, and they seem to be nearly allied to those of the Sáh dynasty of Gujarát. The only clue we can give to what their coins may have represented, is the figure of a four-armed deity (? Śiva) confirming the Khárepátan[3] grants, as shown in the annexed woodcut. Similar to this are the figures in relief, but they are not very distinct, on the seals of several copper grants such as those of Dantidurga, I. A. vol. xi. pp. 110-13; of Govinda III., in which the hoods of the snakes form a canopy over the god, *ib.* 126; of Prabhutavarsha, xii. 11; of Dhruva III., *ib.* 179.

From the above indications, the inference is, that this family were worshippers of Śiva. But it is remarkable that Amoghavarsha's inscription mentions that he "had the sign, or mark, or banner of Garuḍa," which indicates a tendency to Vaishnaism.

## 4. THE KALACHURIS OF KALYAN.

The founders of the first of the minor states before mentioned belong to a distinguished race, of whom an incidental notice will be found at p. 11 *ante*, as having been considered by Col. Wilford[4] to be the representatives of the Haihaya tribe. They became celebrated as Kings of Chedi in Bandelkhand, and were the founders of Kálanjarapura (Kálinjar), from which most of the principal families claim to be derived. They are widely, though sparsely, distributed, and are found in Jabalpur in Ságor, Ratnapúr in Berár, etc., etc.

The branch now to be considered were chiefs (Mahámaṇḍaleśvares) of Taddevádi in North Maisur, and probably had charge of the neighbouring districts of Hángal, Banawási, Nonambavádi, etc. The head of the family in the twelfth century was Permádi. He was succeeded by his son Bijjala, who in addition held high military command at Kalyán under the Chalukya king. We know not how his disloyalty to his sovereign arose, but it is certain that he drove Tailapa III. from his capital about the middle of the twelfth century. He did not, however, immediately declare his independence. Following his sovereign to the south, we find him still using the subordinate style and designation, but in an inscription at Annigeri before 1162 A.D., which was about the date of Tailapa's death, he threw off the mask and proclaimed himself supreme. Among his titles he uses those of "Tribhuvanamalla," and "Lord of Káḷañjarapura,"[5] with the

[1] J. Bo. Br. R. As. Soc. vol. xii. p. 213.
[2] Arch. Reports, vol. ix. p. 30.
[3] J. B. As. Soc. vol. i. pp. 209-16.
[4] As. Res. vol. ix. 8vo. p. 105; Cun. Arch. Rep. vol. ix. p. 101.
[5] Ind. Ant. vol v. p. 48.

standard of the golden bull, the *damaruka* drum, etc.[1] Little is known of the events of his reign. He had four sons, of each of whom we find grants within very few years of each other. In fact, their usurped authority was never consolidated.

The son of Tailapa, Somesvara IV., continued to make head against them in the south for twenty years after his father's death, and finally succeeded in obtaining a precarious hold on the dominions of his family about 1182 A.D., the year at which we lose sight of the Kalachuri rule. His success was greatly promoted by the dissensions which prevailed at Kalyán on the introduction of a new religious sect called Lingáyats, which sprang up at this time. The Kalachuris were said to have been Jainas, and are so represented in the Basava-purána, the sacred book of the Lingáyats, although in their insignia is included the banner of a golden bull, which is also found on the seal of a grant of Siṇghaṇa Deva, and, with the phallus-like representation of Mahádéva, heads the inscription on a stone tablet at Balagami.[2] The new creed was a form of Saivism, known as the Jangama or Víra Śaiva sect. Between them and the old sect a mortal enmity existed. Some account of the new religion will be found in the Jour. Roy. As. Soc.[3] It is sufficient to state here that Basava, its founder, an Áradhya Bráhman, was the minister or Dewan of Bijjala, whose power he undermined, and compassed his death, an event of which conflicting accounts are given. The exact date of Bijjala is unknown, but he is supposed to have reigned about eleven years. He was succeeded by his eldest son Somesvara, who ruled for eight more, after which his three younger brothers, in all of whose names inscriptions are extant, struggled to maintain the falling fortunes of their house for a short time longer. The latest record of Siṇghaṇa, the youngest, is dated 1183 A.D., which would show the duration of the Kalachuri rule to have lasted only about thirty years.

Short as is this term, I have met with two coins, a pagoda with a standing figure advancing to the left, and on the reverse the words Sovi Murári Ráya Déva,[4] and two or three fanams with the same device, which I refer to Bijjala's eldest son. As stated above, the seal on a copper grant of Siṇghaṇa has the figure of a bull couchant, which may therefore have been also used on their coins. A genealogical list of the family follows.[5]

**Jógama or Krishṇa.**

**Permádi (A.D. 1128).**

**Bijjala (A.D. 1156-1167).** — **Siriyádevi, married Chávunda II. of the Sindas of Erambarage.**

Sons of Bijjala:

**Sómeswara (A.D. 1167-1175).** — **Saṇkama (A.D. 1175-1180).** — **Áhavamalla (A.D. 1176-1183).** — **Siṇghaṇa (A.D. 1183).**

[1] The *damara* or *damaruka* is a small double drum shaped like a sand-glass, a distinction like the *noubat* (*pancha mahá śabda*), the right to carry which is conferred by the sovereign on men of rank. It is represented on the seal of Vishṇuvardhana Chalukya VII., pl. ii. fig. 1. Num. Ol. Madr. Journ. N.S. vol. iv.

[2] Ind. Ant. vol. iv. p. 274, and vol. v. p. 46.

[3] Vol. iv. O.S. pp. 20, 22, Madr. Journ. vol. vii. pp. 212-214.

[4] Inscriptions recording grants made by him are exant at Ingleswar and Kukkanur in the neighbourhood of the Nizam's territory, and extending southwards into the western parts of Dhárwáṛ. My coins were from the Sátárá district.

[5] Int. Ant. vol. iv. p. 274.

## 5. THE YÁDAVAS OF DÉVAGIRI.

Another of the minor States before mentioned was that of the Yádavas of Devagiri, who drove the Kalachuris out of Kalyán, and gained possession of the northern Chalukya districts. Its principal station was at Dévagiri, the modern Daulatabad, a remarkable fortified hill of great strength, a few miles south of Élurá.

At this time the head of the family was named Bhillama, who does not appear to have descended from distinguished ancestors, but is simply stated to be of the Yádu (*vamsa*) stock. No mention of him is found in the few inscriptions that have been copied, but one recently met with gives the names of his father Mallugi, and his grandfather Siṇghaṇa. After him we have nine successors, but only seven generations. The duration of the family as rulers did not exceed 124 years (or from 1187 to 1311 A.D.), when it was subverted by the arms of 'Alá-ud-dín Muhammad Sháh, the Mahommedan Emperor of Delhi.[1]

Coins of this family are rare. Their device was a golden *garuḍa*, a bird sacred to Vishnu. On a recent copper-plate edited by Mr. Fleet[2] the seal has the form of the god either seated or kneeling. If the latter, it may be meant for the semi-human form of Garuḍa. I have also two or three pagodas, representing Garuḍa, half man half bird, but cannot assign them with certainty to this dynasty.' The use of the designation Dvárávatipur-varadhiswara would seem to connect them with the family next to be considered, although no other proof of affinity appears. The following is a genealogical list.

**Siṇghaṇa I.**
|
**Mallugi.**
|
**Bhillama (A.D. 1187-1191).**
|
**Jaitugi I. (A.D. 1191-1209).**
|
**Siṇghaṇa II. (A.D. 1209-1247)**
|
**Jaitugi II.**

- **Krishṇa (A.D. 1247-1260).**
  - **Rámachandra (A.D. 1271-1308).**
    - **Saṃkara (A.D. 1309-1311).**
    - **Bhíma.**
    - **A daughter (married to Harapála), whose tragical end at the hands of Kutb-ed-din Mubárik Sháh Khilji (A.D. 1317, the son of Alá-ud-dín), the King of Delhi, is described by the Mahommedan historian.**
- **Mahádéva (A.D. 1260-1271).**
  - **Amana.**

[1] J.R.A.S. vol. iv. pp. 28–31; Brigg's Ferishta, vol. i. p. 365; Thomas's Pathán Kings of Dehl., pp. 156, 188.

[2] Journ. Bom. Br. Roy. As. Soc. vol. xv. p. 383.

## 6. YÁDAVAS OF DVÁRASAMUDRA COMMONLY CALLED HOYSALA BALLÁLAS.

The other family deducing their descent from Yádu just mentioned, rose to celebrity at Dváràvatipura, now called Dvárasamudra and Halabidu in Maisur. Now as the dynasty we have last been considering included among their titles that of Dváràvatipur-varadhisvara, we may fairly conjecture that they were an offshoot from this family, since according to the well-known practice of other great houses, such epithets were always derived from some place of note, the earliest seat of the race. Be this as it may, it had not the effect of producing relations of amity between them. The obscurity of their origin is veiled under a legend of a native of Shásákapura, named Sala, having protected a Jaina priest from the attack of a tiger, which animal, thenceforward, became their cognizance, and is represented on their seals. The exploit is also perpetuated in a group of statuary on the roof immediately in front of the tower, on a temple in the *táluk* of Raṭṭihalli in the Dhárwaṛ district, and repeated with variations on two other temples in the same *táluk*. They are of considerable merit and are the only instances I have met with of free sculpture. The figure of the man is bold, and well shaped, but the animal more resembles the mythological *sirja* or *yáli.*[1] He is the reputed ancestor of Vinayáditya, the first of the family of whom we have authentic mention, who was a feudatory (Mahámaṇḍaleśwara) of the Kalyán Chalukyas. From him is deduced the following genealogy:

Vinayáditya (A.D. 1047-1076).
|
Ereyanga.
|
Ballála I. (A.D. 1093.) — Vishṇuvardhana (A.D. 1117-1137). — Udayaditya.
|
Narasimha I.
|
Ballála II. or Víra Ballála (A.D. 1191-1211).
|
Narasimha II. (A.D. 1223.)
|
Somesvara (A.D. 1252).
|
Narasimha III. (A.D. 1254-1286.)
|
Ballaḷa III. (A.D. 1310.)

From the name of Vinayaditya's grandson, which was likewise borne by others of his descendants, they are sometimes styled Hoysaḷa Balláḷas. Although the family had been growing in importance for some time previously, as appears from Vishṇuvardhana, his grandfather, having taken Talkád, the capital of the Koṅgu Chéras, seizing part of their territory, and having added the country north of Dvaravati as far as the Tungabhadrá to his possessions, it was not till the close of the twelfth century that the second Ballaḷa (or Víra Balláḷa) assumed regal titles. He seems to have been a warlike prince, and boasts that he had "despoiled the warrior race of Kaḷachuri," and overcome Jaitrasimha (probably

[1] Ind. Ant. vol. v. p. 179.

the second prince of the Devagiri line).[1] As this was coincident with the fall of the Kalachuris, and as previous to that time all the members of the family bore the subordinate title, we may conclude that this event encouraged them first to declare their independence. Their power now rapidly increased and overspread the greater part of Kuntala. The tide of success however was turned in the reign of Singhaṇa, Jaitugi's successor.

On the death of Ballála about A.D. 1211, the Hoysaḷas were driven back within their former limits of the Tungabhadrá river. Narasimha then appears to have assisted the Choḻa in his contests with the Paṇḍya king, obtaining considerable influence to the eastward, and residing much at Vikramapúr in the Choḻa country.[2]

Nothing of importance is recorded of the three following princes, the last of whom, Ballála III., was crushed (1310 A.D.) by the generals of 'Alá-ud-dín,[3] who, having completed the conquest of Worangal in the previous year, captured Dvarasamudra, and made Ballála a prisoner. He was afterwards liberated, and allowed to make a show of sovereignty at Belur until the final destruction of Dvarasamudra in A.D. 1326. After this, they retired to Tonnúr, in the north of Seringapatam, where they maintained an independent position with the modest style of *Danda-náyakas*, equivalent to the European title of General.

Copper coins issued by them are still extant, having on the obverse the figure of an elephant facing to the right, surmounted by the Canarese Śrí, and a legend in the same characters on the reverse.

I have not succeeded in meeting with any Hoysaḷa coins, but the seal[4] on the ring of a set of copper plates dated A.D. 1252, recording a grant by Someswara, in which he is called "Víra Soma," "during his residence in his favourite city of Vikramapur in the district of Kulakani-naḍ in Choḻa-desam," etc., which I saw in the office of the Chief Commissioner of Maisur, bears the figure of a tiger, which, as above mentioned, was adopted as the cognizance of the family, as represented in the accompanying woodcut, and some such symbol will probably be found on their coins. This people continued to profess the Jain religion till the time of Vishṇuvardhana. He was converted to Saivism by Ramanuja Charya,[5] who had fled from the court of Tanjore to escape the persecutions of Kerikala Choḻa.

**Note.**—Since the above was written my friend Gen. Pearse has made me acquainted with a gold coin in his collection, of which the following is a description, and which will be represented in our plates.

The coins are of extreme rarity, two only being known, his own obtained in 1882, and a second in the Museum at Bangalore. The obverse has a maned lion advancing to

[1] Ind. Antiq. vol. ii. p. 303.
[2] Inscription at Bangalore dated A.D. 1250. See Mysore Inscriptions, p. 322.
[3] Briggs's Ferishta, vol. i. p. 373; Zia-ud-din Barni, in Sir H. Elliot's Historians of India, vol. iii. p. 203.
[4] See Mysore Inscriptions, p. 322.
[5] Cald. Comp. Gram. Introd. pp. 129, 143; Hist. of Tinnevelly, p. 30.

right, above his back and loins a smaller lion rampant, both facing what the General calls an altar or *stambha*. In front of the smaller lion is a sun. On the reverse three lines in old Canarese characters, reading on the one Śrí Nonambavádi Dóná, and on the other Śrí Talakadoo Dona,[1] the latter proving the date of the coin to be subsequent to the time of Vishṇuvardhana, the conqueror of Talkáḍ. The Mackenzie Collection is also said to have contained a copper coin of the same Vishṇuvardhana, on which was a figure of Ramanuja.[2]

## 7. KÁKATIYA OR GANAPATI DYNASTY OF WORANGAL.

The decay of the Chalukya empire favoured the rise of another small dynasty at Orugallu or Woraṇgal, but the original seat was at Anumakoṇḍa, in its immediate neighbourhood, where the family had previously been settled. The materials for their history are few, viz. an inscription on stone at Anumakoṇḍa, three versions of which have been published.[3] I have also an unpublished inscription on stone, from the Mangaligiri *taluḳ* in Guntúr.[4]

The first individual of this line of whom we have an authentic record was a chief named Próla, whose origin is not very clear. He is called the son of Tribhuvanamalla in the inscription at Anumakoṇḍa, but this is a mere title assumed by several kings.[5] and we must therefore consider Próla as the founder of the family. He is said to have professed the Jaina faith,[6] and is styled a Mahamandalesvara, from which it is inferred that he was a feudatory of the Chalukya king. During the troubles that arose soon after the accession of Taila III., Próla openly rebelled and made captive his royal master. He appears, however, to have returned to his allegiance, released the king "through devotion by his goodwill,"[7] and acted against his enemies. He incarcerated one named Góvindarája for a time, replacing him by a chief named Udaya; quelled the outbreak of another named Gunḍa of Mantrakúṭa; and drove back a third called Jaggadéva, who had advanced to attack Anumakoṇḍa. Taila, however did not long survive, and the death of Próla, which took place about the same time, probably 1160 A.D., threw upon Rúdra, his son and successor, the further prosecution of the war. He followed up his father's successes with vigour, subduing Bhima, Rája of Vardhamánanagari, and his ally Chódóḍaya, who, perhaps, was the Chola-Chalukya king of Vengi, or his general. Bhima was driven from

[1] Nonambavádi, the seat of the Kalachuris of Kalyán (see p. 77), is a district in Chitaldrug division, south of the Tungabhadrá, in the kingdom of Maisur. I can find no such word as *Dóná* for a pagoda in any Dravidian Dictionary.

[2] Cat. vol. ii. App. p. ccxxxv.

[3] J.A.S.B. vol. vii. p. 901; Bom. Journ. Roy. As. Soc. vol. x. pp. 46-49; Ind. Antiq. vol. xi. p. 9.

[4] On a pillar opposite the temple of Viveswara Swámi in the Malkapúram Agraharam in Mangalagiri *táluḳ*.

[5] Chalukyas, Hoysaḷas, and Kalachuris.

[6] Mackenzie's Cat. vol. i. p. cxxviii.

[7] Ind. Ant. vol. xi. p. 17.

his territory to the forests, probably of the Eastern Gháts, and then with other rebel chiefs submitted to Rúdra's authority. During these successes, which are more fully detailed in the Anumakoṇḍa inscription, he enlarged and consolidated the Kákatiya dominions. Several additional particulars are found in two vernacular histories, summarized in Taylor's Catalogue.[1] Wilson also briefly notices them, but I refrain from quoting them because they rest on no sufficient evidence. We have no further account of Rúdra's proceedings, nor of the date of his death. He was succeeded by his brother Mahádéva, of whom still less is known, although some legends of his acts are embodied in the local traditions. After him came his son Ganapati, said by some to have been his nephew, and the son of Rúdra; but the Mangalagiri inscription expressly calls him the son of Mahádéva. Prof. Wilson states that the inscriptions of this prince in the Mackenzie Collection range from 1223–1261 A.D.,[2] but few authentic records of his doings remain, although traditionary statements are not wanting. He is said to have been a zealous votary of Śiva,[3] and to have persecuted the Jainas, displacing the hereditary village accountants or *karanams* (karnams), and substituting in their stead Niyogi Bráhmans, who still retain possession of the office. That he was a prince of vigour and ability is established by the fact that from him the family is called the Ganapati as well as the Kákatiya dynasty. He died, about 1257 A.D., without male issue, leaving an only daughter, married to a scion of the Chalukya house. Rúdrama Dévi,[4] the widow of Ganapati, then assumed the direction of affairs. There is an inscription[5] dated S.S. 1191 = 1269 A.D. in the twelfth year of her reign, which would place her accession in 1257 A.D.; so that the date of her husband's death, above mentioned, may be accepted with confidence. She is said to have held the regency for twenty-eight years, and then to have made over the government to her grandson Pratápa Rúdra. The early part of his reign appears to have been prosperous,[6] and marked by successes over his neighbours, but these were obscured by the disasters of its close. The tide of Mahommedan conquest had now reached Telingana. We learn from Ferishta that an expedition against Worangal was despatched from Bengal in 1308 A.D., which proving unsuccessful, Malik Káfur was sent against the place with a second army by way of Dévagiri in 1309 A.D. Advancing rapidly, he besieged the city before Pratápa Rúdra's allies could come to his assistance. The king capitulated, purchasing peace by the payment of a large sum, and the surrender of his horses, elephants and jewels, at the same time engaging to pay an annual tribute for the future. This he appears to have done in good faith, but the other Hindu chiefs having withheld their tribute, Malik Káfur proceeded for the fourth time to the Dakhan in 1312 A.D. to enforce their

[1] Taylor's Or. Cat. MS. vol. iii. pp. 480–84; Mackenzie Cat. vol. i. pp. cxxviii. cxxix.

[2] Vol. i. p. cxxxi.

[3] Vol. i. pp. cxxix, cxxx.

[4] In her Colonel Yule recognized the "Queen of Mutfili" (Motapilli), whose able and virtuous administration of her country is eulogised by Marco Polo (vol. ii. p. 295). It does not appear that Marco Polo visited her country, but the fame of her rule may have come to his ears and the dates agree pretty well.

[5] At Durgi in the Palnáḍ *táluk* of the Kistna Division. Sewell's List of Antiq. vol. i. App. xx. 1882.

[6] Mackenzie's Cat. vol. i. p. cxxxii; Taylor's Cat. Or. MSS. vol. iii. p. 483.

submission. He marched from Dévagiri and ravaged the greater part of Maháráshtra and Carnatica, but spared Telingana. No particular change occurred till 1322 A.D., when, on the accession of Gheias-ud-dín Tughlak, Pratápa Rúdra attempted to free himself from the Delhi yoke. An army under the king's son was despatched to Worangal, but after a protracted siege he was compelled to retire with great loss. In the following year a second expedition proved more successful. Pratápa again offered terms similar to those accepted by Malik Káfur, but they were rejected. The city was taken with great slaughter, and the Rája and his family, with all his treasures, were sent to Delhi. At the same time the name of the city was changed to Sultánpúr, which, however, it did not long retain.[1]

Of the future fortunes of Worangal few authentic particulars have been recorded. Pratápa Rúdra is said to have been allowed by the Sultán of Delhi to return to his capital, where he died, probably before or about 1325 A.D.[2] He was succeeded by his son Virabhadra. During the troubles which prevailed in Mahomed Tughlak's reign, the people of the Dakhan on several occasions rose against their Mahommedan conquerors. It was during this period that the kingdom of Vijayanagar was founded,[3] offering an asylum to refugees from the subverted Carnatic and Telingana States. Worangal was more than once the scene of successful insurrection, the last recorded occasion being in 1344 A.D. Subsequent to this no certain information regarding its history is forthcoming. Pratápa Rúdra's son is said to have retired to Kondavid, and the family disappears from history. Ultimately Worangal passed under the dominion of the Bhamani kings, on the dismemberment of whose territory it fell to the Imád Sháhi rulers of the Golconda principality.[4]

The following is a genealogical list of the Kákatiya line:—

Bhuvanaika malla, or
Tribhuvanika malla, or
Kákati Prolaya or Púla (A.D. 1110-1160).

Rúdra Déva (1160 ?). Mahádéva (? 1223.)

Ganapati (A.D. 1223-1257.) = Rúdrama Dévi (A.D. 1257-1285.)

Umaka or Mumaka = Vira Déva, or Virabhadra.

Pratápa Rúdra (A.D. 1285-1323.)

Virabhadra.[5]

Although the line of succession above given is tolerably correct, the dates are ten-

[1] There are two if not more gold coins of Muhammad bin Tughlak extant of the Sultánpúr mint, both dated A.H. 729. Pathán Kings of Delhi, pp. 210, 211.

[2] The above facts are derived from Briggs's Ferishta, vol. i. pp. 371, 372, 378, 405; Elphinstone's India, vol. ii. pp. 46, 48, 56-7, 63; Zia-ud-dín Barní in Elliot's Historians of India, vol. iii. pp. 204-233.

[3] Briggs' Ferishta, vol. i. p. 427; Elphinstone's India, vol. ii. p. 63

[4] Mackenzie's Cat. vol. i. p. cxxxiii.

[5] Mackenzie's Cat. vol. i. pp. cxxvii-cxxxiii; J.A.S.B. vol. vii. p. 901; Journ. Bom. Br. Roy. As. Soc. vol. x. pp. 46-49; Ind. Ant. vol. xi. p. 9.

tative only, there being nothing to mark the duration of each individual's reign. The Mackenzie Collection contains a number of dated inscriptions which Professor Wilson gives in the introduction to the Catalogue, but the results obtained from them are so unsatisfactory that I am inclined to think they have been incorrectly copied from the originals. There are two dates, however, which may be accepted with confidence; that of Tailapa Déva's succession to his brother in 1150 A.D., and that of Rúdra's inscription at Anumakoṇda, 1162 A.D. The death of Taila, that of Próla, and the accession of Rúdra must all have occurred within a space of twelve years, and probably, as already stated, about 1160 A.D.; for Próla's rebellion and repentance, followed by his exertions to put down the king's enemies, in the midst of which he seems to have died, must have occupied a considerable time. Although the exact date of his accession is nowhere recorded, tradition assigns him a long reign of fifty years, which, according to the year we have assumed as that of his death, would place it in 1110 A.D. Rúdra is also credited with a long reign, but, as already stated, we have no date of his death. Nor is any date in the line met with on which we can rely, until that mentioned before of the twelfth year of Rudramá Dévi,[1] which is supported by a second inscription of the same year. From these we obtain the date of Ganapati's death, and the succession of his widow. The devolution of her authority in the year 1285 A.D. on her grandson rests on tradition only, but is not improbable. The dates of the closing scenes of Pratápa Rúdra's reign are related by the Mahommedan historians.

The duration of this small dynasty would be about 215 years, giving to each of the seven princes an average reign of 30·5 years—a result in excess of probability. Yet, except with regard to the commencement of Próla's era, which is uncertain, and the fact that two of the princes, viz. Ganapati and his grandson Pratápa, succeeded, if not as minors, at a very early age, the duration assigned to the dynasty is within the limits of possibility, and does not lack the support of contemporary records.

I have not had the opportunity of meeting with many coins of this family, but have made some notes of a few that I have seen, as well as of seals of their grants. Their cognizance appears to have been a bull couchant, which is seen on several of the seals, between two candelabra, with an umbrella above, and on each side a chowrie. One seal had a four-armed figure seated under the umbrella, instead of which on another was a bell, and on a third is the appearance of a snake (?) or undulating line under the bull. A copper coin, now lost, had on the obverse a bull couchant, and on the reverse a legend, not very clear, in a somewhat old form of Nágari, of which the following is a tentative reading, Srimat . . . Ka . . . Kakati . . . Pratápa Ra . . . ya . . (Q. variya) Kataka . . . Saka . . . 2 . . . I had also a large handsome gold coin, with a well-executed bull couchant on the obverse, which must have belonged to this dynasty, and I have still one or two gold fanams with a sitting bull from Rowáda in the Northern Circars.

[1] Sewell's List of Antiq. vol. i. p. 57, 1882.

## 8. EASTERN CHALUKYA DYNASTY.

Having now disposed of the main branch of the great Chalukya empire and the short-lived states which sprang out of its ruins, we turn now to the other branch of the family distinguished from it as the Eastern Chalukya. It was founded, as above stated, by Kubja Vishṇuvardhana, brother of Pulikési II., who, fixing the seat of his power at Rájamahendri *circa* 605 A.D., ruled over Vengi and the greater part of Kalinga. He was followed by fifteen successors, as shown by the accompanying genealogical list, who reigned till about 920 A.D.

About this time an intruder named Táḷapa or Táṛapa pushed aside Vijayáditya, the rightful monarch, and a period of revolutionary changes and disputed successions prevailed for about twenty-five or thirty years. This was followed by an interregnum of about the same duration, after which a prince named Danárnava, whose descent is not clear, restored order and reigned for three years, leaving the throne to his son Kírttivarmá. He was succeeded by his brother, Vimaláditya, the last of the line. The unsettled state of affairs above described appears to have attracted the attention of Rája Naréndra,[1] the then reigning Choḻa king, who, being unsuccessful in a contest with Someswara I., the Chalukya prince of Kalyán, now turned his attention to Vengi-désam. The Rajámahendri kingdom fell an easy prey to the invader, and became incorporated with the empire of the Choḻas, of which it continued to form a part until they were expelled by the Kákatiyas of Worangal at the end of the thirteenth century.

I have not met with any coins of this dynasty, although I was in charge of the provinces which formed their dominions for five years. A few small gold fanams of the Choḻa period were the only result of my enquiries.

The following is the genealogy, slightly modified from that published by me in the Madras Journal.[2] It is still imperfect, but will doubtless be corrected hereafter as fuller details are obtained.[3]

[1] This name taken from the Chélin *Śásanam*, I take to be another appellation of the great Rajendra Chola, who had many titles. Burnell gives him those of "Vira Çoḷa, Kulottuṅga-Çoḷa (i), Rájarájendra (Rájarája) Koppákesarivarmá." The first name, however, I believe to be that of Vira Déva Choḻa, Kulottunga Chola (ii), Tribhuvana Chakravarti, Saptama or seventh Vishṇuvardhaṇa, who succeeded his brother Rája Rája as Viceroy of Vengi-désam.

[2] Vol. iv. n.s. pp. 81-2, 1858.

[3] Ind. Ant. vol. vii. p. 16, and Sewell's List of Antiquities.

Pulikési I.

- Kirttivarma.
- Mangalísa.

(Sons of Kirttivarma:)

- Pulikési II. or Satyasraya I. (Western Line.)
- Vishṇuvardhana I. or Kubja Vishṇuvardhana (A.D. 605, 18 years). Eastern Line.

(Sons of Vishṇuvardhana I.:)

- Jayasimha I. (33 years)
- Indra.

Vishṇuvardhana II. (9 years)

Yuvarája Mángi. (25 years)

- Jayasimha II. (13 years)
- son or brother — Vishṇuvardhana III. (37 years)
- Kokkili (stepson ?). (6 months)

Vijayáditya-Bhaṭṭaraka I. (18 years)

Vishnuvardhana IV. (36 years)

Naréndra Mrija Rája or Vijayáditya. (48 years)

Kali Vishṇuvardhana V. (2 years 6 months)

- Guṇánka Vijayáditya III. (44 years)
- Yuvarája Vikramáditya I.

Chálukya Bhíma I. (30 years)

- Kolabhiganda Vijayáditya IV.
- Vikramáditya Rája (11 months) expelled Tálapa.

Amma Rája I. (7 years)

- Vijayáditya or Kandagachitya. A minor, dethroned by Tálapa or Tárapa (1 month)
- Bhíma Sena II. (8 months)

Malla Nripati or Yuddha Malla (7 years) ........ Bhíma Nripati III. (16 years)

Vijayáditya VI.

Vishṇuvardhana VI.

Amma Rája II.

Interregnum

Danárnava

- Kirttivarmá.
- Vimaláditya.

Daughter = Rája Narendra Chola.

These last details are derived from a very fine copper-plate *sásanam*, in possession of the *karaṇam* of Chélúr,[1] of Víra Déva Choḷa, surnamed Kulottunga Choḷa, Tribhuvana Chakravarti, and Saptama, or seventh Vishṇuvardhana, of Rájamahendri, dated s.s. 1001, conferring the village of Kaléru for maintaining two *mantapams* at Pithápur and Draksharámam, and a tank at Chélúr, supplemented by a smaller copper-plate. He had just been appointed to the Viceroyalty of Vengi, in succession to his brother Rája Rája, whose presence was required at Tanjore, after having held the office for one year only. His inscriptions range from s.s. 1001 to s.s. 1057=A.D. 1079 and 1135.

My only copy of the first, and most interesting document, is with Mr. Fleet in India, and I can only refer to it from the incidental notices in the Madras Journal above quoted, assisted by my memory, which will account for any inaccuracies that may have crept in. The particulars differ in some respects from those given by Burnell at page 22, and again at page 40 of his Palæography of Southern India.

## 9. LAST GREAT HINDU KINGDOM OF VIJAYANAGAR.

The increasing power and importance of the Choḷa state during the eleventh and twelfth centuries would seem to point to it as that in which we might expect to find the next important class of coins, but such is not the case. The inscriptions of Someswara Déva Chalukya I. and his two sons show, it is true, that the Choḷa kings were engaged in frequent warfare with them during the latter half of the eleventh century.[2] This is also confirmed by the narrative in the Vikramanka Charitra,[3] proving that the Choḷa power was then growing in importance. But further hostilities were checked by the long and prosperous reign of Káli Vikrama (Vikramáditya VI.), and afterwards the predominating influence of the Mahommedans prevented any further hostilities on that side. This, however, did not hinder them from advancing along the coast, and from occupying the Rájamahendri kingdom in the early part of the eleventh century, when their power was at its highest, as will be seen when we come to treat of the Dravidian coinage.

In the fourteenth century the foundations were laid for the last great Hindu dynasty, which exercised an important influence on the history of Southern India, both in its political and numismatic aspect. This was the kingdom of Vijayanagar. Like the minor states we have lately been reviewing, its founder boasts of no ancestral lineage, but declares himself simply to be of Yádu race, an origin which deserves fuller consideration.

We have before adverted to the ethnological importance of two great predominating

[1] Madras Journ. vol. iv. N.S. p. 94.  [2] J.R.A.S. vol. iv. pp. 13, 14.  [3] Introd. pp. 27-8, *note* 7.

classes in the early population of India, the pastoral, and predatory or martial.[1] The former exist under many different names, their best known title in the north being that of Ahirs. They are widely distributed, and hold an important position from the earliest times. Sir Henry Elliot describes their wide distribution from the north-west provinces[2] towards Bengal. In the Vishṇu-purána they are included as Abhíras[3] among the people inhabiting the west; and their names occur on two or three other occasions in the enumeration of countries and peoples, from which Prof. H. Wilson takes the opportunity of identifying them with the Abiria, whom Ptolemy places above Patalene on the Delta of the Indus, and also of referring to the mention of them in the Mahábhárata and Rámáyána. They are further specified in the same purána as the dynasty[4] immediately following the Andhras. Sir H. Elliot again refers to them as the Ahir princes who were at one time "Rájas of Nepál, about the beginning of the Christian era, and as perhaps connected with the 'Pála,' or shepherd dynasty, which ruled in Bengal from the ninth to the latter part of the eleventh century."[5] Nor were they confined to Upper India only, for Sir Henry further points out that the name of Aseergurh, which Ferishta says is derived from Asa Aheer, shows that they held an important place in the Dakhan also, where they are best known by their Dravidian name of Kurumbars or Kurubas, with various synonyms in the different dialects.

In early days the Kurumbars occupied a no less conspicuous position in the south than the Ahírs did in the north. The greater part of Drávida then bore the name of Kurumba-bhúm,[6] which extended across the whole peninsula from the Coromandel to the Malabar coast. Occasion has already been taken to notice the eastern portion of it, which on its conquest by the Choḷas received the name of Tondamandalam. Until late years the principality of Kurumbenáḍu existed in North Malabar near Calicut under its own chiefs, the last of whom, according to Buchanan, became extinct in A.D. 1778-79.[7]

When the great officers of Kéraḷa threw off the yoke of the Chéras in the fourth century, the Kurumbar Rája is found among the Sámantas or minor chiefs who declared their independence. At the present day the name still lingers in the Kurumbar *táluk* of Malabar, and in a class of predial (Wilson's Glossary, *s.v.*) slaves in the same district; and although the territorial name in its full extent is lost, the people are found scattered throughout the country in many places.[8] All these, whether Ahírs, Kurumbars, or by whatever name they are called, are sections of a great pastoral race, formerly holding an important place in the political constitution

[1] Journ. Eth. Soc. 1869, vol. i. p. 112.

[2] Supp. Gloss. p. 7, *v.* Aheer.

[3] Vol. ii. p. 168, *note* 4, and p. 185, *note* 2.

[4] Vol. iv. p. 202.

[5] Supp. Gloss. p. 6.

[6] Madr. Journ. vol. vii. p. 312, etc.

[7] Buchanan's Journeys, vol. ii. p. 499.

[8] They are found both in the mountains and in the plains; in the former they fell the timber, at which they are very expert; and in the latter they pasture their flocks, leading a semi-nomad life, in the waste land and jungles, and weaving the black blanket (*kambala*) in general use. Occasionally they engage in agriculture, and are distinguished for their probity and love of truth, so that their word is accepted without hesitation. Those in Arcot and the Tamil provinces generally speak the Canarese language amongst themselves, and may be seen frequenting the market of Madras with their buttermilk and dairy produce. In some parts of Maisur a Kurumbar is required to turn the first furrow for the farmer in spring, indicative of their former hold on the soil; and on the Nílagiri plateau the proud Toḍa, who exacts a tribute in token of superiority from all the other cultivating classes,

of India, of which they have been deprived by subsequent events. Mythologically they are classed as belonging to the Yádu *vamsa*, descended from Yádu, the progenitor of the Yádavas, who were essentially a race of herdsmen. Hence many of the indigenous dynasties have thought it no discredit to deduce their origin from the Yádu *vamsa*, and in doing so may be considered to be derived from the pastoral stock. This, as we have seen, was the case with the Dévagiri and Dvárasamudra families. It was also that of the Raṭṭas or Ráshṭrakúṭas of Mányakhéṭa,[1] and is now seen to be the origin attributed by themselves to the house of Vijayanagar, an origin also claimed for the present dynasty of Maisur. However uncertain the source of the other families may be, the correctness of that assigned to the earliest Vijayanagar dynasty cannot be questioned, for it has always been known as the Kuruba line.[2]

The political state of the South of India in the fourteenth century offered opportunities favourable to the rise of a new power. The raids of Mahmúd of Ghazni and 'Alá-ud-dín Chilji effectually broke down the older Hindu dynasties and established the authority of the Muhammadan empire of Delhi in the northern Dakhan. Its further extension to the south was checked by the revolt of its officers, who, throwing off their allegiance to Delhi, established their independence. In course of time the Báhmani state of Kalburga, the most important of these, in like manner fell to pieces; and this, as well as the subdivision of its territory into four minor principalities, contributed to divert the attention of the Muhammadans from pushing their advances further south at that time. It was in this unsettled period that the kingdom of Vijayanagar arose, and had a lengthened career, which, if its princes had avoided interference in the quarrels of their Musalman neighbours, might have continued to flourish longer than it did. Early in the fourteenth century an adventurer from the south named Sangama, crossing the Káveri, possessed himself of Seringapatam,[3] and with his five sons[4] gradually obtained possession of the Hoysaḷa dominions. The eldest son,

himself presents an offering of the firstfruits to the despised and hated hill Kurumbar, whom at other times he dreads, for his supposed magical powers, and sometimes inflicts on him, in secret, a bloody retribution for visitations of small-pox, cholera, or murrain among their buffaloes attributed to their spells (Rice, Gazetteer of Mysore, vol. iii; Trans. Third Preh. Congress, 1868, p. 253; Proceedings Criminal Courts of Coimbatore, on the slaughter of three Kurumba villages). They take a prominent place in the primeval festival celebrated annually in honour of the village *numen* (the *Gramadevatá*) (Journ. Ethn. Soc. vol. i. N.S. 1868-9, p. 97), under the direction of the Pariahs (*Paraiyar*). On these occasions a general licence prevails. All distinction of caste is suspended; Bráhmans even take part in the bloody rites. After the Pariahs, the Kurubas, or Dhángars as they are also called (Wilson's Glossary, pp. 135, 305), are the leading celebrants, conspicuous, like their probable congeners the Santáls, by their great drum. The saturnalia ended, all revert to their usual status. Notices of the Kurumbars are frequent in the Tamil MS. collections, references to some of which will be found below. Madras Journal, vol. vii. pp. 10, 18, 28, 305-312, 321, 350; vol. viii. pp. 17, 31-2; vol. x. p. 16, etc.; also in the appendices not published in the Journal.

[1] Witness the copper-plate grants of Kardla, J.R.A.S. vol. ii. p. 379, vol. iii. p. 100; of Khárepátan, Journ. Bom. Br. Roy. As. Soc. vol. i. p. 209; of Wana-dindori in Nasik, J.R.A.S. vol. v. p. 350.

[2] They have also been called by some the Narapati dynasty, which, with similar names, as the Gajapati, Aswapati, Chhatrapati, etc., applied to other princes, seems to be a modern practice for which there does not appear to be any good authority.

[3] Inscription at Chitrakaldurg. Colebrooke's Essays, vol. ii. p. 228, and Journal Bombay Branch Royal Asiatic Soc. vol. xii. p. 372.

[4] In the inscriptions translated by Colebrooke the five brothers stand as follows:—Harihara, Kampa, Bukkaraya, "who was sovereign of the earth," Marapa and Mudgapa. Their early title of Mahámaṇḍaléswara is equivalent to that of Count or Palatine in the middle ages applied to the head of a principality, but not necessarily implying submission as a feudatory to a higher power. They have also the title of *Voḍeya* (*sic*) (Journ. Bom. As. Soc. vol. xii. p. 340-1), Odeya or Udaiyár *vulgo* Wodeiyar—a lord, a chief, a ruler—a title borne by some Hindu tribes, and still employed by the sovereigns of Maisur and Kurg (Coorg) (Wils. Glos. pp. 381, 529).

Harihara, and the third, Bukka, are mentioned in inscriptions under the modest title of Mahámandaléśwara, but Bukka was the first who assumed regal style and titles.[1] This is shown by the way in which his name is mentioned as compared with those of his four brothers. Assisted by his celebrated minister Mádhava, also called Vidyaranya, he fixed his capital near the ancient town of Ánegundi, giving to it first the name of Hosapaṭṭaṇa, "new city," afterwards of Hastinávatí, perhaps the Sanskrit equivalent of the Canarese Ánegundi,[2] and finally, as his power extended, that of Vijayanagara, "the city of victory," which became its permanent designation, sometimes exchanged for Vidyanagara, "the city of learning," in honour of his great minister. The date of Bukka's assumption of royalty and the foundation of the city have not as yet been accurately ascertained, but may safely be placed in the period between the third and fifth decades of the fourteenth century. His oldest inscription with which I am acquainted is the copper-plate[3] from Harihar (s.s. 1276 = A.D. 1354), with the seal of a god, before the family adopted the *varáha* or Boar *avatar* of the Chalukyas; and in an inscription on stone at Banawási, the minister is said to rule the Banawási province under Bukkaráya in A.D. 1368 (s.s. 1290). This was probably near the end of his reign, which lasted, Wilson states, according to some accounts, thirty-four years, and if so, would agree with the date (A.D. 1334) assigned for its commencement by Mr. Ravenshaw.[4] It is evident therefore that the chronology and order of succession of the dynasty have yet to be cleared up.

It will be sufficient now to give a nominal list only of the ruling princes as far as they can be ascertained, none of the coins struck by them having dates. Before doing so, however, a few remarks may be offered on the character of the minister Mádhava, to whom much of the celebrity enjoyed by the Kuruba dynasty is due. Of his early history we know comparatively little. He is popularly stated to have aided Bukka both by his counsel and the wealth of which he is reputed to have been possessed. He is known to have been a profound scholar, and, notwithstanding the cares of state, to have written, or caused to be written, voluminous commentaries on the Vedas. In these it is stated that he was assisted by his brother Sayaṇa, regarding whom great differences of opinion prevail. Despite the declarations to the contrary recorded in the commentaries, southern Paṇḍits maintain that Mádhava and Sayaṇa were one and the same person, and further, that he professed the *Vedantist* doctrines of Sankaráchárya, and ended his days at Sringeri as the head, or *Jagadgúru* of the *Smárta maṭha* sect, which post he held for some years, dying in 1386, aged between 80 and 90.

These assertions are scarcely reconcileable with facts derived from other sources. The inscription on stone at Banawási, before mentioned, edited by Fleet, the authority of which has never been questioned, states precisely that in A.D. 1368 the *Máhapradhána* (or

[1] Ind. Ant. vol. x. p. 63, also Journ. Bom. Br. Roy. As. Soc. vol. xii. p. 340–1.
[2] From the word for elephant, *áne*, Canarese = Sanskrit *hasti*.
[3] Journ. Bom. As. Soc. vol. xii. p. 338.
[4] As. Res. vol. xx. p. 7; also pp. 18, 19.

Prime Minister), Mádhavánka, was ruling the Banawási Twelve Thousand under Bukkaráya. This is supported by a copper inscription obtained by Le Grand Jacob[1] in the Southern Konkan, where it is said that in A.D. 1391 the Prime Minister Mádhava, still holding under Harihara the government of Jayantipúr (or Banawási), led an expedition against Goa, expelled the Moslem garrison, and annexed it to the Vijayanagar state.

This contemporary record makes it very improbable that he could have become an ascetic, and ended his days in a *maṭham* at the time stated (A.D. 1386). We may rather conclude that he held his high office of Prime Minister to the last. So much for his history. As regards his opinions, he appears to have had a mind of a high order. His love of letters is proved by his study of the ancient literature of his country, and his cultivation of it, by the important works written by him, or under his superintendence. Among his administrative reforms was the improvement of the mint, and the introduction of the Nágari alphabet in the public records and on the legends of the coins. These, with the *varáha avatar* adopted on the coins and on the state seal, differing only from those of the Chalukya dynasty by the addition of a sword in front of or above the animal, evince a leaning towards Vaishnava rather than Saiva opinions.

The age was one of religious[2] excitement. The teaching of Sankara, Rámánuja, and Madhwácharya; the doctrines of the *Vedánta*, *Adwaita* and *Dwaita* schools; the creed of the *Jangamas* or *Lingáyats*, etc., led to interminable discussions, all urging their respective tenets with a zeal only surpassed by their persecution of the Jainas and other sects, and especially their extirpation of the Buddhists, in which Sankara and his followers were conspicuous. We would fain believe that the tolerant spirit of the wise and learned minister stood aloof from the extremes of bigotry, and that he lent his influence rather to compose differences,[3] and to revive the old simple Vedic theology.

The large number of inscriptions on stone and copper extant should have furnished a reliable narrative of the fortunes of this dynasty, and certainly a trustworthy chronological list of its rulers, had they been critically examined. In the absence of such a work, we can only state the line approximately.

The principal lists available are those published by Professor Wilson,[4] founded mainly, it would appear, on inscriptions of fifteen princes, contained in the Mackenzie Collection,[5] and compared with what he calls the "Chronological statement most generally received," printed in the above-mentioned Collection, and in the Asiatic Researches, vol. xx.; and a list prepared by Colonel Mackenzie himself for the use of Mr. A. D. Campbell, and published in the preface to his Telugu Grammar. From these it would appear that the original Kuruba family was superseded about 1490–1500 A.D., by Narasinga or Víra Narasimha, represented as of

[1] Journal Bombay Br. Roy. As. Soc. vol. iv. p. 107; vol. ix. p. 27.

[2] See Wilson on Religious Sects of the Hindus, As. Res. vol. xvii. These essays have been republished in vols. i. and ii. of Wilson's collected works, by Trübner, in 1861-2.

[3] See an instance, Inscription of Bukkaráya at Belligola, As. Res. vol. ii. p. 270, 8vo. ed.; also Mediation between Jains and Vaishnavas, As. Res. vol. xx. p. 8.

[4] As. Res. vol. xx. p. 7.

[5] Vol. i. p. 293; *ib.* pp. 291–2.

Tuluva extraction,[1] from whom the line has been called the Narasinga dynasty.[2] He and his immediate successors, especially Kṛishṇaráya, appear to have been men of enterprize and ability, and to have extended their dominions considerably to the south, adding to them the whole of Drávida-désam, and placing their lieutenants in Trichinopoly, Tanjore, Madura, Maisur, etc. Ráma Rája[3] is said by some to have been the relative and minister of Sadásiva, the fourth from Narasiṁha, and to have been the *de facto* ruler himself. Ultimately he is represented as setting aside his principal altogether. However this may have been, Ráma Rája provoked the enmity of his Muhammadan neighbours in the Dakhaṅ. He was defeated and slain in the fatal battle of Talikota, A.D. 1564.[4] His brother Trimala, after a futile attempt to resume his authority at Vijayanagar, then removed to Penakonda, a strong position about a 100 miles south of Ánegundi, where, and at Chandragiri, and occasionally at Vellore,[5] his successors resided for some years with greatly diminished power.

After this it is doubtful whether this the third line did not become extinct, but those who claimed to succeed (whoever they might be) were expelled by the Muhammadan King of Golconda, in A.D. 1646,[6] some taking refuge in Ánegundi, calling themselves Polygars only, while others of the family sought an asylum in Bednur. In A.D. 1801, on the cession of that part of Tipú (Tippoo) Sulṭán's dominions to the British Government, the family in Ánegundi, being found in a state of destitution, received a pension from the East India Company. The list of names thus derived, but for the accuracy of which I can in no wise vouch, is given tentatively as follows: to which I further append that prepared by Dr. Burnell, apparently from other sources, and published in his Palæography, pp. 54-5.

| Kuruba Line. | | |
|---|---|---|
| Bukka Ráya[7] | A.D. | 1334—1368-70 |
| Harihára ... | ,, | 1370—1400 |
| Déva Ráya[8] | ,, | 1400—1424 |
| Vijaya? ... | ,, | 1424—1445? |
| Mallikárjuna | ,, | 1445?-1465 |
| Virupaksha | ,, | 1473—1488 |

| Narasimha Line. | | |
|---|---|---|
| Narasimha... | A.D. | 1488—1508-9 |
| Krishna Ráya | ,, | 1508-9—1530 |
| Achyuta Ráya | ,, | 1530—1542 |
| Sadásiva ... | ,, | 1542— ?? |

| Third or Usurping Line. | | |
|---|---|---|
| Ráma Rája | A.D. | 1550?-1564 |
| Trimala ... | ,, | 1564—1571 |
| Sriranga I. | ,, | 1572—1586 |
| Venkatapati | ,, | 1586—1608 |
| Viraráma ... | ,, | 1622—1626 |
| Sriranga II. | ,, | 1615—1628 |
| Venkata ... | ,, | 1628—1636 |
| Rámadéva ... | ,, | 1636—1643 |
| Ánegundi Venkatapati | ,, | 1643—1646 |

but he having been expelled in A.D. 1646, the line virtually ceased.

[1] In the inscription of his son Kṛishṇa Ráya, dated S.S. 1434 = A.D. 1512, edited by Fleet, in the Bombay Journ. vol. xii. pp. 391-3, he is called Narasa, Nṛisiṁha, and S'rí Nárasiṁha, descended from "Timma, famous among the princes of Tuluva." But Ferishta repeatedly refers to him as the Telinga Rája. The recent destruction of Woraṅgal, with the events which followed, doubtless sent many to seek their fortunes in a new country. In the same grant Kṛishṇa Ráya is called his son by Nagaládévi, by some said to have been a concubine.

[2] Wilkes's History of Mysore, vol. i. p. 15. Inscriptions of Virupaksha, the last of the Kurubas, extend from 1473 to 1478 A.D. Mackenzie Cat. vol. i. p. cxliii.

[3] Ferishta makes him son-in-law of Sheo (Sadásiva). According to the Persian account, a powerful minister, named Timráj, took advantage of the minority of Sadásiva's grandson, whom he poisoned on his attaining manhood, and setting up another minor, administered the affairs of the kingdom till his death, on which his son Rámrája, who had married Sadásiva's daughter, openly usurped the throne. Briggs's Ferishta, vol. iii. p. 80-1; Mackenzie Cat. vol. i. p. 294.

[4] After the battle Bijanagar was taken and sacked by the conquerors, a blow from which it never recovered. Its wealth and prosperity have been described in glowing terms by several travellers. One of them, Abd-or-Razzak, ambassador from Sháh Rokh in 1442, says, "The city is such that the pupil of the eye has never seen a place like it, and the ear of intelligence has never been informed that there existed anything to equal it in the w rld." His accounts are confirmed by the Venetian traveller Nicoló Conti, who visited it in the early part of the fifteenth century (Hakluyt Soc., India in the Fifteenth Century, p. 23; *ib.* p. 6), and by Cæsar Frederick, who saw it three years after its fall.

[5] Wilkes's History of Mysore, vol. i. pp. 12-19.

[6] *Ib.* p. 19.

[7] Mackenzie Coll. i. cxlii. and Ravenshaw, As. Res. xx. 7.

[8] Burgess and Fleet, Inscriptions, p. 22. Date of his installation, 1400 A.D.

*List according to Burnell.*

Sangama, of the Yádava family and Lunar race ! !

- Hariyappa (1336-1350)
- Bukka I. (1350-1379), m. Gaurambiká
  - Harihara (1379-1401)
    - Bukka II. (1401-1418) m. Tippámba.
      - Devarája, Víradeva, or Vírabhúpati (1418-1434) married Padmámba and Mallámba, Vijaya (? 1434-1454), and others, ? Prauḍha Deva (? 1456-1477), Malikárjuna (1481-1487), Rámacandra (1487), Virúpáxa (1488-1490), Narasimha (1490-1508).
        - (Víranarasimha)
        - Krishnarája (1508-1530)
        - Acyuta (1534-42)
          - Sadáçiva (made an alliance with Viceroy J. de Castro in 1546).
      - Krishṇaráia

This Sadáçiva succeeded as a child: "Thirty yeares was this Kingdome governed by three brethren which were Tyrants, the which keeping the rightfull king in prison, it was their use euery yeere once to show him to the people, and they at their pleasures ruled as they listed. These brethren were three captaines belonging to the father of the king they kept in prison, which when he died, left his sonne very young, and then they tooke the gouerment to themselves" (C. Frederick, in "Purchas His Pilgrimes," vol. ii. p. 1704; *cf.* Couto, Dec. vii. 5, 5, f. 93*b*).

Vírappa Náyak

- Rámarája (killed in 1565)
- Timma (Tirumala Bómma). Transferred the seat of government to Pennakoṇḍa in 1567; Purchas, vol. ii. p. 1705.
  - Rangarája (?1572-1585).
  - Venkatapati (? 1585-1614) at Candragiri (Purchas, vol. ii. p. 1746).
- Bengatre (*sic* in Purchas. He was killed in 1565. According to Couto, Decada vii. 2, 8, his name was Venkataráya.)

The history of Ferishta,[1] who wrote during the end of the sixteenth and the beginning of the seventeenth century, throws considerable light on the events we have just been considering. He resided at the court of Ahmadnagar with his father,[2] in the reign of Murtuza Husain Nizám Sháh. During the troubled times which followed the death of that prince he repaired to Bijapúr, and found an asylum with Ibrahim 'Ádil Sháh II., A.D. 1579-1626, and must, therefore, have been familiar with the events he describes.

According to his narrative, the Rájas of Vijayanagar[3] early came into unwise and

[1] Ferishta who was born in the end of the sixteenth century, completed his history in 1609 at Bijapúr.
[2] Brigg's Ferishta, vol. i. pp. xl, xli
[3] Ferishta, vol. ii. p. 301.

unprovoked collisions with the Báhmani kings and their successors, but the facts as related by him for the possession of Moodgul[1] appear to be exaggerated, and the name of Kṛishṇa given to the Bijanagar king nowhere occurs in the generally received lists. It is found, however, in that of Dr. Burnell. Other cases of ill-judged interference on the part of the Hindus are mentioned, one of which, in 1520 A.D.,[2] was attended with partial success, but generally the Muhammadan historian shows them to have been worsted. An interesting summary is given of the events ending in the battle of Talikota,[3] and of those that forced Ráma Rája's successor, here called Venkatadri, to seek for refuge in Penakonda and Chandragiri,[4] together with the steps taken by 'Ali 'Ádil Sháh to follow up the victory.

The adoption of the boar symbol of the Chalukyas by Mádhava, with the use of the Nágari alphabet, should have appeared more prominently on the new coinage; but I have only met with it on the copper money, in which the boar is distinguished from that of the Chalukyas by the addition of a sword. This, however, does not apply to the gold coinage, in which I have met with no instance of the employment of the same symbol, but only with mythological forms of their deities: in all, the legends are Nágari. The employment of this character was continued, so far as our present knowledge extends, by the princes of the three successive sections of the dynasty. But the coin figured by Wilson[5] from the Mackenzie Collection implies that the practice of the first prince of the Narasinga line forms an exception. As described it represents on the obverse the Narasinga *avatar*, while the legend on the reverse exhibits, in Canarese characters, the name Narasimha. In the absence of other examples, it cannot now be determined how long this innovation lasted, but it would appear from the readings given below that it did not continue. Probably it owed its appearance to the foreign extraction of Narasinga, derived, according to some accounts, from the Malabar coast, but, according to all the Muhammadan historians, from the Telugu country. The Kuppelúr inscription describes him as the son of Isvara, and a coin bearing this name may be explained in this connection. It represents the figures of Ráma and Sita, seated, with Hanumán, and, on the reverse, the word Isvara, in Canarese. as will be noticed when treating of the *Ráma-ṭanka* medals further on.

There are, besides these, copper coins having the boar and sword on the obverse and Canarese legends on the reverse, which must be attributed to the same period.

In a paper on the pagoda or *varáha* coins in the Journal of the Asiatic Society of Bengal, vol. lii. mention is made of a gold coin in the Madras Government Museum, weighing fifty-one or fifty-two grains, bearing the figure of Hanumán seated, on the obverse, and an imperfect legend on the reverse, in which the name "Bukka" is said to have been read. For this reason it has been assigned to the founder of the Kuruba line. The description given is very short. The figure exhibits none of the characteristics of the monkey

[1] Ferishta, vol. ii. p. 310.
[2] *Ib.* vol. iii. pp. 48–50.
[3] *Ib.* p. 80.
[4] *Ib.* p. 141.
[5] As. Res. vol. xvii. p. 595, pl. iv. fig. 90.

deity, and the character of the letters in which the single word "Bukka" is read is not stated. As represented in fig. 9, plate ii. it looks like Canarese, or Telugu.

The same paper contains a notice of two coins taken from Moor's Hindu Pantheon,[1] of which the Museum does not appear to possess examples. They are represented in plate i. figs. 10, 10a. The obverse is described as exhibiting a "two-headed bird, like the Russian national ensign, but holding a small elephant in each beak and in each claw." On the reverse, *S'ri Pratápa Déva Ráya*, as read by Dr. Burgess (but only, it would appear by the context, from Moor's figure, and not from the coin), which he attributes to the third Kuruba prince. Before, however, accepting this assignment, it is proper to examine the matter a little further.

Gold coins with this device are by no means rare. Moor figures four; Wilson gives representations also of four; and I myself possess seven. Among all these are two types: one with a two-headed insessorial bird advancing to the left; the other exactly resembling the spread eagle of the Russian and Austrian arms. Wilson suggests the name on the legend to be Śrí Víra, which a friend (Mr. Fleet), well known for his skill in palæography, reads Śrí Pratápa Chatura Ráya. Mr. Thomas reads Śri Pratápá Chatuta Ráya, which he thinks may stand for Achatutya, and be identified with Achyuta, the third name in the second or Narasinga family.

It is difficult, amongst such varying statements, to decide on the paternity of these coins. Dr. Bidie figures a second exemplar as 10 among his gold coins, but refers to it as a copper piece in plate ii. It has the reverse of what appears to be a trisula, or trident. I have a number of copper pieces (upwards of thirty), all of them with the double-headed bird, some with Nagari legends on the reverse, others with Telugu or Canarese, much worn, and none of them intelligently read. One has apparently a figure seated on an animal on the reverse; others are quite plain, and many show signs of considerable antiquity. For a long time I attributed these coins to Kṛishṇa Ráya, the greatest prince of this dynasty, who, in the copper-plate inscription at Kuppélúr, in the Raṇibennur[2] *táluḳ* already referred to at p. 93, is described as "a very Gaṇḍabhéruṇḍa to the herds of elephants that are his foes." Under the diverse readings of the reverse, this identification will not stand. The conclusion to which I now come is that the symbol is not indicative of a particular dynasty, but may have been assumed by any prince in token of his military prowess. I am strengthened in this view by the fact of the figure of Garuḍa having been adopted as the cognizance of several of the dynasties of which I have treated above, viz. the Yádavas of Devagiri, the Raṭṭas or Ráshṭrakúṭas, the Siláharas of Kolhapur, and being, moreover, a favourite emblem of all votaries of the Vaishnava creed.[3]

[1] Plate 104, p. 434.

[2] Journ. Bom. Br. Roy. As. Soc. vol. xii. p. 393.

[3] Moor and Wilson likewise suppose the bird to represent *Garuḍa*, and Col. Yule also considers the strange relations of Marco Polo regarding the *Gryphon* to have had a similar origin. Whencesoever derived, it is undoubtedly the monster popularly known in South Indian mythology under the name of *gaṇḍa bhérunda*. In the Tamil dictionary it appears as *gaṇḍa* or *kaṇḍa bhérunda pakshi*, meaning, "a double-headed monstrous bird." Brown, in his Telugu dictionary, under the word *gaṇḍa*, gives a not well-authenticated meaning, "a lump of flesh"; and the Malayálim word, according to Dr. Gundert, signifies "the

It is remarkable that no coin of Krishṇa Ráya himself has yet, as far as I am aware, been found. A representation of the youthful Krishṇa on a very well-executed coin, I believed would be found to pertain to him, but neither does this hold good, when the legend is read. The fame of his style and superscription (viz. Śrí pratápa Krishṇa Ráya) has caused it to be largely assumed by subsequent usurpers of the royal prerogative, who asserted their independence on the fall of the empire.

My collection contains a considerable number of coins unread before I left India, which, as now interpreted, appear to belong to this dynasty. Several of them have figures of Śiva and Parvati seated, and others exhibit the semblance of Vishnu standing under an archway, or canopy. Being unable, from loss of sight, to describe these and some others more minutely, Mr. Thomas has kindly offered to decipher them for me, and I now append the conclusions to which he has arrived in his own words, as shown in the subjoined note.[1]

temple of the elephant." Dr. Rost considers that *gaṇḍa* may be a southern corruption of *Garuḍa*, and *bhérunda* or *bhairunda* a *tadbhava* form meaning "terrible."

Eastern romance contains many allusions to a monstrous two-headed bird holding elephants in its beak and in its claws, the elephant in the former sometimes replaced by the *sarabha*, or fabulous lion. We are all familiar with the part it plays as the Roc in the story of Sindbad the Sailor, and his adventures with the gigantic egg, and also with the bird, as told in Lane's Arabian Nights, where both its figure and its attack on Sindbad's ship are vividly portrayed (vol. iii. pp. 90, 52; also vol. ii. p. 60, *note*). It appears to be the *'angka* of the Arabs, the *simurgh* of the Persians, the *bar yuchre* of the Talmud, the *gryps* of the Greeks, and the *griffin*, or *gryphon*, of European heraldry.

[1] [As we may eventually, perchance, be unable to exhibit in our Plates facsimile illustrations of the various ramifications of the Vijayanagar currencies, I have compiled the subjoined list of Nágarí legends from the previously published engravings and descriptions of this series of Coins, aided by the extant specimens of the class in Sir Walter Elliot's collection. The identification of the issuers of some of the coins is not always complete.

The alphabet employed does not seem to have reached a very determinate stage, and the die-engravers themselves seem only partially to have understood the original forms of the letters. Hence the Palæographer will detect many anomalous revivals of the normal types of the Nágarí characters—a difficulty in the way of interpretation which will not be lessened by the ignorance of subsequent artists who have had to reproduce the originals for our more modern copper plates.

No. 1.—Gold. Sir W. Elliot. Six coins.

OBVERSE.

Şiva and Parvatí.

REVERSE.

श्री प्रताप हरिहर

*Şrí Pratápa Harihara.*

No. 2.—As. Res. vol. xvii. Nos. 93, 94, 95, 96, p. 595; Moore's Hindú Pantheon, pl. civ. fig. 3; J.A.S. Bengal, 1883, pl. i. 10*a*. Sir Walter Elliot has numerous coins of this type.

OBVERSE.

Two-headed Bird. Garuda? sometimes to the front, at others to the left.

श्री प्रतापाचतुत राय

*Srí pratápa-achatuta Ráya.*

The reading of the name on this class of coins has hitherto remained indeterminate. Prof. Wilson hesitatingly suggested वीर *Vira* (As. Res. vol. xvii. p. 595). Dr. Bidie, under the inspiration of Mr. J. Burgess, prefers *Deva Ráya*—a reading I cannot concur in. A peculiarity is noticeable in those legends in the frequent prolongation of the final *a* in *Pratapá*, which implies a short *a* before the apparently opening *ch*, and authorizes the identification of the name with that of *Achyuta*, No. 8 of Wilson's list of Inscription designations, in the As. Res. vol. xx. p. 7, or that of the eighth king after Bukka. See pp. 93, 94, *ante*.

No. 3.—General Pearse.

OBVERSE.

Siva and Parvatí.

श्री प्रताप सदासिव राय

*Şrí Pratápa Sadá Sivá Ráya*

No. 3*a*.—Marsden, MLXXIV. J.A.S. Bengal, 1883, pl. ii. fig. 13. Sir W. Elliot. Two coins.

OBVERSE.

Siva and Parvatí.

श्री सदा सिवा

*Şrí Sadá Sivá* (the *Ikkeri* king).

No. 4.—J.A.S. Bengal, 1883, pl. ii. fig. 14. Sir W. Elliot. Two coins.

OBVERSE.

Siva and Parvatí.

श्री कँव चरमल राय

*Şrí Kanwa Triramala Ráya.*

The copper coins of this king with the boar obverse read

चलम चरमल तक

*Chalem* (*Chalen*) *Triramala taka* (for *Tanka*)

No. 5.—Marsden, MLXXIII. As. Res. vol. xvii. No. 96; J.A.S.B. 1883, pl. ii. fig. 15.

OBVERSE.

Vishnu.

श्री वेंक ईस्वराय नमः

*Şrí Venka íswaráya namah.*

Marsden read *Deswara*, but Mr. Sewell, more correctly, gives *Eswara*. The initial letter is a near approach to the modern *í*, a counterpart of which we have in the titles of Lankeswára, Dareswára etc.

From the above identifications it appears that representations of Śiva and Parvati found especial favour with several of the princes of the line, which, with reference to their religious proclivities and to the Vaishnava names of several, is somewhat remarkable. The same device is found on the coins of the Rájus of Ikkeri and Bednur, who were worshippers of Śiva, and with whom they have hitherto been supposed to have originated.

The not uncommon coins called Venkatapati *húns*, having the effigy of Vishṇu, standing under an archway, probably originated with the later Chandragiri princes, three of whom bore that appellation. Which of them first struck the pieces now bearing the above name it is difficult to say; not improbably it was retained by all three. They are well executed, and continued in circulation to a late period, especially on the east coast and in the province of Arcot. In Ráidrug (Ráyadurga), a district of Bellary, Major (Sir Thomas) Munro states that they were the only gold coins current at the end of the last and beginning of the present century, although not accepted in the neighbouring districts.[1] This is accounted for by the fact that on the dissolution of the Vijayanagar government, the then military commander, or *Dalawái*,[2] of the place, made himself master of Penakonda, from which he was ejected by the king of Bijapúr, and was then established at Raidrug, paying a considerable tribute, in addition to stated military service, to the 'Ádil Sháhi dynasty, and afterwards to Aurangzeb.[3]

The Nágari legend on the copper coins with the figure of the boar is, according to Mr. Thomas, *Chalam* (current) *Triramala taka* (for *ṭanka*), which he therefore assigns to Tirumala, the brother of Ráma Rája; that in the Canarese character is read by my friend before mentioned, *aisakha mása* with the numeral 1. followed by another, perhaps a fraction (?), above it, apparently having reference to the exchangeable value of the piece. A number of these coins were figured in the Numismatic Gleanings, where the epigraph was read as *Sálava* or *Chálava Tiramal Ráya*,[4] and the Canarese legend on another, fig. 11, as Śriman Ráma, with the numeral 15 above it.

No. 6. OBVERSE.

Dancing figure of Kṛishṇa—Sir W. Elliot; two specimens.

श्री चिक देव राय

*Şri Chika Deva Ráya.*

"*Chakka Deva Mahárúya*" is mentioned in Mr. Ravenshaw's Inscription, No. 7, of s. 1442 (As. Res. vol. xx. p. 28), as of the "tribe of Casyapa . . . strong as the *Garuda Bharunda*." He is supposed to be the *Chak dás*, No. 116 of the Pedigree list, p. 19. But the device on this coin seems to remove it from the Vijayanagar list proper.

No. 7.—Marsden, No. MLXX. and MLXXI. As. Res. vol. xvii. No. 88. Journ. Asiatic Soc. of Bengal, 1883, No. 12*a* and 12*b*, Dr. Bidie's paper.

OBVERSE.

Durgá seated.

श्री प्रताप कृष्ण . .

*Şri Pratápa Kṛishṇa Ráya.*

Sir W. Elliot considers that these coins represent a class of later date, and of a different locality.

No. 8.—Dr. Bidie gives an engraving of a coin (pl. i. fig. 11) with an obverse of Siva and Parvati, as in No. 1 of this list, with a reverse which reads clearly

श्री प्रताप दाव राय

*Şri Pratápa Dáva Ráya.*

This piece he classes under a series otherwise supposed to belong to *Deva Ráya*, or the next in succession to *Harihara*. The Nágarí transcript in the Ravenshaw inscription, No. 3, p. 38, adheres to the देव *Deva*.—E.T.]

[1] Letter to Bd. of Rev. 25th January, 1806.

[2] *Dalawái* is the title of a military commander, or minister of state, and is still borne in that sense by the ministers of Maisur and Travancore.

[3] Appendix to the Report of the Principal Coll. of the Ceded Districts, dated 20th March, 1802, quoted in V. Report H. of C. 1812, p. 839–40.

[4] The word *Sálava* before *Tiramal* may be the family name of the third dynasty, and may perhaps also have some connection with the second dynasty (Ind. Ant. vol. xiii. p. 155). The old family of Sálva or Saluva was of some distinction, and flourished for several centuries at Karwait or Karveti Nagara. See *ante*, p. 43, *note*. Also Mad. Journ. Lit. and Sc. vol. iv. N.S. pl. i. figs. 12-17, pp. 91 and 96-99.

To this era I would assign the large cup-shaped gold medals, the form of which may have been taken from the concave *padma-ṭankas* before described, as struck at Banawási, of which Mádhava was so long governor. These medals, with elaborate representations of Ráma and Síta sitting in state surrounded by numerous attendants, among whom Hanumán is conspicuous, are known as *Ráma-ṭankas*,[1] and are greatly prized by Vaishnava Bráhmans as objects of household worship at the present day, so much so, that they are now often manufactured for that purpose. Flat pieces, with a similar representation of Ráma and his court on the obverse and a Nágari reverse, weighing from 167 to 180 grains and upwards, are occasionally met with. I have only seen them in the British Museum. Both these appear to be medals. In connection with the above I may advert to the coin mentioned before with that of Narasimha, the founder of this second dynasty, in which Ráma and Śita are represented seated on the obverse with Hanumán, and the words Śri Isvara on the reverse. They weigh 58 grains. In addition to these I have two spheroidal specimens, somewhat resembling Mr. Gibbs' coin described at page 53, but only weighing from 18 to 18½ grains. They have on the concave side what appears to be Hanumán holding a flower, and on the convex reverse apparently one or two figures seated, but much worn and indistinct. The cabinet of the late Col. Guthrie contained two gold pieces, of which he kindly gave me casts, connected apparently with this class of medals. The larger exhibited on the obverse, Ráma and Sita seated in profile with Hanumán before them, and behind them a figure holding a *ch'hatra* or umbrella. On the reverse were four erect figures supporting a canopy (?) and in the exergue two indistinct letters. The other is similar, but smaller. The obverse is the same, but the three figures on the reverse appear to be moving to the right. The casts are too indistinct to allow of a more minute description. Having been purchased, their origin is not known. The whole collection is believed to have gone to Berlin.[2]

The characters impressed on the gold coins of the Vijayanagar dynasty survived its decay, and continued to be exhibited in a class of pagodas, mostly associated with the figure of Durga and the legend of Kṛishṇa Ráya, struck by numerous local chiefs and princelings who, after the fall of the empire, established themselves on its ruins as noticed before. Some account of these will be found in the concluding section of Part III.

NOTE.—After the foregoing was in type, Dr. E. Hultzsch's paper on a copper grant of Ranga II., s.s. 1566 (=A.D. 1644), appeared in the June number of the Indian Antiquary, vol. xiii. p. 153, which throws some further light on the succession of the later princes, subsequent to the Narasinga line, after their supersession by the descendants of Ráma Rája.

In this paper the learned Doctor refers to a grant of Sadásiva in his possession, received from

[1] *Ráma-ṭankas* occur in different sizes, the largest ought to weigh four *tólas* or 720 grains, perhaps a double *Ráma-ṭanka*, and is very rare; the next, 360 grains; the third, 180 grains. These appear to be the normal weights, which have been reckoned according to the standard *tóla* of 1833 = 180 grains, but the bazaar *tóla* of twelve *mashas* is somewhat less, and varies in different places.

[2] The same subject is likewise engraved on seals, of which I have a good specimen cut in a piece of lapis lazuli.

Dr. Burgess, bearing the date of s.s. 1478 (=A.D. 1556–7), which does not appear to have been published. This grant gives the genealogy the same as that in Mr. Fleet's Kuppélúr inscription of Kṛishṇa Ráya, with the additional names of Raṅga, Achyuta, his son Venkata, and his nephew Sadásiva. Then the substantive grant of Raṅga II. goes on to show the genealogy of Ráma, who married the sister (?) of Sadásiva, and eventually usurped the throne. This Ráma is shown to be derived from a family of subsidiary princes styled Rájas of Karnata.[1] He and his brother Tirumala are said to have been the sons of Raṅga, who was the son of Ráma, and he the son of Bukka, "protector of Saluva Nṛisiṁha (of Vijayanagar?)," whatever this may mean. But this Bukka has no connexion with the founder of the Kuruba line. The succession of the remaining Karnata princes, which is somewhat confused, concludes the paper. The grant is dated A.D. 1644, only two years before the taking of Chandragiri by Abdullah Kutb Sháh, of Golconda, which extinguished the monarchy.

The following are the names of the reigning Karnata kings, as taken from the grant of Ranga II. mentioned above, showing their descent, but omitting the names of those who did not reign, and being a succession of six princes from 1564–1644, which gives an average reign of 13·2 years each.

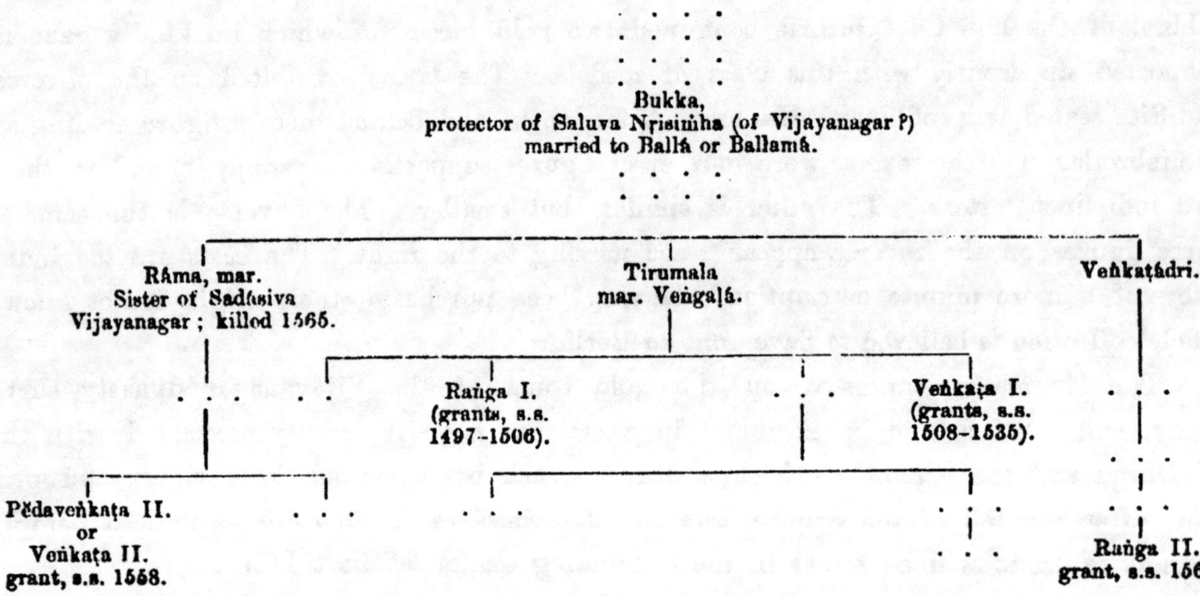


[1] According to an inscription given by Rice in the Mysore Inscriptions, they are called "Lords of Aravîṭipura" (p. 254). Grant of S'ri Raṅga Rája at Devanhalli, dated s.s. 1506 = A.D. 1584.

## 10. THE VEMA REḌḌIS OF KONDAVIḌ.

A family of this name attained to some distinction after the fall of Worangal. I had obtained some inscriptions concerning them, in the Kṛishṇa division of the Northern Circars which, with the rest of my collection, having been lent to Mr. Fleet, are now in India. I am, therefore, only able to give a very meagre account of the family. My chief reliance is on a copy of an inscription[1] from the pagoda of Amareswara, at Amarávati, neár the Krishna in Guntúr, dated s.s. 1283=A.D. 1361, recording the dedication of a temple to Amareswara, which was re-established by Ala Véma Reḍḍi in the year 1361 A.D., some twenty or thirty years after the fall of Worangal; and on some local records, which cannot be accepted with much confidence.

In these it is stated that the family first came from Anumakoṇḍa, the original seat of the Kákatiyas, where a wealthy farmer named Permál, Perumálla, or Prolaya Reḍḍi, resided. He had five sons, with whom he established himself at Kondaviḍ, a place of great strength, and extended his possessions over the neighbouring country. He was succeeded by his son Allanda Reḍḍi, and he by his brother Dodaya Reḍḍi. The latter had three sons, of whom the youngest, Allada Bhúpati, succeeded him. His son was Véma Reḍḍi, the only possessor of the name found in the manuscript, and if the family took their designation from him, he must have been a personage of some importance. But the only authentic mention of the name is in the above inscription. He was followed by his brother Virabhadra, in whose time Kondaviḍ is said to have been taken by Kṛishṇa Ráya of Vijayanagar. Other accounts, however, attribute the fall of Kondavid to the Muhammadan ruler of Golconda. But this must be a mistake, for Kṛishṇa Ráya reigned from 1508-9 to 1530 A.D. It is quite impossible to reconcile this with the date of the inscription above mentioned, which is not only clear in the manuscript copy which I possess, but agrees with Professor H. H. Wilson's mention of it in the Introduction of the Mackenzie Catalogue; and is further irreconcileable with the Professor's statement that "the number of descents is uniformly stated at seven, and this is apparently correct,"[2] and on the previous page that "they sunk under the ascendency of the Vijayanagar dynasty, after an independent reign of about a century."[3] I can find, however, only the names of six princes, which are shown in the accompanying genealogical table. It is probable, therefore, that Véma Reḍḍi either had at least six or seven successors of whom no mention is made, or rather, which is more probable, that we must attribute the establishment of the Kondaviḍ principality to the Véma Reḍḍi of the inscription, or his immediate progenitors, before the middle of the fourteenth century. This agrees with the final subjugation of Worangal about the same period, when some of the fugitives from that place are said to have found a refuge at Kondavid, where, in virtue of their common origin, they would be favourably received.

[1] Given to me by Colonel Mackenzie's employé, Cavelly V. Lutchmiah.

[2] Mackenzie Cat. vol. i. p. cxxxv. [3] *Ib.* cxxxiv.

I have seen few, if any coins, as far as I know, belonging to this family; but I have three copper pieces bearing a bull couchant with a *lingam* over the back, which may perhaps be attributed to it; for they adopted the cognizance of the Worangal Kákatiyas, namely, that of a bull (or Nandi) couchant. I have a facsimile of a figure of this animal, which I saw on the ring connecting the plates of one of their copper grants. It is neatly modelled, and represents a recumbent bull covered with trappings, having a small *lingam* and *yoni*, the emblem of Mahádéva, or Siva, in front of its bended knees.

### *Véma Reḍḍi Genealogy.*

From a Manuscript headed "Ancient Princes of Reddiwár Family of the Kondavid Dynasty in Telinga." Also Mackenzie Catalogue, Vol. I. p. 309.

Permál, Perumálla, or Prolaya Reḍḍi = Annamamba.

- Allanda Reḍḍi.
- Pedda Cóta Reḍḍi.
- Anna Prala Reḍḍi.
- Dodaya Reḍḍi.
  - Pola Bhúpati.
  - Cóta Bhúpati
  - Allada Bhúpati.
    - Véma Vibhunda, or Véma Reḍḍi.
    - Virabhadra Reḍḍi.
    - Dadaya Reḍḍi.
    - Annaya Reḍḍi
- Penna Cóta Reḍḍi.

Another List from Taylor's Catalogue Raisonné Or. MSS. Vol. III. p. 513.

| | | | |
|---|---|---|---|
| Potaiya Véma Reḍḍi, reigned | | 12 | years. |
| Cómti Véma Reḍḍi | ,, | 27 | ,, |
| Anupota Véma Reḍḍi | ,, | 30 | ,, |
| Rája Véma Reḍḍi | ,, | 4 | ,, |
| Dherma Véma Reḍḍi | ,, | 12 | ,, |
| Cumara Giri Reḍḍi | ,, | 14 | ,, |

## 11. SILAHARAS.

Before leaving the table-land it may be worth while, here, to notice another small state in Western Kuntala, although I have no acquaintance with their coins. It is that of the Siláháras of Kolhápur, connected with which are branches below the Ghâts in the Konkan. They never attained to great eminence, but an interest attaches to one of their titles as deriving their origin from Tagara, a place known to the Greek geographers, the identification of which has given rise to much ingenious speculation.

The family claim to belong to the Vidyádhara Jimutaváhana *kula*, distinguished by the ensign of a golden *Garuda*, with the style and title of a Mahámaṇḍaleswara, and the distinction of the *noubat* (five *mahásabdas*). The several divisions of the family have been fully treated by Paṇdit Bhagvanlál in the thirteenth volume of the Bombay Journal.

A Kolhápur copper grant has the impression of a *Garuḍa* on the seal, while that of a grant from the Konkan bears a sitting figure, probably *Garuḍa*, with the hands joined in the attitude of devotion. The following are the genealogies of the two principal families:

1st.—Kolhápur, Journal Bombay Branch Roy. Asiatic Soc. Vol. xiii. p. 16 (Paṇḍit Bhagvanlal's).

- **Jatiya I.**
  - **Nayavarman or Nagimma.**
    - **Chandarája.**
      - **Jatiga II.**
        - **Gonka Gonkala.**
          - **Marsinha (A.D. 1058)**
            - **Guvala II.**
            - **Gangadéva.**
            - **Bhojadéva I. Balláladéva.**
            - **Gandaráditya (A.D. 1110, 1118, 11136).**
              - **Vijayáditya, Vijayárka (A.D. 1143-51).**
                - **Bhojadéva II. (A.D. 1100, 1131)**
        - **Gúvala I.**
        - **Kirttirája.**
        - **Chandráditya.**

2nd.—Kharepatan Plates (Ind. Ant. Vol. ix. pp. 33-46).

- **Kapardi I.**
  - **Pulaśakti.**
    - **Kapardi II. (A.D. 853-877).**
      - **Vatpuvanna.**
        - **Zanza (A.D. 916).**
        - **Goggi.**
          - **Vajjaḍadéva I.**
            - **Aparájita.**
              - **Vajjaḍadéva II.**
                - **Chhittarája (A.D. 1026).**
                - **Nágárjuna.**
                  - **Anantadéva (A.D. 1094).**
                    - **Aparáditya (A.D. 1187).**
                - **Mummuṇi (A.D. 1060).**
              - **Arikesarí (A.D. 1017).**

## 12. WODEIYAR DYNASTY OF MAISUR.

The only State of importance which established itself permanently after the fall of Vijayanagar in south Kuntala was that of Maisur. When the greater part of Southern India was annexed to that empire by the Narasinga dynasty in the sixteenth century, the charge of the south-western districts was entrusted to a viceroy located at Seringapatam, who collected the revenue, or tribute, from a number of local chiefs, or Wodeiyars, as they were called, according to Wilkes thirty-three in number.[1] As the paramount authority declined, these chiefs, or Polygars, assumed a more independent position, and even adopted, when they dared, the title of Rája.[2] Tradition relates that among these were two brothers named Vijaya and Krishṇa, who are said to have constructed the fort of Maisur, in the district of Hadana, early in the sixteenth century. One of their successors, named Cháma Rája, went so far as to withhold his tribute and set the viceroy at defiance.[3] It was, however, paid with more or less regularity by his successors till early in the seventeenth century. Ráj Wodeiyar, the then chief of Maisur, who appears to have been a man of capacity and energy, and had great influence with the viceroy, assumed possession of the whole province on the death of that functionary.[4] The importance of the family as an independent power may be held to have begun with this Ráj Wodeiyar. He was followed by eight successors:—

| | |
|---|---|
| Ráj Wodeiyar .. .. .. .. .. .. | 1578—1617. |
| Chama Rája IV. .. .. .. .. .. | 1617—1637. |
| Immaḍí Rája .. .. .. .. .. .. | 1637—1638. |
| Kaṇṭhiráva Narasa Rája .. .. .. .. | 1638—1659. |
| Kempa Déva Rája .. .. .. .. .. | 1659—1672. |
| Chikka Déva .. .. .. .. .. .. | 1672—1704. |
| Kaṇṭhiráva Rája II. ("Múkarasu," or the dumb) .. | 1704—1714. |
| Doḍḍa Krishṇa Rája .. .. .. .. .. | 1714—1731. |
| Cháma Rája V. .. .. .. .. .. | 1731—1733. |

with the last of whom the line seems to have ceased in 1733 A.D., during a period of anarchy caused by disputed successions which enabled Haidar 'Ali to seize upon the throne. He died in 1782, and on the death of his son Tipú, who was slain in 1799, the old line was restored in the person of Krishṇa Rája Wodeiyar, a child of five years old. After a long reign of sixty-nine years, he was succeeded by his adopted son, the present Rája, in 1868.

[1] History of Mysore, vol. i. p. 20. [2] *Ibid.* [3] *Ibid.* p. 35. [4] *Ibid.*

I have heard that gold coins of a Cháma Rája have been found, but this is doubtful. The name occurs five times in the lists, three antecedent to Ráj Wodeiyar, and two subsequent to him, the former of these last two being probably the prince referred to. A Rája of the same name is said, with what truth I know not, to have struck the copper coins bearing a series of Canarese numerals, from one to upwards of thirty. The reverse exhibits three or four pairs of double lines crossed by similar pairs at right angles, the square interstices either plain or containing a dot or small symbol. One of my smallest pieces has a six-pointed star in the central square. My specimens extend from one to thirty-two, but those of the British Museum go still further. They are of different sizes, weighing from thirty to fifty grains, or even more.[1]

The princes of this dynasty seem to have inherited the cognizance of the elephant from the Koṅgus and the Chéras, for it appears on numerous copper coins which are still current in the form of the *áne paisa* or small elephant cash, and even Tipú, notwithstanding his love of innovation and contempt of everything Hindu, continued to use it on his copper coins, many of them large and handsome, which are still frequently met with.[2] But according to Buchanan the Maisur princes never coined pagodas, and the first authentic record of a gold coinage is that of Kaṇṭhíráva Narasa Rája, who, in the middle of the seventeenth century, issued the gold fanams bearing his name, which became the standard denomination of the currency.[3] This fanam bears the image of the Narasinga *avatár*, and varies in weight from six to eight grains, but in the Calcutta mint tables it is entered at $5\frac{8}{10}$ grains, and containing fifty-eight per cent. of pure gold.[4] Ten of these formed a nominal pagoda of account, in which the revenue of the northern provinces was kept, as appears by Sir Thomas Munro's Report on the settlement of the Ceded Districts for 1806-7.[5] But Although no gold pagodas were struck by the Maisur princes, they were issued by the Rájas of Ikkeri, who were votaries of Śiva under the form of Aghoreswara. The first of these, Sadásiva Náyak,[6] struck pagodas with the figures of Śiva and Parvati, and his own name in Nágari on the reverse, a device which was used by his successors until their expulsion by Haidar, who still continued their issue in the same form, merely substituting his own initial ح on the reverse. The Bedar Polygar of Chitaldrug coined Durga pagodas in the same fashion and

[1] This design of a chequered reverse is common, and does not appear to be peculiar to Maisur, if indeed it is rightly attributed to Chāma Rāja at all. The figures on the obverse of the other varieties are very various, comprising Hanumán, Durga, an elephant, horse, peacock, *padma* or *lotus*, *śankha* shell, bell, etc., which cannot be identified with any special family or locality. I believe them to be quite modern, and therefore devoid of historical importance. Marsden describes a similar reverse on the gold fanams of Tanjore and Madura. I have never met with such. The numerous examples which have come in my way have been all of copper.

[2] Marsden's Num. Or. vol. ii. pl. xlvi.

[3] Buch. Journ. vol. iii. pp. 257-8.

[4] Prinsep's Useful Tables, p. 40.

[5] See his Report, dated 18th April, 1806.

[6] Although of no great historical importance, a list of these Rájas of Keladi, as they were first called, or Ikkeri and Bednur, may be useful to further enquirers. I have two lists, which do not agree in dates, and show other discrepancies.

*According to the Maisur Gazetteer.*

| | |
|---|---|
| Sadásiva Náyak ... ... ... ... | A.D. 1559—75 |
| Bhadrayya o. Bhadrappa ... ... ... | ,, 1575—84 |
| Dodda Sankana ... ... ... ... | ,, 1584—91 |
| Chikka Sankana ... .. ... ... | ,, 1591—92 |
| Siddhappa ... ... ... ... ... | ,, 1592—93 |
| Venkatappa ... ... ... ... ... | ,, 1593—1625 |
| Bhadrappa ... ... ... ... ... | ,, 1625—48 |
| Sivappa Náyak ... ... ... ... | ,, 1648—70 |
| Bhadrappa ... ... ... ... ... | ,, 1670—80 |
| Hucha (Mad) Somasek'hara ... ... ... | ,, 1680—85 |

character as those so generally employed by the Polygars and Zamíndárs of the upper Carnatic and the valley of the Krishṇa. These supplied a sufficient circulating medium not only in Maisur but in the neighbouring provinces. On the fall of Tipú, the Maisur Government, having found it convenient to coin pagodas of the same value as the Kaṇṭhíráya *hún*, previously only employed in accounts, issued them from the mints at Maisur and Nagara, at the same time restoring the old Ikkeri.[1] This, as already stated, had been adopted by Haidar under the name of the Baháduri pagoda, until its supersession by the Sulṭáni *hún* of Tipú. The revised pagoda was called the new Ikkeri, which eventually merged into the Kṛishṇa Rája *varáha* or pagoda now in use.[2]

The restored dynasty also coined silver fanams, double and single, with the figure of Bala Kṛishṇa, the youthful form of that god, and replaced the traditional elephant of their copper pieces by the mythological lion or *sarabha*.

I do not here propose to notice the coinage of the Muhammadan usurpation. They have been described and figured in Moor's Account of Little's Detachment and Marsden's Numismata Orientalia, plates xlv. and xlvi., and would form a fitting sequel to a description of the coins of the Muhammadan kings of the Dakhan from the Báhmanis downward.[3]

| | |
|---|---|
| Chinnammaji | A.D. 1685—97 |
| Basavappa | „ 1697—1713 |
| Somasek'hara | „ 1713—39 |
| Budi Basavappa | „ 1739—54 |
| Chikka Basavappa | „ 1754—57 |
| Somasek'hara Virammáji (Queen-regent) | „ 1757—63 |

*According to the Keladi Rája Pattam, No.* 1920, *in Taylor's Cat. Rais. vol. iii. p.* 650.

| | |
|---|---|
| Chelvapa Náyak pattam | — |
| Sadásiva Náyak | A.D. 1514 |
| Dodda Sancara vijaya | „ 1546—1559 |
| Chicka Sancara pattam | „ 1559—68 |
| Rama Náyak | „ 1568—83 |
| Vencatapati Náyak pattam | „ 1593—1630 |
| Virabhadra Náyak pattam | — |
| Sivapapa Náyak pattam | — |
| Chicka Vencatapati Náyak | — |
| Bhadrapa Náyah pattam | — |
| Sóma sec'hara Náyak pattam | — |
| Hari Basava Náyak pattam | — |
| Sóma sec'hara Náyak pattam | — |
| Basavapa Nàyak pattam | — |
| Sóma sec'hara Náyak pattam | A.D. 1758 |

[1] Buch. Journ. vol. iii. p. 258.

[2] Buch. Journ. vol. iii. p. 25.

[3] This would be a desirable contribution to the I. N. O. if coins could be found, as I doubt not they will be now as times are more settled. I endeavoured, when in the Southern Mahraṭṭa country, to make a collection of these, and although in charge of a considerable portion of the 'Ádil Sháhi territory, failed in procuring more than a few insignificant copper pieces. I have, however, a tolerable collection of their seals, copied from impressions on their *sanads*.

## PART III. SECTION i.

# COINS OF DRAVIDA.

We come now to consider the moneys of the Dravidian dynasties, the relations of which lay more often with each other than with those of their northern or western neighbours. That they were early recognized as distinct powers appears from the mention of them in Asoka's edict, where they appear as the Codas[1] (Choḍa), Páṇḍyas, . . . . and the prince of the Kéraḷas. But beyond this, the political history of Drávida is very imperfect; the native writings, which are numerous, are altogether untrustworthy, and the attempts to found historical narratives based on them are consequently unsuccessful. The large collections, made with so much care by Colonel Mackenzie, have never been fully analyzed. A Catalogue Raisonné of his MSS., prepared for the Madras Government by the Rev. William Taylor, and printed in the Journal of the Madras Literary Society, affords some fragmentary notices,[2] and more extended portions of them, which have been published from time to time without the means of verification from other sources, have yielded no certain results.

Such are the sketches of the Paṇḍyans by Professor Wilson in the Journal of the Royal Asiatic Society, vol. iii. p. 199; such, also, those of the Chéras by Professor Dowson in vol. viii. p. 1; and the incidental notices by Dr. Burnell in his South Indian Palæography have supplied a few facts. The late F. W. Ellis would probably have thrown much light on these, as well as on most other subjects of Dravidian literature, had he lived to utilize his materials; but the large and valuable collections he had made perished on the occurrence of his untimely death. The latest reliable work, by competent authority, bearing on the subject—Dr. Caldwell's History of Tinnevelly[3]—shows how much remains still to be accomplished. Professor H. Wilson alludes to the obscurity in which the whole subject is involved, observing that, although a large number of inscriptions is still extant,[4] they are either without dates, or have only those of the reign of the donor, whose name is given with

[1] Dr. Bühler's late trans. of Asoka's edict; Khalsi version, p. 12, in Zeit. Morg. Ges. for January, 1883.

[2] Mr. Taylor afterwards published a fuller catalogue of them, and of MSS. in the College Library at Madras, in three volumes, 1857–62, but they have added little more to our knowledge.

[3] Caldwell's History of Tinnevelly, p. 27.

[4] Mackenzie's Catalogue, vol. i. p. lxxxi.

perplexing variations. To which, moreover, it may be added, that many more, as yet unnoticed, still remain to be transcribed. It is to these contemporary records that we must look for more certain data, and meantime, I can only throw together a few general statements to illustrate as far as possible the coins that have come to hand.

Of the three predominant states before mentioned, the most northerly—Cholamandalam, the country of the Cholas—lay between the Pennár on the north and the Vellár[1] on the south, the sea on the east, and Kutakeri on the west; but afterwards, by the conquest of Tondamandalam, its northern limit was pushed to the Eastern Gháts, and to Śrí Harikotah on the coast. From the Vellár to Cape Comorin in the south, and from the eastern sea to an ill-defined line separating it from the Chéra territory on the west, constituted the boundaries of the Paṇḍyan state. All the country to the west of the latter, and both sides of the Sahyádri hills as far as the sea, including Kéraḷa, formed the most ancient Chéra limits, but when it was dismembered, and Kéraḷa became independent, they were restricted to Koyimbatur (Coimbatore) and the southern parts of Maisur and Salem, after which, the name of the Chera dynasty was merged in that of the Koṅgani rulers of Koṅgu-desa.[2] These, which are the received boundaries, varied from time to time, and, as Dr. Caldwell remarks, "shifted," as one or other was in the ascendant.[3]

Each of the three had its particular symbol, or standard, that of the Cholas being a tiger, of the Páṇḍyans a fish, and of the Chéras a bow, to which the Koṅgani dynasty added that of an elephant, still retaining the bow. These emblems are represented on the most ancient coins, that of the predominant power of the time holding the middle place, with those of the other two on either side. The earlier coins bear representations of these figures, but about the eleventh century a remarkable change occurs, by which the currency became largely composed of a new type, described by James Prinsep under the name of the Ceylon series,[4] having a rude human figure, standing on the obverse, and seated on the reverse. Previous to this change, the oldest Choḷa coins which I have seen exhibit their own device of a tiger between the bow and fish, and the legend in an old form of Nágari, showing them to have been then in the ascendant; but in the later examples, which are very numerous, the tiger is exchanged for the Ceylon type, with the name of the king in more modern Nágari, under the arm of the seated figure. In like manner the earlier Páṇḍyans have the impress of the fish symbol only, and the epigraph in old Nágari; but after the change above mentioned, the fish is seen under the arm of the sitting figure on the reverse, or of larger size, in various combinations, occupying the whole field, the legend in Tamil character, while the standing figure on the obverse remains unaltered. The change did not affect the Western money till a recent date, but an approach to it was, in some rare cases, observable.

How this change from the more ancient forms arose is hard to discover. I was long

[1] Of the two rivers of this name, that referred to is the most southerly, which falls into the sea to the south of Point Calymere.

[2] Mack. Cat. vol. i. pp. lxxiv, lxxxii, xcii; Taylor's Hist. MSS. vol. i. pp. vi, xi, xii; vol. ii. App. D. pp. 25-28; Cald. Hist. of Tinnevelly, pp. 24, 25, 26.

[3] History of Tinnevelly, p. 24.

[4] Essays, Thomas' edition, vol. ii. p. 419.

under the impression that it was introduced from Ceylon during the successful invasions, and protracted occupation, of the northern part of the island by the Tamils, which took place, according to Turnour, in the tenth century.[1] But Mr. Rhys Davids' statements do not coincide with this view. Admitting that a more ancient coinage might have once existed, but of which no examples have come to light, he finds that the earliest specimens known, date from the middle of the twelfth to the end of the thirteenth century.[2] All these exhibit the same character to which, as before stated, Prinsep has given the name of the Ceylon type, a designation which it is convenient still to retain. The device on the obverse is a rude standing figure, which has been described by some as that of Hanumán, or of a *rákshasa* according to others, but which in reality is a degraded figure of the king, by whom, as I think and shall explain hereafter, the coin was originally struck. It has the left arm upraised, holding what seems to be a flower, and below the elbow four or five flattened globules or pellets, the right hanging down, and under it a weapon, or sceptre. The drapery is represented by a straight line on each side of the legs, and another line between the latter, making with the legs, five parallel lines. On the reverse, a similar rude sitting figure, with a legend or characteristic symbol under the left arm, the right hanging down over the knee, with fingers extended.[3]

Nothing similar to this is found in any Indian coinage before the eleventh century, when it came into general use in Drávida only, at the time the Choḻa-Páṇḍyan dynasty were masters of the whole of it. Before this, the relations of the Choḻas and Páṇḍyans, while still separate, with the Singhalese, had become very complicated. The Mahawanso states that from the eleventh century the island was under the control of the Solleans (Choḻians),[4] who held the administration in their own hands till they were expelled by Vijaya Báhu. His nephew, Parákrama Báhu the Great, not only completed[4] the humiliation of the Tamils, but, resolving to punish Kulasek'hara, the Páṇḍyan king, "for the countenance and aid he had always afforded to all invaders of Ceylon," he sent an army under his minister to the mainland, who defeated Kulasek'hara and his Choḻian allies, and seated his son, Víra Pandu, on the throne.[5] Here, then, we have a period of revolution and conflicting authority coinciding with the change in the character of the coinage.

The legend on the earliest of these Singhalese pieces is Lankeṣwara=Lord of Ceylon, a term which, in its Páli form, Lankissara, Mr. Rhys Davids observes, was only applied to three kings before the reign of Parákrama the Great. Of these, the first two lived before

[1] Turnour's Mahawanso, App. pp. lxiv, lxv.

[2] Inter. Num. Or. Vol. I. Part VI. p. 1.

[3] Mr. Rhys Davids' researches lead him to the conclusion that, although he has found no evidence of the existence of coined money proper in the island before the fifth century A.D. (Inter. Num. Or. Vol. I. Part VI. p. 13), it is not impossible that such may have existed. "There is sufficient evidence," he says, "of the use of pieces of metal of certain weights as mediums of exchange, and probably marked or stamped," like, I conclude, the *purdnas* or *eldl'gs* of the mainland. But it does not appear, as far as I can learn, that examples of these have been found.

[4] App. p. lxiv.

[5] Mahawanso, App. p. lxvi. Another account states that he was invited by the Páṇḍyan king to oppose Kulasek'hara Déva, whose relation to the Páṇḍyan family is involved in much obscurity, and will be further noticed when we come to treat of that dynasty.

the fourth century A.D., "in whose time coins were unknown in Ceylon." The third was Vijaya Báhu I. (1071 A.D.), and "it is not known that any were struck in his reign." The use of the epithet he supposes to have been applied, not to him individually, but in its general sense, as to all kings of the island. He then states that the Singhalese form, Lankeṣwara, came into use in Parákrama's reign, and in his opinion, therefore, that the coin bearing it belongs to that prince. He further observes that "he conquered the south of India, and thence introduced the art of coining into Ceylon;" adding that "he is the only king of Ceylon who struck several coins," [1] though his successor continued the use of the same title, with the addition of Kalinga. Thus, in Mr. Rhys Davids' opinion, the Singhalese obtained the type in question from India, instead of having been the means of introducing it into that country. Whence, then, could it have originated? From whatever source derived, it made its appearance in India in the same degraded form as we now see it. Rude as it was on its first appearance, it made little change during a considerable period, some of the later specimens being, if anything, rather an improvement on their predecessors, although, eventually, they became so altered as to be scarcely recognizable. Notwithstanding Mr. Rhys Davids' high authority, I am disposed to believe that stamped coins must have existed in Ceylon before the time of Vijaya Báhu, for I cannot imagine that a people who had reached a comparatively high state of civilization could carry on the ordinary transactions of daily life without having recourse to a monetary system already in use among the people around them.

Frequent intercourse was carried on between the Buddhists of the north and those of Ceylon during five or six centuries before the period in question, and, doubtless, they must have brought stamped money with them, an art which a people so far advanced as the Singhalese would not be slow to imitate.[2] They would thus become acquainted with the elegant coinage of the Guptas,[3] which I have always believed to have formed the prototype of the coins in question.

Without pursuing the subject further at present I will notice such particulars as I can find regarding each of the three states above-mentioned, beginning with Chéra.

[1] Inter. Num. Or. Vol. I. Part VI. pp. 26–7.

[2] Cunningham, Ancient Geography, pp. 534–7.

[3] See Ariana Antiq. pl. xviii. figs. 11, 12, 22, 23, etc.; Prinsep's Essays, vol. i. pp. 227, 374, plates xxii. xxiii. xxix. xxx.

## PART III. SECTION ii.

# DYNASTIES OF DRAVIDA.

## 1. CHERA AND KONGU DYNASTIES.

THE Chera power seems to have been at the highest before the Christian era, when it is found under the name of Kéraḷa in Asoka's edict, and has been recognized by Professor H. Wilson in the Carei, and in the Carura Regia Cerebothri of Ptolemy,[1] terms which, making allowance for inaccuracies of sound and transcription, may be held to represent the city of Karúr, the capital of Chérapati, or Lord of Chéra. Up to the separation of Kéraḷa, described in a former section (p. 61 *ante*), but little is known of its history. The severance of so large a portion of territory must have seriously affected its influence as an independent state,[2] and, as we have seen, the importance of the Chéras as a substantive power waned from that period, the western portion being split into numerous principalities, while the eastern continued, with diminished influence, under a different name. Among the dynastic lists collected by Colonel Mackenzie, a series of twenty Chéra kings, purporting to have reigned in the *Kali-yuga*, is found; but they seem to be so apocryphal that I have not thought it necessary to transcribe them,[3] and this I do the more readily because I have never heard of the existence of any Chéra coins; nor, when we consider the early date at which the dynasty was subverted, does it appear probable that any improvement on the *eldling* had taken place. But, if any piece should be discovered hereafter, it would probably bear the impress of the bow, still found as an adjunct on later Dravidian coins.

The obscurity in which the Chéra dynasty is involved continues to be felt in tracing the fortunes of the eastern remnant of its territory, which, under the name of Koṅgu-déśa, comprised the western portion of Maisur as far as Nandidrúg, together with Koyimbatur (Coimbatore) and Salem.[4] Here a new dynasty arose, for the history of which, the authority hitherto followed, with too much confidence, is a native chronicle called the Koṅgu-déśa Charitra (or Rájakal), of which an abstract has been published by Professor Dowson, and a

[1] Mack. Cat. vol. i. p. xciii.

[2] See Burnell's Palæog. Second Edition, p. 33.

[3] See MS. volume, noted in the App. to the Mack. Cat. vol. ii. p. cxxviii, from which Dowson obtained the list quoted in the J.R.A.S. vol. viii. p. 26.

[4] To this Dr. Burnell adds Tondainâḍu, of which there is no proof. It was too far removed from the seat of their authority, and continued more probably in the possession of the independent Kurumbars, until its subjugation by a Choḷa conqueror.

fuller translation given by the Rev. William Taylor.[1] It professes to give a succession of twenty-eight princes, according to which the first seven were said to belong to the Reḍḍi or Raṭṭa race, of whom nothing more is known than that their capital is said to have been at Skandapúra, a site not identified.[2] A careful examination of the contents of this work, however, will show that it is not to be trusted as an authority, although it quotes inscriptions in support of its statements; for these, instead of adding strength to the narrative, only show its weakness. A grant conferred by the fifth prince on a Jaina (priest?) is dated s.s. 4—long before that era was known in the south; and the seventh is said to have been converted to Saivism by Sankara in s.s. 100, centuries before that teacher was born. After the seventh prince a change in the succession occurs, which appears to mark the introduction of another dynasty, whether following the preceding immediately, or at an interval greater or less, is not stated, but resting on better established grounds.

Quitting, therefore, this guide, we turn to a series of inscriptions emanating from princes of this latter race. The first of these was Koṅgani Varmá, whose capital, according to the Chronicle, still continued to be Skandapúra, wherever that was; but the true seat of their power was Talavanpura, or Dalavanpura, now Talkáḍ. From him the line became known as the Koṅgani dynasty. They originally professed the Jaina religion; were of the Kánváyanasa *gótra*, and Jáhnavi *kula*. From the latter circumstance, they are sometimes called the Ganga dynasty, Jáhnavi being another name of the sacred river. As before stated, they took for their cognizance an elephant, in addition to the Chéra bow, the latter being that by which they continue to be recognized by their Choḷa and Páṇḍyan neighbours. Koṅgani Varmá was followed by some twenty successors, according to the Rájakal, fifteen of whom are found in inscriptions published in the *Indian Antiquary*. But even these records are not free from contradictions and discrepancies, which seriously damage the authenticity of some of them. The earliest published, under the names of the Merkara and Nagamangala copper plates,[3] attracted considerable attention, and were accepted by Dr. Burnell on palæographic grounds. A third copper plate, bearing a strong family resemblance to the other two, was obtained by me from Tanjávúr (Tanjore), an impression of which led Dr. Burnell to reject it at once as a forgery. It was subsequently edited by Mr. Fleet[4] from the original, when he not only confirmed Dr. Burnell's verdict, but was led to throw doubts on the authenticity of the other two, founded on the discrepancy of the dates, and on the fact that the engraving of all three purported to be the work of one and the same individual. The genealogy in the Merkara and Nagamangala plates agree as far as they go. The date of the former plates, in the reign of Kongani III., is given as 383, of what era is not stated; while Prithuvi Koṅgani

[1] J.R.A.S. vol. viii. p. 2; Mad. Journ. vol. xiv. p. 4.

[2] Lassen places it at the Gajalhaṭṭi pass in Salem, but others have supposed it to be identical with the modern Udipi on the coast. If it is the site of the ancient Chéra family, it may be found in the vicinity of Karúr, near Pálghát, and may not improbably be identical with Karúr itself, the Karoura of Ptolemy (Κάρουρα βασίλειον Κηροβόθρου). According to the Imperial Gazetteer, Karúr has likewise borne the names of Vanji and Gardhapuri.

[3] Ind. Ant. vol. i. p. 360; vol. ii. p. 155.

[4] *Ib.* vol. viii. p. 212.

(the sixth of the name), in the Nagamangala plates, sanctions, in s.s. 698, the fiftieth year of his reign, the grant of a village to a Jaina temple at the request of a dependent, whose wife was the daughter of a Pallava chief (see *ante*, p. 42).

Supposing the year 388 to refer to the Saka era, as proposed by Professor Bhandarkar, the interval between these two grants would be 310 years. This apportioned among the six intervening princes, would give an average of 51·4 years, a supposition not to be thought of. But as the year 388 may refer to some other era, it is possible that a solution of the difficulty may hereafter be found. Again, if Mr. Fleet's supposition is correct, that the Viswakarmá, who executed the Merkara plates, is the same individual as the engraver of the Nagamangala plates, our confidence in both is destroyed. But it may be observed that Viswakarmá was originally an epithet of any great god, and ultimately was restricted to the personification of the creative power.[1] As such, he became the especial deity of all classes of artificers, so that the name, in these instances, may have had a general, rather than an individual application, which would also account for its use in the undoubtedly spurious Tanjore grant: this, however, is a very forced solution of the difficulty. Four more copper grants have been published by Mr. Rice in the Antiquary, two of which were found in the village of Mallohaḷḷi, near Bangalore. One of these has the usual elephant seal, on the other it is missing. They refer to grants of land, one in the twenty-ninth year, or Jaya *samvatsara*, of Kongani Rája (II.), the son of a Kadamba mother, and the donor of the Merkara plates; the other by his son Avinita, Srimat Kongani Vriddharája, or Durvvinita in Vijaya, the thirty-fifth year of his reign. Their genealogy is given in detail and agrees with all the inscriptions, which makes the former, who is the second of the name (or, if we include Márasimha Satyavákya Kongani Varmá, the third), the sixth in succession to the founder. The date assigned to the first grant by Mr. Rice is s.s. 376, computed by him from a comparison of the cycle year Parábhava, corresponding with the assumed s.s. year 388 of the Merkara plates, and, as Jaya is twelve years earlier than Parábhava, he thus gets s.s. 376 as the corresponding Saka year of that (Jaya) cycle year. But then comes the difficulty of his son's grant being placed in the year of the cycle preceding that of his father, and in the thirty-fifth year of his reign. To escape from this dilemma, he is therefore obliged to place Avinita's grant in the Vijaya of the following cycle, which corresponds with s.s. 435, placing fifty-nine years between them, and involves the further difficulty of assigning reigns of unusual length to Kongani and his son. To account for the long reign of the former, he infers, from an incidental expression in the second deed, that he was crowned in his infancy; and for that of his son, that he was the same person as the Datta Avinita, called also Avanita Mahádhirája Bhadatta, the *mantri* or minister, of the king,[2] who, having obtained the village, the subject of the Merkara charter, gave it, etc., etc., and thus was contemporary, and ruling jointly with his father. It is remarkable, however, that this person is nowhere

[1] Dowson's Classical Dictionary, *s.v.*

[2] Ind. Ant. vol. i. p. 365.

called the son of Koṅgani III. in the Merkara grant, nor is a son mentioned at all, but the prefix *Datta*, attached to his name, may imply that he was an adopted son.[1] In the Mallohaḷḷi grants his son is distinctly called Avinita, and Srimat Kongani Vriddharája, with the surname of Durvvinita, implying that he was an unjust or tyrannical prince.[2] All these circumstances considered, together with the uncertainty of the era, and the careless notation of the date pointed out in the *Indian Antiquary*, vol. i. p. 363, leave an impression of doubt as to the amount of credence to be accorded to these documents, although the documents themselves have the appearance of being genuine.

Of the two remaining grants, one having the elephant seal, was produced in support of a claim, before the court at Harihar. It relates to a gift of land made by Rája Malla, lord of Koḷáḷapúra (? Kolár), to one Ráma Déva of the Yarakula caste,[3] for service rendered to his wife and her attendants. The date has not been clearly ascertained owing to the ambiguity of the characters in which it has been expressed, but it corresponds with the cycle year Sadharana, and which Mr. Rice conjectures may be s.s. 272. This Rája Malla's name does not appear in any of the other inscriptions, but his father's name, Vishṇu Gopa, is found in all the lists. The last plate of the set, the seal of which is missing, was found among the old records in the Commissioner's office. It is dated in the third year of Koṅgani Mahárája, the son of Koṅgani Maharaja (III.), deduced in regular succession from the founder. The description given in the grant is somewhat obscure, but seems to make him the same person as the Avinita, surnamed Koṅgani Vriddharaja (IV.) and Durvvinita, of the Mallohaḷḷi grant. The date is not given, and the rest of the grant is imperfect.

Turn we now to the stone inscriptions, the first of which is that obtained by me at Lakmeshwar, and edited by Mr. Fleet,[4] in which Márasiṁhadéva, who had also the titles of Ganga-Kandarpa and Satyavákya Koṅguni Varma, gave a grant of land to a Jaina priest in s.s. 890. The stone on which it is inscribed is a large and fair slab in the Jaina temple, and in itself is free from suspicion; but below it, and on the same stone, follow two other inscriptions, the first of which being undated, and as derived from a family of no great note, need not be noticed now. The third, however, and the last on the stone, which records a benefaction to the Jaina temple, on the occasion of its repair by Vikramáditya Chalukya II. (whose genealogy is correctly given), in the Saka year 656, involves the difficulty of a more ancient record coming in succession to the later deed. The only possible explanation that occurs to me is that the older grants might have been transferred to this stone at a later period, for the unification of the titles. On the other hand, a second grant of the same prince (Marasiṁhadeva), in the same year, is found on another stone in the temple, and this, on the above hypothesis, should have been added in succession if there was room for it.

[1] Ind. Ant. vol. v. p. 140.

[2] Koṅgu-désa Rájakal, J.R.A.S. vol. viii. p. 4. The terms Avinita and Durvvinita are nearly synonymous; the first meaning unmannered or mannerless, the second has the more intensified signification of evil mannered.

[3] A nomad caste of this name is still found wandering over the plains of Southern India, earning a subsistence by catching birds and weaving mats.

[4] Ind. Ant. vol. vii. p. 101.

Márasiṁha, whose name occurs nowhere else, is called the younger brother of Hari Varma, which places him near the beginning of the line, and makes the settlement of his date of the greater importance. He is further distinguished in the inscription by the epithets Ganga-Kandarpa, and Satyavákya Koṅguni Varmá (*i.e.* the cupid of the Ganges, and the truth-speaking Koṅguni Varmá). The last appellation is that of the author of the three inscriptions on stone, found by Mr. Kittel in different villages of the Kodagu (Coorg) district, which will now be noticed. The first of these conveys an endowment to the Jaina temple at Pergga by Satyavákya Koṅgini Varmá (so read). The date of the grant is somewhat doubtfully read by Mr. Kittel as s.s. 780. Mr. Fleet, finding the name Satyavákya to be the same as that in the Lakmeshwar inscription, inclines to the opinion that both were made by the same person, whom he therefore identifies with Márasiṁha; and to get over the otherwise irreconcileable difference of date, which involves a space of 120 years,[1] for reasons stated, reads that at Pergga as s.s. 900. And it is remarkable that both these dates correspond with the Isvara *saṁvatsara* of their respective cycles. The second inscription procured by Mr. Kittel relates to a Jaina grant of a Satyvákya Koṅguni Varmá in s.s. 809, and there seems no reason to cast any suspicion on the accuracy of this date. But if Mr. Kittel's reading is the right one, the interval between the two grants would be twenty-nine years, and might easily refer to the same person. The last grant is a deed of investiture by a Satyavákya Koṅgunivarma, fixing the quit-rent of certain lands in kind and money, but being undated it requires no further notice. All three have one or all of the following titles: lord of Koḷáḷapura or Kovaḷáḷapura, protector of Nandagiri, Ráchamalla, Permmanaḍi, which it will be remembered were also borne by Rája Malla of the Bangalore copper plate.

Having thus examined all the inscriptions hitherto published, together with the native Chronicle, there is found to be a considerable agreement, both as to the names and the order of succession. Neither of them, however, afford reliable chronological data to determine either the beginning or end of the dynasty. We are thus driven to seek for its place in history from such indirect mention of it as can be found elsewhere. The most important notice is the statement in the documents relating to the Yádavas of Dvárasamudra that Vishṇuvardhana, the fourth prince, captured and burned Talkáḍ, and annexed the Ganga territory. The name of the Koṅgu king is not mentioned, but as it is given as a simple fact, unaccompanied by the usual laudatory ascription of victories over surrounding potentates, it may be received as correct. This would place the extinction of the dynasty between the second and third decade of the twelfth century Now, seeing that there were twenty-one Koṅgu kings, according to the Rájakal, although fifteen or sixteen only are found in the inscriptions, at twenty years to a reign we obtain a period of four centuries (420 years) for the duration of the dynasty, or at an average of fifteen years, three centuries (315 years).

[1] Ind. Ant. vol. vii. pp. 102-3.

The former of these would place the rise of the family about the beginning of the eighth century, and the latter to the beginning of the ninth, an approximation to the date of the Lakmeshwar grant, for Hari Varmá's brother, Márasimha, is the fourth in the list, and his inscription is dated S.S. 890 (=968 A.D.). A further confirmation is obtained by taking the period between Márasimha, A.D. 968, and the close of the dynasty in A.D. 1125, which embraces 157 years. This distributed among his eleven successors, according to inscriptions, would give an average of 14·3 to a reign. This conclusion differs so entirely from the views hitherto entertained, which rest chiefly on the Koṅgu-désa Charitra, that I offer it with some diffidence.

Mr. Foulkes, in his sketch of the dynasty published in the Manual of the Salem Collectorate,[1] gives the date of the first Koṅgani Varmá as S.S. 111 (=A.D. 189), and its extinction by the Cholas about S.S. 800 (=A.D. 878), being a period of 689 years, and giving an average of nearly 33 years (32·8) to a reign, after which they held it for 126 years.[2] Of this Chola conquest I have been unable to find any proof; while of that of the Hoysaḷa Balláḷas the evidence is clear and consistent. How the Chola supremacy ended, or how the Ganga power revived, as it clearly must have done during the century that intervened before its so-called second extinction by Vishṇuvardhana, we are not told. It is for those who hold that view to explain the difficulty. Granting, however, these statements to be correct, it must have become once more very powerful, as Vishnuvardhana seems to have considered its destruction one of the most glorious acts of his reign.[3] In addition to this it must be noted that the Chola ruler, so far from subduing the Koṅgu country, was aided by Narasimha II. of the Hoysaḷa Balláḷas in his conquest of the Páṇḍyan kingdom;[4] as a result of which Somesvara, his son, obtained a portion of the conquered territory, where he frequently resided at the town of Vikramapúra.[5]

The cognizance adopted by the Koṅgani dynasty, in addition to the bow of the Chéras, was an elephant, and was taken with much propriety from that noble animal, the principal haunts of which in the south are the hills and forests of Koṅgu-désa. The only coins on which it appears in gold are those known as *anai kásu, anai milti* or *gajapati kásu,* which are found both in the form of *húns* and *fanams,* and are not uncommon on the Malabar coast. They have an elephant caparisoned on the obverse, and what I have called the floral reverse, seen on many of the earliest pagodas and fanams, with sometimes a Canarese letter above the elephant's back, of the meaning of which I am not aware, but conjecture it may be the first letter of the king's name, or of the cycle year in which

[1] vol. i. p. 37. [2] *Ib.* p. 39.

[3] Inscription at Belúr (Velapúra) dated S.S. 1039 (=A.D. 1117). . . . "Having by the might of his arms first acquired the wealth of the Hoysaḷa kingdom, taking up the circle of the points of the compass, he gained possession of Talakáḍu, and of Ganga Rájya, being *the first to rule them*" (*i.e.* in supersession of the ancient race), "this Vishṇu Bhúpála, the raiser of the fortunes of the Yádu race. The Lakshmi of victories gaining great increase by the power of his arms, he burnt the capital city of the Gangas this powerful king Vishṇu, called *Bhujabala Ganga*, possessor of the city of Talavanapúra (Dalavanpúra), subduer of the *Konkonga* country, gained possession of Koḷáḷapúra," with the titles Bhujabala, *Vira Ganga*, and Vikramaganga, importing his conquests over the *Gangas*.—Rice, Mysore Inscriptions, pp. 262, 263; also inscription at Sindigere, *ib.* p. 330.

[4] MS. inscription at Harihar.

[5] Compare *Sásanam* at Bangalore; Rice, Mysore Inscriptions, p. 322.

it was issued. Copper coins are often met with of considerable variety, and have a character specially their own. They are small and irregularly shaped, without a raised edge, weighing from 50 to 55 grains, but one was as much as 68. Another of only 23 grains I take to be a half. The symbols on the obverse are very various, and neatly executed, that in the centre, sometimes an elephant, sometimes a weapon, etc., is generally, though not always, flanked by a bow; and some other forms difficult to name, and which, owing to my blindness, I will not now attempt to describe. Some thirty years ago I had a large collection of these, from which a selection was depicted and partly engraved for my Gleanings, but I left India *re infecta*. They will be found represented in the plates. From their simple, not to say rude forms, I at first attributed them to some earlier Chéra dynasty, of whom no clear record survives; but seeing that they are die-struck, the outcome of an art of which there are no ascertained specimens anterior to the fifth or sixth century, I hesitate to assign to them a date earlier than the Kongu age.

I may add that I have one coin with the Ceylon sitting figure on what I here take to be the obverse, and the usual Kongu altar on the reverse, but it would be unsafe to assign to this dynasty the adoption of an innovation which was recent at the time of its fall.

## GENEALOGIES.

### ACCORDING TO INSCRIPTIONS.

S'rimat KONGANI Varmá Dharma Mahádhirája I. or Mádhava I.

- S'rimán MÁDHAVA Mahádhirája II.
  - S'rimad HARI VARMÁ Mahádhirája
    - S'rimán VISHNU GOPA Mahádhirája
      - S'rimán MÁDHAVA Mahádhirája III. (married a Kadamba princess, sister of Krishna-Varmá).
        - Srimán KONGANI Mahádhirája III.
        - AVINÍTA DURVVINITA KONGANI Vriddharája IV.
        - MUSHKARA
        - S'ri VIKRAMA
        - BHU VIKRAMA
          - VILANDA Rája S'ri Vallábhákya
          - NAVA KÁMA (? the same as Kongani Maharaja V., surnamed S'imeshvara).
            - Son, name not given.
            - PRITHUVI KONGANI Maharaja VI., a Bhima Kopa and Rája Kesari.
      - Rája Malla (?)
  - MÁRASIMHA Ganga Kandarpa-Satyavákya Kongani Varmá II.

## ACCORDING TO THE KONGU-DESA CHARITRA.

- S'rimat KOṄGANI VARMÁ Dharma Maháthiraya I.
  - S'rimán MÁDHAVA Maháthiráya I.
    - S'rimat HARI VARMÁ[1] Maháthiráya
      - VISHṆU KOPA[2] Maháthiráya
        - MÁDHAVA Maháthiráya II. (adopted son)
        - KṚISHṆA Varmá Maháthiráya (son)
        - daughter — married to DINDICARARáya, or Hari Chandra-Dindicararáya (son of Pari-kulattiráya)
          - S'rimat KOṄGANI Maháthiráya II.
            - DHRUVANITIRÁYA
              - MUSHKARARÁYA,[3] or Brahmahariráya
                - TRI VICRAMARÁYA[4]
                  - BHÛ VICRAMARÁYA, or Gajapati
                    - Vallavákyaráya
                      - Rája Govindaráya[5] Nandi Varmá
                      - S'IVA RAMARÁYA, S'iva Maháráya
                        - . . . . . . . . . . . . . . . . . .
                          - PRITHUVI KOṄGANI, Maháthiráya IV. S'iva Maharáya
                          - Vijayádityaráya
                            - RÁJA MALLA DÉVARÁYA I., S'iva Maháráya
                              - GANDA DÉVA Maháráya
                                - SATYA VÁCYARÁYA
                                - GUṆÁLUTTAMARÁYA
                                - RÁJA MALLA DÉVARÁYA II.
                    - KOṄGANI MAHÁTHIRÁYA, Bhuvicramaraya II.

[1] Hari Varmá changed the capital to Dalavanpúra.

[2] Vishṇu-kopa embraced the Vaishna religion, and having no child of his own, he adopted a son named Mádhava, who succeeded him. Subsequently a son was born to him, named Kṛishṇa Varmá, after which there appears to have been a disputed succession, ending in Dindicara, a pretender, being set aside in favour of Koṅgani Maháthiráya II. or III. (see Mallohaḷḷi plate), the son of Kṛishṇa Varmá's younger sister.

[3] Mushkara and his father Dhruvanita were wise and warlike.

[4] Trivicrama, ? the S'ri Vikrama of the Nagamangala plate.

[5] Rája Govinda Raya changed to Saivism.

## 2. PÁṆḌYAN DYNASTY.

THE historical obscurity of Dravidian history, already noticed, is equally felt in dealing with the Páṇḍyans. For nearly two thousand years the position of their country kept them much secluded from contact with the rest of India. The mild and inoffensive character of the Jaina religion which prevailed there from the earliest times was favourable to the cultivation of letters and the arts. The many compositions of the former, afterwards leavened by the Vedic literature of the first northern missionaries, unfortunately contain no notice of passing events, and the traditionary writings of a later date supply nothing to make up for the deficiency. The quiet tenor of the Jaina period was first broken by the theological disputes of the ninth to the twelfth centuries, about which time a further light breaks in from the Singhalese annals. It is by a comparison of these with native traditions, and such help as can be obtained from inscriptions, and other casual notices of contemporary events, that we must endeavour to elucidate the changes that have taken place in the development of the coinage.

It has already been observed that two essentially distinct types are found, the first of which bears the distinguishing Páṇḍyan figure of the fish only, with ancient Nágari letters. The only specimens that are known, and all of gold, are of this type, and very rare. One is in my own possession, weighing 58·8 grains; another has been figured by Prof. H. Wilson[1] from the Mackenzie Collection, and a third is found in Moor's Hindu Pantheon.[2] This kind, undoubtedly the oldest, probably belongs to that period when the capital of the Páṇḍyans was at Kólkói or Kórkói (*Κόλχοι*), long the seat of the pearl fishery, and the emporium of the trade of the south, the ancient site of which, still retaining the same name, was discovered by Dr. Caldwell[3] near the modern village of Máramangalam. How long it continued to be the capital is uncertain, and it was perhaps not till the seat of government was removed to Madura that the elegant coins above mentioned were struck. The characters on the reverse, from their

[1] As. Res. vol. xvii.

[2] Plate 104, figs. 9 and 11. Two coins are represented, one of which resembles mine.

[3] Ind. Ant. vol. vi. pp. 80-83.

greater resemblance to Nágari than to Tamil, favour the supposition that the dies were cut by Jaina artists after the alphabet had been modified by Aryan intercourse, and the establishment of the Madura *Sangam* or College, placed by Dr. Caldwell in the eighth or ninth century. But there is no reason why they should not be dated a century or two earlier, or on the other hand, that they may not have been struck as late as the tenth century. After this the character of the coinage underwent the complete change by the introduction of what in the previous section has been called the Ceylon type. This I suppose to have been owing to the intercourse between Ceylon and Madura, our accounts of which are derived exclusively from Singhalese writers. The inhabitants of the latter, called Solleans, settling in the island in considerable numbers, provoked the enmity of the natives, which led to their expulsion, and to invasions of Madura in retaliation, two of which are recorded to have taken place, the last only being very successful. But it is remarkable that no mention whatever is made of them by Tamil writers.[1] That these invasions actually occurred, the character of the Ceylon histories do not allow us to doubt, but it may be questioned whether they, especially the last, were of so decisive and important a character as asserted. If the Singhalese chronology is undisputed, they must have taken place about the twelfth century. But this, as will be seen, is open to question.

Previous to this change, the kingdom of Madura had fallen under the dominion of the Cholas, whose power had been carried to its highest point by Rajendra Chola, between 1064 and 1113 A.D. The few coins I possess of his time all belong to the old type of that dynasty, exhibiting their own symbol of the tiger between the Páṇḍyan fish and the Chera bow, with the legend in old Nágari. It was not until the time of Rája Rája that the so-called Ceylon type appeared. It then at once came into general use. Coins with the name of Rája Rája flooded the country; those of copper are still numerous, and examples in silver, though rare, and one or two in gold, have also been met with. From that time they constituted the prevailing character of the Dravidian currency. We may, therefore, safely conclude that the change took place somewhere about the eleventh or twelfth century, and that the names of the kings on the coins of that type now found with Tamil legends, the letters of which, it may be observed, differ little from those now in use, are also subsequent to that time.

I have given Rajendra Chola's date on data furnished by the Chalukya inscriptions, but the establishment of its accuracy is so important that I will mention some additional evidence derived from Tamil records. Dr. Caldwell has found inscriptions of his in every part of Tinnevelly. Two of these near Cape Comorin, are dated in the fourth and fifth years of his reign.[2] They are confirmed by the inscription at Gangondaram quoted by me in the Madras Journal, vol. xiii. pp. 37–44 (1844). All these take credit for a so-called victory (?)

[1] I may also observe that the Madura chronicles, such as they are, are significantly silent as to the Chola conquest, showing their unwillingness to record any facts tending to the disparagement of their own country.

[2] At Kótár, in South Travancore; Hist. of Tinnevelly, p. 28.

gained by him over Ahavamalla at Kudala Sangam, the junction of the Kṛishṇa and Tungabhadra rivers. This Ahavamalla we know from the Western Chalukya inscriptions, was Someswara I. surnamed Ahavamalla, the second who assumed that title, and reigned from 1042–1068 A.D. He it was who in the passages of the inscriptions at Annigeri and Lakmeshwar cited by me in 1836,[1] states that he repelled the invasion of the Choḻa king, who could be no other than Rajendra.

I will now examine the value of the native accounts of the Páṇḍyan dynasty. These are recorded in nominal lists containing names varying in number from thirty to seventy-seven, of which five have been published by Professor H. Wilson, and two by Mr. Nelson.[2] Almost all these begin and end with the same names (viz. Kulasek'hara, and Kúna or Sundara Páṇḍya), and it is manifestly impossible that they can be accepted as correct. Professor Wilson indeed says that "the conflicting statements they contain are not likely to afford much satisfactory information;"[3] and Bishop Caldwell adds that "such lists, until confirmed by inscriptions, are of no conceivable historical value."[4] Even then, the light they afford is very doubtful, so many of the inscriptions being without dates. Moreover, the brief legends on the coins, as before stated, and the names likewise, are Tamil, while the names in the lists are Sanscrit. Nevertheless, Dr. Caldwell cites one instance in which the name on a coin is found in the lists, and, as I have three or four more besides, I have appended these lists to this section for purposes of comparison.

It is more difficult, amid such discordant elements, to assign the Chola conquest to its proper place among them. Tradition associates Rajendra Choḻa with Sundara or Kúna Páṇḍya, the last name in the lists, whom he reinstated in his hereditary dominions, making him his vice-regent, and giving him his sister in marriage. But Rajendra's conquest of Madura having taken place before the change in the coinage, it is clear that the individual so distinguished could not have been the last of a line of princes, all of whom adopted that change. Still, I cannot reject a tradition so generally received as a myth, but prefer to associate it with an earlier Sundara. It has occurred to me that the name Sundara, which is found on many of the coins, with or without addition, may be a dynastic title, like Śátakarṇi of the Andhras, derived from Sundara, the husband of *Mínáṭchi*, the tutelary goddess of Madura. His name stands third in all the lists published by Wilson, except the third, which it heads, and is conjoined with that of *Mínáṭchi* in the second. It is repeated several times in Mr. Nelson's shorter list, and recurs in inscriptions and on coins, with nothing to mark the particular ruler referred to. Dr. Caldwell himself doubts "whether Rajendra gained the sovereignty of the Páṇḍya country by conquest or by voluntary cession,"[5] and certainly the traditionary statements import the conditions on which Rajendra reinstated the Sundara, whom he admitted into the closest family relations, to have been liberal and lasting. This

[1] J.R.A.S. vol. iv. notes at pp. 13 and 14.
[2] J.R.A.S. vol. iii. pp. 236-239; Madura Man. pp. 39-41, 74-5.
[3] J.R.A.S. vol. iii. p. 202.
[4] Hist. of Tin. p. 27.
[5] *Ib.* p. 28.

would enable that Sundara to transmit his dignity to his descendants, and when the Choḷa power began to wane, would encourage them to throw off their dependence on it, as they appear to have done. It accounts, likewise, for the way in which their names are written in some of the stone inscriptions, as Sundara Páṇḍya-Choḷa.[1] These inscriptions boast undisguisedly of their victories over the Choḷas, and the inscription on one coin has reference to the capture of Kánchí by a Páṇḍyan prince.[2]

There is nothing to show at what period the superiority of the Choḷas became seriously impaired. It is known from the recorded interference of the Hoysaḷa Ballála princes, Balláḷa II. and Narasimha II., in disputes between the Choḷas and the Páṇḍyans about this time (see p. 81 *ante*), that the authority of the former was by no means unquestioned, and it was probably further shaken by the Singhalese invasion, and by the appearance in the political horizon of a new competitor for power in Drávida, who bears the name of Kulasek'hara, but whose proper name has not been ascertained. Nor do we at present know the circumstances under which he attained that power and influence which the events of the period show him to have possessed. Dr. Caldwell has seen many of his inscriptions in Tinnevelly,[3] and the celebrity to which he attained may serve to account for the place his name holds at the head of all the lists except the two shorter ones. Parákrama Báhu, 1153-1186 A.D., according to the Mahawanso, sent an army to attack him for the assistance he had given to previous invaders of Ceylon;[4] but another account states that the Singhalese monarch was invited by the then king of Madura to repel an enemy named Kulasek'hara, who was preparing to attack him.[5] Parákrama Báhu accordingly sent his general, Lankápura-dandu-nátha, with an army to his assistance, ordering him to establish the rightful king upon the throne. Kulasek'hara seems to have espoused the cause of one Sundara, who is called the Pandu king. This would imply that a dispute was now pending for the throne of Madura, between two competitors, the pretensions of one being backed by the Singhalese, and those of the other by Kulasek'hara. After several battles, Lankápura claims to have succeeded in placing the other claimant, named Víra Páṇḍya, on the throne.[6] The latter version receives support from the statements of two or three Muhammadan historians; but according to the dates given by them the chronology presents considerable difficulties. The most reliable of these writers is Amír

[1] Inscription at Karuvúr (Karúr) (Hist. of Tin. p. 32), a practice which Caldwell observes was very common in subsequent reigns. One instance is given in which Rajendra himself is said to have assumed the name of Rajendra-Choḷa-Páṇḍyan (Hist. of Tin. p. 28) and probably others will be found.

[2] Extracts from an inscription on the rock at Thiruipparan-kunram, near Madura (Nelson's Mad. pp. 56-7). . . . "Who terrified the flags bearing respectively the emblems of the furious tiger and the strong bow, and compelled them to hide themselves. . . . . Who destroyed the power of the tiger-flag in the country surrounded by the Kávéri river; and made the fish-flag of the Páṇḍya kingdom, which is bounded by Cape Kumári, to fly everywhere; and marched and spread abroad his forces, furnished with high couraged horses and elephants; set Tanjore and Uriúr on fire. . . . Who in his anger drove the Choḷa from his dominions into a barren place; took away his crown of pure gold . . . anointed himself with all proper ceremonies in the *mantapam*, which was the Choḷas anointing hall at Ayirattali." The coin referred to in the text is of the true Ceylon type with the fish crossed, and crozier, and the legend *Kacchi Vaḷungum Perumán*, meaning the "Conjeveram giving king," referring to the taking of Kánchí and its restoration, but affording no key to the name of the king.

[3] Hist. of Tin. p. 30.

[4] Turnour, App. p. lxvi.

[5] Rhys Davids, from native statements, purporting to be derived from the Mahawanso.

[6] Bengal Journal, vol. xli. pp. 191 201 (1872).

Khusru, who died in 1325 A.D. In describing Malik Káfur's campaigns in the Dakhan, he says that two claimants for the throne of Madura, the one named Bír Páṇḍya and the other Sundar Páṇḍya, who had hitherto been on friendly terms, were now in opposition to each other. On learning this, the Muhammadan general attacked and plundered Mathra (Madura), "the dwelling place of the brother of the Rái Sundar Páṇḍya," who forsook it and fled.[1] Another historian, 'Abdu-llah Wassáf, gives a somewhat different account of the same event. He states that Sundar Pandí, the Dewar or ruler of Ma'bar, who had three brothers, each ruling an independent country, died in A.H. 692 (1292-3 A.D.).[2] Afterwards, he says that "enmity prevailed between the two brothers, Sundar Pandí and Tíra Pandí, after the murder of their father."[3] In a third place he describes Kales Dewar as a prosperous and powerful ruler of Ma'bar for upwards of forty years. He then states that he had two sons, Sundar Pandí and Tíra Pandí, the latter of whom, though the younger, and illegitimate, was declared by his father to be his successor. The elder, Sundar, enraged at this supersession, killed his father 1310 A.D., and seized the crown. But the son of Kales Dewar's daughter, Manár Barmúl, taking the part of Tíra Pandí, he was ultimately successful, and Sundar Pandí fled for protection to Delhi, where he not only found an asylum, but 'Alá-ud-dín ordered his general Malik Káfur to afford him assistance, which appears to have been the cause of the expedition of that general against Madura above mentioned.[4] All these narratives appear to refer to the same historical event, viz. a disputed succession[5] between the two sons of the king of Madura, Sundara and Víra Páṇḍya, in which an individual named Kulasek'hara, who perhaps may be the same person as the Kales Dewar of Wassáf, plays a conspicuous part.[6] Memorials of him have been found in the shape of copper *śásanams*, the seals of which have the fish symbol in the centre, flanked by the tiger and the bow, as represented in the annexed woodcut, showing that he had assumed the paramount position of the Cholas, or in other words, of the whole of Drávida. The copper plates to which the seals above described were attached were translated by Dr. Caldwell,[7] and purport to be issued in the "13th year, 4364th day of the lord of the earth, Śrí Kochchadei Varma, emperor of the three worlds, Śrí Kulasek'hara Déva," etc., etc. If this is the year of the *Kaliyuga*, it would correspond with 1263 A.D. Should this date be accepted, it brings his era near to that of the Muhammadan writers, and as his reign is said by Wassáf to have been

[1] Sir H. Elliot's Historians, vol. iii. pp. 88, 91.

[2] *Ib.* pp. 32, 34.

[3] *Ib.* pp. 49, 50.

[4] *Ib.* pp. 52-4. See also p. 81, *ante*.

[5] Nelson in his Manual of Madura characterizes the period from 1100 A.D. to 1324 A.D. as "one of numberless invasions and constant internecine strife," during which the ancient race of the Pâṇḍyans came to an end, and those who assumed the name at a later period he styles "Pseudo-Pâṇḍyans" (Part v. p. 111).

[6] Amír Khusrû wrote the life of 'Alá-ud-dín, and is said to have been his contemporary, and to have participated in some of the events he describes; whilst 'Abdu-llah Wassáf, who published four volumes of his history in A.D. 1300, and a fifth in 1328, appears to have been introduced by the Wazír Rashíd-ud-dín, who was his friend, to the Persian court, and to have presented his history to the Tartar king Uljáítú. Rashíd-ud-dín also composed a history of his times; and, quoting from Al Biruni, gives nearly the same account as that of Wassáf above noticed. Elliot's Hist. vol. i. pp. 69-70. See also Colonel Yule's paper on "Rashíd-ud-dín's Geographical Notices of India," J.R.A.S. vol. iv. N.S. pp. 345, *et seq.*

[7] Ind. Ant. vol. vi. p. 142.

a long one, it is so far confirmatory of their narratives; but then comes the difficulty of the earlier Ceylon date, for it is not probable that two such contentions for a precisely similar object between two brothers of the same names should have taken place so soon after each other, although the dates differ so materially as the middle of the twelfth, the middle of the thirteenth, and beginning of the fourteenth centuries. Perhaps an explanation may be found in assuming, as Dr. Caldwell has suggested, that some confusion has taken place in the Singhalese records.[1]

I have a drawing and facsimile of the seal of another *ṣásanam*, which, to the best of my recollection, was deposited with the preceding at Tiruppûvaṇam, and referred to the grant therein mentioned by the chief of Madacolam, a feudatory of Kulasek'hara. This seal differs somewhat from the above marginal woodcut in having the tiger and the fish placed upright, opposite each other, in the middle of the field, with the bow transversely below them: round it a legend, which has been read doubtfully as Páṇḍya Narendra Varmanaha samasta lókásrayaha = The Páṇḍya Narendra Varma, lord of the whole world. Two inscriptions deposited in the University of Leyden were exhibited during the meeting of the International Oriental Congress in September 1883, the seals of which lead, presumably, to the supposition that they were granted by the same ruler, the Kulasek'hara above mentioned. One of them is described to me by General Pearse as an exceptionally fine specimen, consisting of twenty-one plates of unusually large size. On the seal, of which he had a photograph, the disposition of the figures resembles that of the Madacolam grant just mentioned, a representation of which will be found at the end of this section, but it is more than double the size, and has the addition of a tall lamp on either side, behind the tiger and the fish. The smaller *ṣásanam* consists of three plates, and has a seal more nearly resembling my drawing. We may expect that the translation of these will throw much light on this vexed question.[2]

Before quitting this subject, I must advert to the Sondar Bandi mentioned by Marco Polo as ruler of the south in 1292 A.D. He sailed with the embassy from the Mongol emperor of China to the Tartar king of Persia in 1292 A.D. The voyage was tedious and difficult, and when they reached the coast of India, the south-west monsoon had set in. This obliged them to put into the port of Kayal, which had succeeded Kórkói as the emporium of the south. The information gathered by him regarding that country does not appear to have been committed to paper at the time, but was dictated by him some years later in Genoa, to a fellow-prisoner whilst he was in confinement after the battle of Curzola in 1298 A.D.[3] The historical part of his testimony is very short, merely stating that the great province of Ma'bar (Drávida) is ruled by five kings who are own brothers, of whom the one at this end is a crowned king named Sonder Bandi Davar.[4] In

[1] Hist. of Tin. p. 30.
[2] Since the above was written a notice of these seals has appeared in the Ind. Ant. vol. xiii. p. 59.
[3] Yule's Marco Polo. vol. i. pp. lii. liii. lxxx.
[4] *Ib.* vol. ii. p. 267.

another place he states the king of Kayal to have been the eldest of the five brothers, and named Ashar,[1] an inexact form of the true name, whatever it may have been. This hardly coincides with his former statement that Sonder Bandi was one of the five brothers who reigned over this end of the province. This is probably an incorrect version of the old tradition that Drávida was first settled by four brothers, named Kola, Chola, Paṇḍya and Chéra. His use of the name Sonder Bandi does not enable us to apply it to any particular individual of that name. If not connected with the dynastic use of the term, it may have had reference to the disputed succession adverted to above, in which a Sundara bore a conspicuous part. It is remarkable, however, that Marco makes no allusion whatever to a contention of such surpassing interest to the whole province. His silence, therefore, may be taken to imply that it took place after his departure, and this adds strength to the doubt cast on the accuracy of the Singhalese Chronicles.

In conclusion, I will now notice some of the more remarkable specimens of the coinage of this dynasty of which I was able to make a considerable collection. Gold coins, as before stated, are very rare. The only addition to those mentioned in the beginning of the section is a gold piece, very recently obtained by General Pearse in London, which he has described to me as remarkable from exhibiting what he calls a crocodile above two fishes, upright, in the centre of the field, below them a third fish placed horizontally. On the reverse three lines of bold archaic Nágari.

Copper coins are met with in considerable numbers, but I cannot assign to any of them a date beyond the tenth or eleventh century, because they all exhibit the Ceylon type, and have legends exclusively in Tamil, differing little from the letters in present use. Most of them, however, exhibit the figure of the fish (*min*, Sans.)[2] in various combinations, which, as before stated, is the special cognizance of the Pâṇḍyan lines. From this the sovereigns took the title of *Minavan*=*the fish one*, and from this also the tutelary deity worshipped in the great temple at Madura is called *Mináṭchi*,[3] whose union with the god Sundara has already been noticed. One of these which had the name of Kulasek'hara, has been lost; but I have an exact drawing of it. This goes to prove that although he heads the native lists, he was subsequent to the eleventh century. Kulasek'hara is an epithet rather than a proper name, and means head ornament or crown of the race. It occurs in three of the inscriptions noted by Mr. Sewell in his Collection of Antiquities,[4] viz. one of Tribhuvana Chakravarti Kulasek'hara Dévar, in A.D. 1402, and two of Kulasek'hara Perumál Dévar, dated A.D. 1536, and 1550, all in Tinnevelly.

I have also a coin of Malaya *ketu*, the Malaya *dhvaja*, second in the lists, who is called

[1] *Ib.* p. 305, *note* 2, p. 310.

[2] A species of carp or barbel found in the larger rivers, the Tamil name of which is *kayal*: the *Barbus tor* of Buchanan, the *mahasir* of English sportsmen; and also celebrated in the heraldry of northern India.

[3] Popularly, but incorrectly, as I am informed by Dr. Caldwell, the name of the goddess is often written *Mináksh* or *fish-eyed*, having reference, perhaps, to other names of Dévi, as *Kámákshi* or *wanton-eyed*, *Visalakshi* or *large-eyed*. The true meaning of *Mináṭchi* is *fish rule*, not *ruler*, formed from the Tamil root *áḷ* to rule.

[4] p. 306.

the son of Kulasek'hara.[1] It exhibits the figure of a mountain and a crescent, and below the word *ketu*, synonymous with the Sanscrit *dhwaja*, a standard. Malaya is the name of a well-known mountain in the Madura district, sometimes called the southern Meru. To these may be added a coin of Vira Páṇḍya, fourth and fifth in the lists. The reverse of this has the two fish with crozier between; a lamp on either side, and the name *Vira Páṇḍya* above. According to Dr. Caldwell there was more than one of the name.[2] The coin read by him as Samara Koláhala, who occupies from the fortieth to the forty-second places in the lists, is remarkable as indicating a change in the religion. I have several varieties of it, suggesting either a long reign of the above prince, or that there was more than one of the name. The most conspicuous exhibits a human figure of Garuḍa on the back of the fish, with the adjuncts of the *ṣankha* and *chakra*, all attributes of Vishṇu; and the meaning of the legend, "din of war," seems to intimate that the change from Saivite tenets had been brought about by violence. Another has *Garuḍa* on the obverse without the fish, and on the reverse two fish facing each other, with a crozier between them. No legend. A third has on the reverse two fish parallel to each other, with or without a candelabra on either side, and the legend round the margin. A fourth has only the word *Koláhala* between the fish on the reverse. The earliest form of religion in the south had probably been that of the Jainas. The Saivite doctrines of the great reformer Sankaráchárya met with a favourable reception at Tanjore,[3] which led to the extermination of the Buddhist sectaries who had obtained a footing from Ceylon.[4] The Choḷa conquest and the marriage of Sundara Páṇḍya with the sister of Rajendra, led to the conversion of that prince, and the extension of the Saiva doctrines into Madura under the guidance of Gnána Sambandha, the religious teacher of the queen. Sundara persecuted his late Jaina co-religionists with relentless cruelty, 8000 of whom are said to have been impaled by him.[5] Confirmatory of these executions sculptured representations are still to be seen on the walls of a neighbouring temple at Trivatúr in the Arcot district. Still later the doctrines of the Vaishnava sect superseded those of Sankara at Madura, as shown by the coins of Samara Koláhala above mentioned, but found no favour at Tanjore, and their author, Rámánuja, fled to Dwárasamudra, where he converted the Jaina king Vishṇuvardhana.[6] An anthropoid figure of Garuḍa appears on another coin holding a bow (?), and above a *ṣankha* shell (?). On the reverse the name *Bhuvanika viran*, a name not found in any of the lists. One coin bears the name of *kúna*, and has the appearance of being older than the rest. On the obverse is the Ceylon standing figure, and on the reverse is a sitting figure, perhaps having reference to Sundara's early attachment to the Jaina

[1] Nelson's Mad. part iii. p. 7.

[2] Hist. of Tin. p. 27.

[3] Caldwell's Comp. Gram. p. 138.

[4] Few traces exist of the hold the Buddhists had in the south notwithstanding the support it must have received from its proximity to Ceylon. We know from Hiouen Thsang that when he was at Kánchi, about the year 639 A.D., a number of Buddhist monks came there to avoid the political troubles in their own country (Cun. Anc. Geo. p. 548), and that it flourished for a time is proved by the monument at Negapatam (Ind. Ant. vol. vii. p. 224), and the tradition that it was persecuted to extirpation by Máṇikka-vúságar in the reign of one of the earlier Choḷas is generally received.

[5] History of Tinnevelly, p. 32.

[6] *Ibid.* p. 30.

faith.[1] Another type has on the obverse two fish with crozier between, and on the reverse the name *Sundara Páṇḍya.*

A somewhat curious specimen has on the obverse a horse galloping to the proper left, with three small symbols above, which I cannot recognize. On the reverse two fishes looking outwards, between them a crozier, and above it a small bull seated between two chowries. I am unable to explain the meaning of these devices, but according to native Paṇḍits they have been referred to the story of Arimardhana Páṇḍya, fifty-fourth or sixty-first in the lists, and his minister Máṇikka-váságar, as told in the *Sthala Mahatmya,* which will be found in Taylor's Hist. MSS.,[2] but with what amount of truth or likelihood I am not prepared to say.

A unique specimen deserves mention from its bearing on General Pearse's description of his recently acquired gold coin, although the Ceylon type shows it to be much more recent. The reverse has the figure of a scorpion and the word *ketu* (= *dhwaja*), under it a crocodile, and below all two fish. This may refer to a name like *Makara ketu,* could such be found. There is a coin with the Ceylon type on both sides, with the addition on the obverse of two fish and a crozier, on the reverse under the arm letters which appear to read *Terumalai,* and may refer to a Náyak of Madura. Another of those with the Ceylon type on both sides has on the reverse under the arm, the crozier and a fish. Another coin has the recumbent bull, and the word *ketu,* and the standing figure on the obverse, but as there is no fish it is doubtful whether a Páṇḍyan origin can be assigned to it.

[1] This close approximation of the Ceylon type to Rajendra Choḷa does not agree with the traditionary statements of the near relationship between him and Kûna.

[2] Vol. i. pp. 104-10. See also his Cat. McK. MSS. in Cat. Rais. vol. iii. pp. 135-138; Madura Man. part iii. pp. 33-36.

SEAL OF MADACOLAM GRANT.

## LISTS OF THE PANDYAN KINGS REFERRED TO AT PAGE THIRTY-FOUR.

| No. | No. 1. Vamsavali. | No. 2. Vol. | No. 3. Mad. Pur. | No. 4. Mad. Pur. | No. 5. Halasya. | Nelson's List. "Hist. of Madura," pp. 39-41. |
|---|---|---|---|---|---|---|
| 1 | Kulasékhara | Kulasek'hara | — | Kulasek'hara | Kulasek'hara | Kula Sék'hara Pándya. |
| 2 | Malaya Dhwaja | Malaya Dhwaja | — | Malaya Dhwaja | Malaya Dhwaja | Malaya Dhwaja P. |
| 3 | Sundara | Minakshi and Sundara | Soma Sundara | Sundara | Sundara | Sundara Pándya |
| 4 | Víra | Wrgra | Wugra | Vugra | Wugra | Ugra Pándya, called Hárad'hári. |
| 5 | Abhishékr | Víra | Víra | Víra | Abhishéka Víra | Víra Pándya. |
| 6 | Vikrama | Abhishéka | Abhishéka | Abhishéca | Vikrama | Abhishéka Pándya. |
| 7 | Rájásek'hara | Vikrama | Vikrama | Vikrama | Sek'hara | Vikrama Pándya. |
| 8 | Anantaguna | R. Sek'hara | R. Sek'hara | R. Sek'hara | Kulottunga | Rája Shek'hara P. |
| 9 | Kulabhara | Kulottunga | Kulottunga | Kulottunga | Anantaguna | Kulóttunga P. |
| 10 | Varaguna | Anantaguna | Anantaguna | Anantaguna | Kulabhushana | Anantaguna P. |
| 11 | Rájá Rájá | Bhushana | Kulabhushana | Kulabhushana | Rajendra | Kulab'húshana P. |
| 12 | Rájá Gambhíra | Rajendra | Rajendra | Rajendra | Rajésa | Rájéndra P. |
| 13 | Chitra Virta | Sundareswara Pada Sekhara | Tari Rájá | Rajésa | R. Gambhíra | Rájésa P. |
| 14 | Chitra Guna | Varaguna | Udalura | R. Gambhíra | P. Vamsapradipaka | Rája gamb'híra P. |
| 15 | Chitra Dhwaja | Rája Rájá | Gambhíra | P. Vamsadípa | Puruhutajit | Pándya Vamsa Pradipa. |
| 16 | Chitra Guna | Vamsa Sek'hara | Vengi Ádi | Purandarjit | P. Vamsa Pataka | Puruhúta P. |
| 17 | Chitra Vikrama | Vamsa Churamani | Purandara | P. Vamsa Vataka | Sundarapada | Pándya Vamsa Patáka |
| 18 | Rájá Martanda | Kula Sek'hara | Kumára | Sundarésá P. Sek'hara | Varaguna | Sundarésha Páda Sék'hara P. |
| 19 | R. Chudamani | Arimarddhana | Vangeya | Varaguna | Rájá Rájá | Varaguna P. |
| 20 | R. Sundara | Chokkanath | Eradana | Rájá Rájá | Chitra Ratha | Rájá Rájá P. |
| 21 | R. Kulottunga | Vírabhadra | Sundarésá Pada-Sek'hara | Suguna | Chitra Bhushana | Suguna P. |
| 22 | R. Sirogicha Gambhíra | Víra | Varaguna | Chitra Vratha | Chitra Dhwaja | Chitra Vratha P. |
| 23 | R. Gambhíra | Prakrama (1370 A.D. Cald. Gr. p. 135). | Rájá Rája | Chitra Bhushana | Chitra Varmá | Chitra B'húshana P. |
| 24 | Pándya Vamsa Dípa | Suravhi | Suguna | Chitra Dhwaja | Chitra Séna | Chitra D'hwaja P. |
| 25 | Purandara Sundara | Kunkuma | Chitra Ratha | Chitra Varmá | Chitra Vikrama | Chitra Varmá P. |
| 26 | Pándya Vamsa Dhurandara | Karpura | Chitra Bhushana | Chitra Sena | R. Martanda | Chitra Séna P. |
| 27 | Jannadeswara | Karunya | Chitra Dhwaja | Chitra Vikrama | R. Churamani | Chitra Vikrama P. |
| 28 | Pandu Sek'hara | Puruskottama | Chitra Varmá | Rájá Martanda | R. Sardula | Rájá Mártánda P. |
| 29 | Varaguna | Chatursasana | Chitra Chéra | Rájá Churamani | R. Kulottama | Rájá Chúdámani P. |
| 30 | Rájá Sardúla | Kúna, or Sundara | Chitra Vikrama | Rájá Sardúla | Ayodhana Pravina | Rájá Sárdúla P. |
| 31 | R. Kulottama | — | Rájá Martanda | Rájá Kulottama | Rájá Kunjara | Dwija Rájá Kulóttunga P. |
| 32 | Ayatana Pravina | — | Sardúla | Pravina | R. Bhayankara | Ayud'ha Pravína P. |
| 33 | Rájá Kunjara | — | Kavi Rájá | Kavi Kunjara | Wugraséna | Rájá Kunjara P. |
| 34 | Pravíra R. Bhayancara | — | Kulottama | R. Bhayankara | Mahásena | Para Rája B'hayankara P. |
| 35 | Varoonajana | — | Tunda Pravina | Wugra Séna | Satrunjaya | Ugra Séna P. |
| 36 | Satrunjaya | — | Rájá Kunjara | Satrunjaya | Bhimaratha | Mahá Séna P. |

**Nelson's Short List. "Hist. of Madura," part iii. pp. 74-5.**

Sóma Sundara Pándya
Karpúra Sundara P.
Kumára Sek'hara P.
Kumára Sundara P.
Sundara Rája P.
Shanmuk'ha Rája P.
Méru Sundara P.
Indra Varmá P.
Chandra Kula Dípa P.
Mína Kétana P.
Mína D'hwaja P.
Makara D'hwaja P.
Mártánda P.
Kuvalayánanda P.
Kundala P.
Satru B'hikara P.
Satru Samhára P.
Víra Varmá P.
Víra Báhu P.
Makuta Vardd'hana P.
Vajra Simha P.
Varuna Kulóttunga P.
Ádi-Víra-Ráma P.
Kula Vardd'hana P.
Sóma Sek'hara P.
Sóma Sundara P.
Rája Rája P.
Rája Kunjara P.
Rája Sek'hara P.
Rája Varmá P.
Ráma Varmá P.
Varada Rája P.
Kumára Simha P.
Víra Séna P.
Pratápa Rája P.
Víraguna P.
Kumára Chandra P.
Varatunga P.
Chandra Sek'hara P.
Sóma Sek'hara P.
Parákkrama P.

**Náyak Dynasty. "Prinsep's Useful Tables," p. 122.**

Visvanátha, 1530.
Krishnappa.
Virappa.
Visvappa.
Kumara Krishnappa.
Kasturi Ranjappa.
Muttu Krishnappa.
Virappa, died 1623.
Terumala or Trimal, 1623-33.
Muttu Virappa, 1633.
Chokkanátha, died 1687.
Krishna Muttu-Virappa, 1687.
Vijaya Ranga, under the regency of Mangammal, 1695
Vijaya Kumára, under the regency of Minaxi ráni, 1731.
Fort seized by the Muhammadans, and Madura became tributary to the Nawab of Carnatic, and afterwards to the British.

## LISTS OF THE PANDYAN KINGS REFERRED TO AT PAGE THIRTY-FOUR (*continued*).

| No. | No. 1. Vamsavali. | No. 2. | Vol. | No. 3. Mad. Pur. | No. 4. Mad. Pur. | No. 5. Halasya. | Nelson's List. "Hist. of Madura," pp. 39–41. | Nelson's Short List. "Hist. of Madura," part iii. pp. 74-5. | Náyak Dynasty. "Prinsep's Useful Tables," p. 122. |
|---|---|---|---|---|---|---|---|---|---|
| 37 | Viraruddanda | — | — | Rájá Bahyamkara | Jayamgonda | Bhima Paracrama | Satrunjaya P. | | |
| 38 | Viraparakrama | — | — | Rudrasena | Parakrama | Pratapa Martanda | B'hímarat'ha P. | | |
| 39 | Pratapa Martanda | — | — | Satrunjaya | Pratapa Martanda | Vikrama Kanchuki | B'hímaparákrama P. | | |
| 40 | Vikramakaryaka | — | — | Vinatar | Vikrama Kanchuka | Yuddha Kolahala | Pratápa Mártánda P. | | |
| 41 | Samara Sek'hara Kolátala | — | — | Viraprakrama | Samara Kolahala | Chaturi Vikrama | Vikrama Kanchuka P. | | |
| 42 | Antala Vikrama | — | — | Pratapa Martanda | Atula Vikrama | Atula Kirtti | Yudd'ha Kólâhala P. | | |
| 43 | Antala Kirtti | — | — | Vikramakanchuki | Atula Kirtti | Kirtti Bhushana | Atula Vikrama P. | | |
| 44 | Vamsa Sek'hara | — | — | Samara Koláhala | Kirtti Bhushana | Vamsa Sek'hara | Atula Kirti P. | | |
| 45 | Pratapa Surya | — | — | Yatula Vikrama | Vamsa Sek'hara | Champaka | Kírti Vib'húshana P. | | |
| 46 | Vamsatulaja | — | — | Yatula Kirtti | Vamsa Churamani, or Chanjpaka | Pratápasurya | Vamsa Sék'hara P. | | |
| 47 | Nipu Marundari | — | — | Kirtti Bhushana | Pratapa Surya | Vamsa Dhwaja | Vamsa Chúdámani, called also Champaka P. | | |
| 48 | Chola Vamsottaraca | — | — | Vamsa Sek'hara | Vamsa Dhwaja | Vamsa Bhushana | Pratápa Shúsaséna P. | | |
| 49 | Kula Churamani | — | — | Vamsa Churamani | Maratakan | Loma Churamani | Vamsa D'hwaja P. | | |
| 50 | Rájá Churamani | — | — | Surya Vanjival Dhwaja | Chola Vamsantaca | Kula Churamani | Ripu Mardana P. | | |
| 51 | Vamsa Siromani | — | — | Marutaká | Chera Vamsantaka | Rájá Churamani | Chola Vamsántaka P. | | |
| 52 | Pándya Gambhira | — | — | Pratapa | Pándya Vamsésá | Bhupa Churamani | Chéra Vamsántaka P. | | |
| 53 | Kuvalatuja | — | — | Sovilanki | Vamsa Siromani | Pándya Kalésá | Pándya Vamshrésa P. | | |
| 54 | Vamsa Vibhushana | — | — | Suvangi Sandha | Pandyeswara | Arimarddhana | Vamsa Sirómani P. | | |
| 55 | Kulésa | — | — | Vamsa Sek'hara II. | Kulodhwaja | Kúnapándya | Pándyéswara P. | | |
| 56 | Chola Churamani I. | — | — | Vamsa Siromani | Vamsa Vibhushana | — | Kula D'hwaja P. | | |
| 57 | Chola Churamani II. | — | — | Pándeswara | Chola Churamani | — | Vamsa Vib'hsúhana P. | | |
| 58 | Rájá Churamani | — | — | Kulutoja | Kula Churamani | — | Sóma Chúdámani P. | | |
| 59 | Bhupa Churamani | — | — | Vamsa Bhushana | Rájá Churamani | — | Kula Chúdámani P. | | |
| 60 | Kulésa II. | — | — | Chola Churamani | Bhupa Churamani | — | Rája Chúdámani P. | | |
| 61 | Arimarundana | — | — | Kula Churamani | Kulésá | — | B'húpa Chúdámani P. | | |
| 62 | Sek'hara Nát'ha | — | — | Rájá Churamani | Arimatun | — | Kulésa P. | | |
| 63 | Vira Báhu | — | — | Bhupa Churamani | Jagannath | — | Arimardana P. | | |
| 64 | Vikrama Bhagu | — | — | Kulésa | Virabahu | — | Jagannát'ha P. | | |
| 65 | Pracrama B. | — | — | Marutan | Vikramabahu | — | Virabáhu P. | | |
| 66 | Durmada | — | — | Jagannath | Pracramabahu | — | Vikrama P. | | |
| 67 | Karunya | — | — | Virabhagu | Suradamaran | — | | | |
| 68 | Sarvasasana | — | — | Vikramabhagu | Bahubala, or Vaguvaler | — | Surab'hi P. | | |
| 69 | Sandhatuta | — | — | Prakramabahu | Kunkumatanya | — | Kunkuma P. | | |
| 70 | Nagarika | — | — | Suratamara | Karpura | — | Karpúra P. | | |
| 71 | Chencalneelyetta | — | — | Vaguvalatu ? | Karunya | — | Kárunya P. | | |
| 72 | Vetteya Vinata | — | — | Kunkumatennen ? | Purushottam | — | Purushóttama P. | | |
| 73 | — | — | — | Karpura | Satrusadhana | — | Satrusása a P. | | |
| 74 | — | — | — | Karunya | Kúna Pándya, or Sundara. | | Kubja P., afterwards called Sundara P. — Beautiful — and known in Tamil as Kún or Kúna P. | | |
| 75 | — | — | — | Purushottama. | | | | | |
| 76 | — | — | — | Chitra Satana ?. | | | | | |
| 77 | — | — | — | Kuna, or Sundara. | | | | | |

## 3. CHOLA DYNASTY.

It remains to notice the succession of the Cholas. That they, as well as the Páṇḍyans, occupied their present position on the coast of Coromandel (Shoramandalam) before the Christian era, is shown by Asoka's edict as before stated, as well as by Ptolemy.[1] But they appear to have been the most important state in Drávida from having given their name to the whole of the eastern coast, and from the practice of the Singhalese historian using the term Sollee for the country, and that of Solleans[2] for the inhabitants, in their relations with the mainland, although their intercourse was more frequent with Madura and the Páṇḍyans. Of their early political status we have no certain information. Their first capital was at Uraiyúr (Warriore = the city of habitation), called also Kóṛi,[3] the oldest part of the modern Trichinopoli (Tirísirappaḷḷi). This Wilson supposes may be the Orthoura (Ὀρθουρα) of Ptolemy.[4] On the destruction of this place by some catastrophe (natural or political?), the capital was transferred about the seventh century to Malaikuṛṛam, the modern Kumbhakonam, which still retains traces of its former celebrity. The seat of government was at one time (about the tenth or eleventh century?) at Gangondaram (Gangaikandapúr, Gunganáḍapúram, Gangáikondu Solapúr), one mile from the southern Great Trunk Road, and about five miles north of the Kollidam (Coleroon), where a magnificent temple and other remains bear testimony to its former importance. This name appears to be connected with that of the Sundara Páṇḍyan, the brother-in-law of Rajendra, and his vice-regent in the south, whose name, according to Dr. Caldwell, was also Gangaikoṇḍa Choḷa, or Gangaikondán. Finally the seat of power was fixed at Tanjávúr (Tanjore). Of the causes which led to these removals no information has as yet been obtained, but they were perhaps connected with dynastic changes in the succession.

The lists of princes are more numerous, more uncertain, and more incomplete than those of the Páṇḍyans. Prof. Dowson has collected ten or twelve of these in his paper on the Chéra dynasty,[5] no two of which correspond, although two or three familiar names recur in all. They are moreover inextricably confused by the practice so frequent in this dynasty

[1] Ellis, Mirasi Right, App. D. ii.; Mack. Cat. vol. i. p. lxxxiv.
[2] Turnour's Mahawanso, App. pp. lxiv, lxv.
[3] Cald. Comp. Gram. Intro. p. 17.
[4] Mack. Cat. vol. i. lxxxiii.
[5] J.R.A.S. vol. viii.

of using titles instead of the proper designations of individuals,[1] and sometimes two or three changes of this kind are found arising out of events in the history of the same person. Dr. Burnell, who had special opportunities in Tanjore for becoming acquainted with their history, has given the results of his inquiries in a note at p. 40 of his Palæography. These are deduced from inscriptions, mostly without dates. More accurate chronological details are derived from the Choḷa-Chalukya inscriptions in the Telugu country, which are invariably dated. A very full copper exemplar[2] of one of these, dated s.s. 1001, gives the following particulars:—

Rája Rája Narendra, called also Rajendra Choḷa, ? A.D. 1023 or 30—1064.
|
Vikrama Déva Kulottunga Choḷa.
|
Rája Rája. — Víra Déva Choḷa, or Kulottunga Choḷa, or Saptama Vishṇuvardhana.[3]

whose inscriptions, as Viceroy of the Rájamahendri or Vengi province are found from s.s. 1001= A.D. 1079 to A.D. 1135. From this Burnell's statement differs considerably, and is as follows:—

Kerikala Chola (? A.D. 950).
Rájarája Choḷa, *alias* Narendra (40 or 41 years) (A.D. 1023-1064).
|
Víra Choḷa, *alias* Kulottunga Choḷa I., or
Rájarajendra (Rája rája),
Koppakesari Varmá (49 years) (A.D. 1064-1113).
|
Vikrama Choḷa (15 years) (A.D. 1113-1128).
|
Kulottunga Choḷa II. (? A.D. 1128), ruled over the whole Tamil country for at least 30 years (Cald. p. 135).
|
. . . . . . .
|
Vikrama Déva,[4] reigning in A.D. 1235.

These discrepancies will doubtless be cleared up hereafter; at present, we may conclude with tolerable certainty that the Choḷa power was in the ascendant from early in the eleventh to the middle of the thirteenth century, and extended from the Godáveri to Cape Comorin. During the latter half of this period the Páṇḍyans appear to have recovered much of their independence, and the affairs of the two states are greatly intermixed.

After the middle of the thirteenth century the Hoysaḷa Balláḷa dynasty under Soma or Víra Somesvara and Víra Narasimha exercised a considerable control over the Choḷa and Páṇḍya states, interfering, according to their own accounts, as the allies of the Choḷas.[5] The

[1] This is noticed by Wilson, Mack. Cat. vol. i. p. lxxxi; Caldwell, Hist. of Tinnevelly, p. 32; Burnell, South Ind. Palæography, 2nd ed. pp. 40, 45.

[2] See *ante*, p. 88.

[3] Saptama, *i.e.* seventh Vishṇuvardhana, the name being repeated so many times in the eastern, from Kubja Vishṇuvardhana the founder, in like manner as that of Vikramáditya was in the western Chalukya branch. He succeeded his brother as Viceroy of Vengi, who only held the office for one year.

[4] Conf. Burnell's Palæography, p. 22. Also Dr. Burgess's list, see additional NOTE, p. 135.

[5] Copper grant of Somesvara (Hoysaḷa) Bangalore, A.D. 1250, and subsequent inscriptions. See Mysore Inscriptions, p. 322, and *post*, p. 134.

confusion of this period is intensified by the Muhammadan raids for the subjugation of Ma'bar, or the south, under the generals of 'Alá-ud-dín, and after them of Muhammed bin Tughlak Sháh, which ended only with his death in A.D. 1350.

I must now endeavour to follow the progress of the Choḷa coinage during this period, as far as materials exist for the purpose. These have not yet been found of an earlier date than the tenth or eleventh century, as I had occasion to remark when adverting to the change of character which I have endeavoured to connect with the existence of relations between the mainland and Ceylon. The oldest specimens I have met with antecedent to that change are pieces of impure silver, showing the power of the Choḷas to have been then paramount in Drávida, after their conquest of the Páṇḍyan kingdom, related in the previous section. Gold coins of contemporary, and of still earlier date, must doubtless have existed, but none have yet, as far as I know, been met with. A solitary specimen once fell into my hands, but I hesitated whether to assign to it a Chola or a Pandyan origin. It was about the size of a sixpence, and might weigh between 50 and 60 grains. The obverse and reverse, which were exactly the same, exhibited a fish on one side to the proper right, and opposite it on the other a sitting tiger, with an implement like a sickle or elephant goad (?), over the head of each; behind the tiger, four characters like Grantham (?) which I could not read. This unique specimen has unfortunately been lost, but I have a faithful drawing of it. The oldest of the silver coins weighs 62 grains, and, like the above, the obverse and reverse are the same, displaying a tiger seated under an imperial umbrella, on each side of it a chowrie, in front of the tiger two fish, and behind it a bow, the emblems respectively of the Páṇḍyans and the Chéras, implying that the paramount authority was now vested in the Choḷas. Below these is a Nágari legend, which has been read as *Ráchó Koṇu Choḷa,*[1] a name I cannot identify with any of those in the lists, unless it be meant for Rajendra. But this can hardly be the case, for in two others communicated to me by General Pearse, and similar in all respects to it, the name on one is distinctly *S'ri Rajendra,*[2] that on the other is not so legible. Four other specimens of silver and one of copper have the same figures as the above on the obverse only, with the words *Uttam Chola* in two lines on the

[[1] The majority of the Nágari letters in the adapted Chola Alphabet seem to follow the main outlines of what Prinsep called the "Kutila" alphabet of the Bareilí Inscription, though this is by no means the uniform result; but it is clearly seen in the consonants क *k*, च *ch*, and in the ज *j*,—acclimatised in Ceylon—as well as in the *test* forms of न *n*, and ल *l*. The र *r* again, is nearer the Bengáli script of 1065 A.D., and creates a difficulty in its similarity to the च *ch*, and the possibility of the opening रा *rá* being taken for a ग *g*. A very curious point may be noticed in the discrimination of the short and long *e*'s, the latter of which, of ancient use, was superseded elsewhere by the Sanskrit sound of *au*. So that all told the limited number of letters we have to account for on our coins, as applied to an unaccustomed language, do not yield such conclusive results as might be desirable. The most satisfactory transcript of the legends I can make—from the repetitions on the obverse and reverse of the two coins before me—is the following:

राचो कोणु चोल:

*Ráchó Koṇu Cholah.*—E.T.]

[[2] Mr. Thomas adds: There is a contrast in the tenour of Rajendra Chola's coin-superscriptions, which seems to me to remove them from the direct association above suggested by Sir Walter Elliot. The Nágari legend runs clearly—

श्री राजेन्द्र:

*Śrí Rájendrah.*

And it is the use of the *quasi* ग *g* for the necessary रा *rá*, in this instance, which determines the purport of the opening *Rá* in the previous example.]

reverse.[1] These words appear to refer to an epithet rather than a name, being generally found in combination qualifying another word, *e.g.* Kulottunga, Kulottama, Purushottama, etc., implying chief, or head, or ornament of a race or family. It may, however, have pertained to an individual of the Chola family, as the following instance shows. In a Tamil MS. in the Mackenzie Catalogue,[2] entitled the Nava Chola Charitra, the author, Panditaradhya, gives accounts of nine Chola princes named—

| | |
|---|---|
| Kerikala. | Varadherma. |
| Vikrama. | Satyendra. |
| Uttunga. | Manujendra. |
| Adivara. | Víra and Uttama. |

and of their attachment to the Víra Saiva or Jangama religion. It is a sectarian work of no authority, as none of these princes, although staunch professors of the Saiva creed, ever conformed to the Jangama or Víra Saiva doctrines; but the list of names appears to include those of veritable Chola princes, and the last seems to agree with that on the coin. All the foregoing, however, must be anterior to the introduction of the Ceylon type, and consequently be older than the tenth or eleventh century. After this date the character of the currency is completely changed, and these archaic forms do not again appear, but give place to the universal adoption of the new type, and so plentiful is it that large numbers are still to be found throughout the south. Copper pieces, the more perfect specimens weighing from 50 to 60 grains, bearing the name of Raja Raja, are met with every day. They are brought in numbers to be melted up by the coppersmiths, and one find within my own knowledge in Tanjore yielded upwards of 4000. One gold piece, weighing 65 grains, found its way from the Southern Mahratta country into Mr. Gibbs' cabinet during the late famine; and I myself obtained half a dozen or more of silver weighing 66 or 67 grains. All these had the name of Sri Raja Raja under the left arm of the sitting figure on the reverse. Smaller copper pieces, half or quarter, of the ordinary type are not uncommon, and I have varieties of the small size displaying a well-formed galloping horseman on the obverse, and on the reverse the usual sitting figure and the name Raja Rája. Another variety has the figure of Krishna as Muralídhara = the flute-player, with a similar reverse, which shows a leaning to Vaishnava opinions. Gold fanams with the Ceylon type on the obverse, and an indistinct Nágari reverse, are occasionally met with. I received from Tanjore two gold pieces, weighing about 8 grains, of later date, because they have the standing figure of the Ceylon type on the obverse. The reverse has three old Nágari letters, which may be read *iraka?* or *daraka?* throwing no light on their origin. Mr. Rhys Davids has figured this form as No. 13 of his Ceylon coins. I was inclined, when I first obtained them, to assign them to the Cholas; as they are not infrequent in the island, their origin is but doubtful.

[1 उत्तम चोल: *Uttam Cholah.*]

[2] Vol. i. pp. xc and 305; Taylor's Or. MSS. vol. iii. p. 646

The Cholas likewise struck coins during their occupation of Rájamahendri or Vengi in the Chalukya territory. Gold fanams with the fish, sometimes one, sometimes two, others with the tiger, and others again with the boar, are found near Pittapúr, Waddáda, and other old places, after heavy rains. They weigh from 6 to 7 grains each. I have likewise two examples of a larger size, one gold and one silver, weighing each alike, viz. $7\frac{2}{10}$ grains, and the device on both precisely the same. The obverse has the central tiger, surmounted by the imperial umbrella, between the bow and fish, and the reverse a Nágari legend, very clear on the silver specimen, which I read as *Udaya Malla.*[1] I have also two copper pieces with a standing figure on the obverse, and a boar on the reverse, weighing fifty-two grains. All the above clearly refer to the Choḷa-Chalukya period, to which I may add the description of a coin in General Cunningham's cabinet, of which he sent me a drawing several years ago, representing on the obverse a boar under an umbrella, with the sun, moon, and four stars, and on the reverse the Ceylon sitting figure, with, as far as I can make them out, the letters Raja Raja under the arm.

A large number of copper coins are found, weighing from fifty to fifty-two grains, which have the Ceylon standing figure on the obverse and a bull on the reverse, with various symbols. I am inclined, though with hesitation, to attribute them to the later Choḷa period. Some of these have the Nágari letter व V in front of the animal, indicating, perhaps, the initial letter of the royal name (Vikrama?). Others have, instead of a letter, a lozenge or diamond-shaped figure, a sword, *ṣankha* shell (?), or crozier (?), etc.; but without more accurate information it is need'less to speculate on the import of these signs. A similar form was afterwards assumed by the Zamíndars of Rámnád and Sivaganga, whose coins exhibit the standing figure on the obverse and an elegantly-depicted bull couchant, with the Tamil legend *Setu* on the reverse, indicating their title of Setupati.[2] Examples of it are not uncommon. I have several copper coins received from the southern districts, with the bull on the obverse, and a tripartite object on the reverse like a fleur-de-lis or the trisula of Śiva, nearly resembling which is a coin figured by Sir Arthur Phayre,[3] with the note that it was struck in Arakan about the eighth century A.D. Sir Arthur gives fuller details of this type in his contribution to the I. N. O., eight varieties in silver of which are figured in Plate II., and shows that they pertain to a dynasty of Chandra princes ruling in Arakan. The intercourse which prevailed between the Coromandel coast and the opposite side of the Bay of Bengal

[1] Mr. Thomas, in describing another specimen, adds—[The edges of this piece (one of Gen.ral Pearse's) are so reduced, and the forms of the letters so eccentric, that I do not think it would be advantageous to speculate on the context beyond the third letter of line one, which may be read as *dads* or *dado*?—E.T.]

General Pearse's cabinet contains specimens of the gold piece which his Paṇḍit read *Yuddha Malla*, a version to which he adheres, but I have found no king of that name in the lists as far as yet made out, the only one being an early Chalukya prince, son of Táḷapa, a usur.per, who flourished before the Chola conquest of Vengi took place. See p. 87, *ante*.

[2] Prinsep long ago figured this coin in his plate (xxxv. fig. 13), and describes it at p. 423 (see Essays, vol. i.). The Setupatis of Rámnád were the chiefs of the Marawár tribe, the most important of the southern predatory classes, and the principal feudatories of the Pāṇḍyans. The office of Setupati or guardian of the approaches to Rameswaram, though claiming a high antiquity, appears to have been conferred or restored on the Zamíndár by Muttu Krishnappa Náyak, the father of Tirumala Náyak of Madura, about A.D. 1605. Nelson's Madura, part ii. pp. 39-41; part iii. pp. 109, 110, 112.

[3] Hist. of Burma, p. 47.

must have been at all times considerable. I have already adverted to the intimate relations between Drávida and Ceylon, where not only numbers settled as colonists, but many were subsidised both as mercenaries and seamen.[1] That similar relations existed between Kalinga and the northern Circars with Arakan and Burma appears from Sir Arthur's statement of coins and medals with Hindu symbols being found in Pegu,[2] and by the fact that the inhabitants of the opposite coast are distinguished by the name of *Klings* to this day. It is therefore by no means improbable that the Chandra dynasty, which flourished in Arakan from the eighth to the tenth century,[3] may have owed its rise to Choḻa influence, then in its zenith. The appearance about the same period of an almost similar currency, distinguished by Saivite emblems, to which the Choḻas were so persistently attached, lends great probability to such a surmise. The founders of the Chandra race are said to have been foreigners from some unknown locality, and the native annals point to disturbances in the country caused by Bráhman and Buddhist votaries struggling for the mastery during this very period.[4]

NOTE.—Since the foregoing was written, Dr. Burgess has published in the last number of the *Indian Antiquary* (vol. xiii. pp. 58-9), a list of Choḻa kings sent to him by the late Dr. Burnell, who, however, said he had no faith in it, "though some of the names were no doubt real ones."

1. Kulóttunga.
2. Déva-Chóḷa.
3. Saśiśékhara.
4. S'ivalinga Chóḷa.
5. Karikála-Chóḷa.
6. Bhíma-Chóḷa.
7. Rájarájéndra.
8. Víramártaṇḍa.
9. Kírttivardhana.
10. Jaya-Chóḷa.
11. Kanaka-Chóḷa.
12. Sundara-Choḷa.
13. Kálakála-Chóḷa.
14. Kalyáṇa-Chóḷa.
15. Bhadra-Chóḷa.

On this Dr. Burnell well remarks that it seems impossible to make this list correspond with the inscriptions, and the editor adds the following list (supplied perhaps by Mr. Fleet?), from inscriptions collected by me; my copies of which, as already stated, being all in India, I am unable to verify them. but as far as my recollection serves me, they do not accord with the results I then obtained:—

Rájarája Chóḷa I. (circa s. 910), A.D. 988.
Rájéndra Chóḷa I. (circa s. 930), A.D. 1008.
Rájarája II. or Narendra Chóḷa (s. 944–985), A.D. 1022–1063.
Rájarájéndra II., s. 985–1034, A.D. 1063–1112, whose *abhisheka* was performed in s. 1000, A.D. 1078.
Vikramadeva Kulóttunga Chóḷa, s. 1034–1049, A.D. 1112–1127.
Rájarája Chóḷa III., s. 1049, A.D. 1127.
Víradéva Kulottunga Chóḷa, s. 1054 to perhaps 1078, A.D. 1132–1156.

[1] Tennant's Ceylon, vol. i. p. 395. [2] History of Burma, p. 31. [3] *Ib.* p. 45. [4] *Ib.* p. 31.

## PART III. SECTION iii.

### TRAVANCORE, COCHIN, AND KERALA.

The only remaining Dravidian state (if indeed it can be rightly included in Drávida proper), which has not been mentioned, is that of Travancore, or Venaḍu as it was first called, and of it I have so slight a knowledge that I am able to say but little of its past and present currency. Shut off by its natural position from familiar intercourse with its neighbours, little is known of its history from the time that it became independent on the partition of Keraḷa, to the time that it was invaded by the Muhammadans. The first Muhammadan inroads took place in 1680 A.D. during the regency of Umayamma Ráni (1677–1684), but the invaders were expelled before her son attained his majority in the latter year. During the three following reigns disputes arose with the Dutch East India Company for frontier territory unwillingly ceded by the Rája, which were finally adjusted by the Treaty of Mávalikara in 1753.[1]

Meantime Haidar 'Alí had been casting wistful eyes on the Malabar coast, but his attempts to add Kéraḷa to his kingdom were frustrated by the English and Dutch East India Companies, the former by the Treaty signed at Madras in 1769, the latter by the refusal to allow the passage of Maisur troops through their territory.[2] In 1762 the then Raja gave effectual aid to the Rája of Cochin in repelling an invasion of the latter by the Zamorin, receiving in return certain frontier villages for the aid so rendered. After Haidar's death in 1782, his son Tipu made renewed efforts to seize on Travancore. Though successfully resisted at first, he would in all likelihood have effected his object had not the war with the English (1789–90) humbled the ambition of the Sultán, and the Treaty of Seringapatam (1792) assured the safety of the Rája's dominions.[3] Since that time the Travancore state has continued in the full enjoyment of its independence.

Believing that the history and progress of a long-established Hindu mint would yield valuable data, I submitted a request to the government of Travancore for information on the subject. From the Dewán (Ṅánú Piḷḷai), and more recently from His Highness the present enlightened Rája, who succeeded in 1880, I received courteous replies; but the hopes I had entertained were disappointed. The Mint, I was informed, had been destroyed by fire, and no early records of the coinage were in existence. I received from the Dewán, however, a list accompanied by fourteen specimens of the different coins of the state, to which the Raja himself

[1] Shanguni Menon's History of Travancore, p. 150.

[2] Wilks's Mysore, vol. ii. p. 124; vol. iii. p. 33.

[3] Wilks's Mysore, vol. iii. pp. 58-66. and pp. 213-244.

very kindly added four old pieces, three of lead and one of iron. Failing to obtain from other sources information regarding the origin and changes of the currency, I must now therefore endeavour to describe them as far as the limited means at my disposal will allow.[1]

According to the general belief of the people, the oldest coin known is the *rasi* (No. 1 in the Dewán's list). They even go so far as to declare that it was struck by Parasu Ráma when he made over the rule of Kérala to Bhanu Vikrama,[2] the first king! Judging from its appearance alone, it must have been subsequent to the four pieces presented to me by the Rája, which probably go back to the earlier years of the monarchy, and would therefore date from a period anterior to the seventh or eighth century. The reverse of all four is smooth, and the obverse, which is much worn, exhibits an imperfect outline of what may have been a *ṣankha* shell, the ancient cognizance of the Travancore state, which it still retains. They, as well as the *rási*, have long given place to a more modern currency, the oldest form of which is the *káli*, properly called the *káli-yugen rajen* fanam, or money of the *káli-yuga*, at one time current over the whole of Kéraḷa. Of this there are two varieties bearing a slight resemblance to the *rasi*. One of these is said to have been issued by the Kolatnáḍ, or Cherakal Raja,[3] which was afterwards imitated by the Zamorin, and called the *vira rayen puṭiya* fanam, or Zamorin's new coin, to distinguish it from that of Kolatnáḍ, which then became the *palaya* or old fanam. Both these were accepted in the northern countries of Kéraḷa as the general medium of exchange, but were not a legal tender in Travancore.[4]

The present circulation consists of the silver *chakram*, in whole and half pieces, and the copper *cash* in four forms — single, double, quadruple, and the double of the last, or eight *cash*, equal to the half silver *chakram*. Report says that *chakrams* of gold[5] had once been coined; but this, though probable, lacks confirmation. Besides these, the silver fanam is stated to have been issued about 1868–9, equal to four *chakrams*.[6] This coin is generally known as the new *velli* (or silver) fanam to distinguish it from the old *velli* fanam, which, as appears from the records in the Calicut Kacheri (Cutcherry), was originally coined tentatively in Bombay in 1730 A.D. It was first issued of the value of $\frac{1}{5}$ of a rupee, as an experiment, when, finding that it was readily accepted by the people of Tellicherri and other towns, a new supply was ordered. These old *velli* fanams had generally the numeral 5 in English or Malayálim, on one side

[1] These consist of the native "Hist. of Travancore," by Shanguni Menon (Madras, 1878), who held the office of Dewán Peshkar of Travancore; "The Land of the Permauls or Cochin," by Francis Day, F.L.S., Mad. Med. Est. (Madras, 1863); "The Land of Charity," by Rev. S. Mateer (London, 1871); and "Letters from Malabar," by Jacob Canter Visscher (Madras, 1862).

[2] History of Travancore, p. 24. See also the notice by Mr. Walhouse, headed *Káshis of Parasurâma*, in his Archæological Notes, communicated to the Ind. Ant., in which he states that they are still found in large numbers in Coimbatore, both buried in the ground, and picked up after heavy rains in the approach to fords of the principal rivers. Tradition says that Parasuráma sowed them broadcast over Kéraḷa, depositing what remained in the *kistvaens* on the eastern slope of the hills, some of which are called by his name to this day and held sacred by the hill Arriyans, or Malaiarasurs = mountain kings. He also mentions a stone circle, much dilapidated, which was known as the *káshi hill of Parasurâma*. Mr. Walhouse states that the natives call them *Shánár kash*, which is an error, that term being confined to the *Venetian sequins*, sometimes called *vil kasu* in Cochin (Ind. Ant. vol. iii. p. 191).

[3] The Cólastri of the Portuguese. It was also called Kólaṭṭiri, p. 63, ante.

[4] Hist. of Trav. pp 82-4. In 1793 the Zamorin is said to have made over his mint to the officers of the English East India Company, on condition of receiving half the net profits (Aitchison's Treaties, vol. v. p. 410).

[5] Hist. of Travancore, p. 83

[6] Land of Charity, p. 110.

whereas the modern fanam has the word *puttu* in Tamil on it.[1] It is not known where the small silver pieces called *târés* (p. 58 *ante*) were coined, but it must have been in North Malabar, probably Calicut. The word *táram* is found in Gundt. Dict. p. 445, meaning a small copper coin, which Buchanan states to be equal to half a *paisa*.[2]

Dr. Day has some pertinent observations on the early coinage of Malabar, in which he refers to the pieces of twisted silver wire, known as hook or fish money, termed *ridi*, as having been introduced by the Portuguese.[3] Although used likewise by the Dutch, it does not appear to have ever obtained a general currency. Sir Bartle Frere told me he had some specimens, found in the Konkan,[4] which were stamped with the name of the 'Ádil-Sháhi princes of Bijapur, thus strengthening the suggestion made at p. 56 *ante* of the temporary adoption of the local currency by that dynasty. But it was not of indigenous origin, and probably owed its introduction to the mercantile ventures of the European and Arab traders. In some remarks of the late Dr. John Wilson on a find at Sangameswar in the Ratnagiri district, they are said to bear the Arabic name of *sáir*,[5] meaning custom or excise duty, which goes far to establish that origin. They were also known as *lári*, from *Lár* south of the Persian Gulf, where they are said to have been invented. Travellers of the sixteenth and seventeenth centuries call them *iarin*; they were long the currency of the Maldive Islands, and though the coins there are now of the ordinary form, the name *lári* is still retained.

The following is a description of the 14 specimens received from the Dewán.

No. 1 *rási* (Gundt. Dict. p. 885) is a gold coin weighing grains $5\frac{8}{10}$, with an obliterated form on the obverse, which may be a degraded representation of the *ṣankha*? The reverse is exactly the same as that of the fanam, so common in the Carnatic under the names of *vir-ráya*, *rati val*, or plough fanam. Though seldom seen in circulation, it is still the denomination used in Northern Malabar for recording the value of lands and the ancient revenue assessed on them; but for all ordinary transactions, it has long been superseded by the *káli* fanam, five of which equal 1 *rási*.

Nos. 2 and 3. The *anandarámen* and its half the *chinna* fanam are gold coins of comparatively recent introduction, weighing respectively grains $5\frac{7}{10}$ and $2\frac{8}{10}$. The obverse has what may be a degraded figure of the *ṣankha* shell, but it is difficult to assign any definite form to the dots and lines on the reverse. The whole coin indeed baffles my powers of description. They appear to have been coined under the direction of the Dewán in the reign of King Ráma Rája (1758–1798), when the finances of the country, which had been somewhat embarrassed, were re-established by the levy of an additional land-tax and the reform of the coinage.[6] It was only retained for a limited period, and has since been discontinued by Dewán Venkata Rao.

[1] Private letter from Dr. Gundert.

[2] Buch. Journ. vol. ii. p. 540. It may be worth noting that *tari* is the name of a coin used, at least in calculation, in the Two Sicilies till 1860. Its value was about half a franc; and the name is generally regarded as a Saracenic survival of *dirhem*. Was the Malabar *târé* and *táram* the same in origin?

[3] Land of the Permauls, p. 574.

[4] They were lost with part of his baggage in the Húglí.

[5] Proc. of Bom. As. Soc. in Journ. vol. iii. p. 138.

[6] Hist. of Trav. p. 250-1.

No. 4 *káli* fanam (Gundt. Dict. p. 219). It is of gold, weighing grains $5\frac{4}{10}$. The device resembles Nos. 2 and 3, but is equally unintelligible. A crescent-like form on all the *anandarámen* fanams I have seen is absent from this single specimen of the *káli* now before me.

Nos. 5 and 6 need no description. They are gold and quite modern, having been struck by the last two Rájas in imitation of the British coinage with the letters R.V., and the date (on this one) 1877 in English.[1] They weigh grains $78\frac{4}{10}$ and $39\frac{2}{10}$.

No. 7 *veḷḷi* fanam, silver, weighing grains $22\frac{9}{10}$ (Dict. p. 602). It resembles in some respects the *káli* fanam, but has a floral wreath round the edge on the obverse, and on the reverse, whatever it may be, a double branch facing right and left, the whole within what appears to be a Tamil legend, probably referring to the value of the coin. It has superseded the former gold (*pon*) fanam, of which there were two kinds — the *palaya* or old fanam, of which 4, 3¾, and the *puṭiya* (or new), of which 3½ went to the rupee.

No. 8 double *chakram* (Dict. p. 340), a silver coin weighing grains $11\frac{6}{10}$. On the obverse a *ṣankha* shell, and on the reverse two equilateral triangles interlaced, forming a six-pointed diagram (commonly known as Solomon's seal), surrounded by a Malayálim legend. In another specimen the shell has some resemblance to the *murex* on No. 14.

No. 9 *chakram*, a small silver coin, which has been compared in size to the split half of a pea. It weighs grains $5\frac{7}{10}$. The device on the obverse resembles that on the *káli* fanam; the reverse a few dots and lines, fancifully compared by the natives to the legs and toes of the national deity Padmanábha.[2]

No. 10 *chinna chakram*. Small silver coin weighing grains $2\frac{8}{10}$. It resembles the double *chakram* in all respects.[3]

No. 11 *kásu*, vulgarly *cash*. The smallest copper coin in use, weighing grains $9\frac{6}{10}$. On the obverse the standing figure of a god, said to be Krishna, and on the reverse the hexagonal diagram.[4]

No. 12 double *kásu*, same as above in all respects, with the Malayálim numeral 2 below the standing figure. It weighs 19 grains.

No. 13, 4-*cash tuṭṭu*, resembles the last two, with the Malayálim numeral 4 under the standing figure, and the addition of a floral sprig under each arm. It weighs grains $39\frac{7}{10}$.

No. 14, 8-*cash tuṭṭu* (Dict. p. 466). On the obverse a different form of the *ṣankha* shell with spines like the *murex*? and the Malayálim legend *ara* (half) *chakram* round it. On the reverse the same diagram within a circle. It weighs grains $80\frac{2}{10}$.

[1] I learn that the present Rája has struck pieces like the English sovereign, with his own head on the obverse, but they do not seem to have been put into circulation.

[2] Land of Charity, p. 110.

[3] The unknown silver coin which I received with the *táré* (*supra*, p. 58) I now find to be a half *chakram*.

[4] Land of Charity, p. 109.

## LIST OF THE TRAVANCORE SOVEREIGNS.[1]

| | | Began to reign A.D. |
|---|---|---|
| 1. | Śrí Víra Ráma Martanda Varmá Rája | 1335—6 |
| 2. | Eravi Varmá Rája | 1375—6 |
| 3. | Kéraḷa Kulasek'hara Perumál | 1382—3 |
| 4. | Chéra Udaya Martanda Varmá Kulasek'hara Perumál Rája | 1382—3 |
| 5. | Vénád Muttu Rája | 1444—5 |
| 6. | Śri Víra Martanda Varmá Rája | 1458—9 |
| 7. | Aditya Varmá Rája | 1471—2 |
| 8. | Eravi Varmá Rája | 1478—9 |
| 9. | Śri Martanda Varmá Rája | 1503—4 |
| 10 | Śrí Víra Eravi Varmá Rája | 1504—5 |
| 11. | Martanda Varmá Rája | 1528—9 |
| 12. | Udaya Martanda Varmá Rája | 1537—8 |
| 13. | Kéraḷa Varmá Rája | 1560—1 |
| 14. | Aditya Varmá Rája | 1563—4 |
| 15. | Udaya Martanda Varmá Rája | 1567—8 |
| 16. | Śrí Víra Eravi Varmá Kulasek'hara Perumál Rája | 1594—5 |
| 17. | Śrí Víra Varmá Rája | 1604—5 |
| 18. | Eravi Varmá Rája | 1606—7 |
| 19. | Uni Kéraḷa Varmá Rája | 1619-20 |
| 20. | Eravi Varmá Rája | 1625—6 |
| 21. | Uni Kéraḷa Varmá Rája | 1631—2 |
| 22. | Aditya Varmá Rája | 1661—2 |
| 23. | Umayamma Ráni (Regent) | 1677—8 |
| 24. | Eravi Varmá Rája | 1684—5 |
| 25. | Uni Kéraḷa Varmá Rája | 1718-19 |
| 26. | Ráma Varmá Rája | 1724—5 |
| 27. | Vanji Martanda Varmá Kulsek'hara Perumál Rája | 1729-30 |
| 28. | Vanji Bala Ráma Varmá Kulasek'hara Perumál Rája | 1758—9 |
| 29. | Bala Ráma Varmá Kulasek'hara Perumál Rája | 1798—9 |
| 30. | Ráni Gauri Lakshmi Bái | 1811-12 |
| 31. | Ráni Gauri Parvati Bái | 1815-16 |
| 32. | Vanji Bala Ráma Varmá Kulasek'hara Perumál Rája | 1829-30 |
| 33. | Vanji Martanda Varmá | 1847-60 |
| 34. | Ráma Varmá | 1860-80 |
| 35. | Ráma Varmá, the present Rája | 1880 |

[1] Trevandram Calendar for 1858.

## COCHIN.

Nearly connected with Travancore is the principality of Cochin. Like the former State it dates its independence from the time that Kéraḷa threw off the yoke of the Cheras, but was inferior to it in size and importance, having only a population of 400,000, while that of Travancore exceeds 1,500,000. Although it has been stated by the Portuguese on their first arrival in 1498 A.D., that none of the native princes, except the Zamorin, were allowed to coin money,[1] this is open to question; for, in the Viaggio di Vincenzo Maria,[2] it is said that when he visited the coast in 1657 A.D., the privilege of coining was confined to four states, viz. Cannanore, Calicut, Cochin, and Travancore. This appears to be more correct, as these places exactly correspond with our information of the four independent states or *swarupas* into which Kerala was divided.[3]

The present Dewán, in reply to my request for information on the subject, states, that owing to the small extent of their territory, they never had a regular mint, resorting to temporary establishments when coin was required. During the Dutch occupancy they had recourse to the Factory mint on several occasions,[4] as 1782–3, 1790–1 A.D., when a large quantity of the coins called *puttans* were struck. After these dates no mint operations appear to have taken place till 1820–1, when, for the first time, 9,62,673 double *puttans* were coined by means of the servants of the State. Between the years 1032 and 1034 M.E.=A.D. 1856 and 1858, 2,08,313 double *puttans*, and 2,05,532 single *puttans* were coined. From this it appears that the authorized currency of Cochin consists entirely of silver *puttans*, which, as the name (=new) denotes, are of no great antiquity. The single *puttan* weighs from 5 (?) to 8 grains, the double 16 grains. Specimens of all these have been kindly furnished to me by the Dewan, of which the following is a description. First, the *káliyamáni* or *ṣankhaláta* (=*without ṣankha*) *puttan*, silver, the oldest form, now rare, so called because the distinctive device of the state, the *ṣankha* shell, is wanting on them. The date of coinage is unknown. Weight $4\frac{9}{10}$ grains. The obverse has been imperfectly struck, a few dots and lines; reverse, part of the device as found on the gold *ram*, *ráti ral* or plough fanams. Second, the *puttans* coined at the Dutch mint, also silver, show that different dies have been used, but all have the *ṣankha* shell on the obverse, and on the reverse the same device above mentioned, which here may be compared to a horizontal letter J, with two or three rows of dots above it. The heaviest of two weighs grains $5\frac{2}{10}$. Third, the double silver *puttans* coined by the late Raja

[1] Land of the Permauls p. 574. [2] Folio. Rome, 1670. [3] *Vide supra*, pp. 62, 63.
[4] Gundt. Dict. p. 675; Wils. Glossary, p. 430.

about 1820-1, weigh 16 grains. The device on both sides is the same as that on the single *puttan*. The latest issue of single and double *puttans* took place in 1856 and 1858. The heaviest of each kind found weigh respectively $8\frac{4}{10}$ and $16\frac{8}{10}$. They have on the obverse the *ṣankha* shell, and the curious device on the reverse is replaced by the sitting figure of the god Śiva according to Dr. Day,[1] as worshipped in the Rája's temple at Tripunathorai, with snakes on either side, a chaplet of skulls, etc., etc., as usually depicted. Others, however, state it to represent Vishṇu, and the reverse the *ṣankha* shell. This would be more appropriate to the Vaishnava symbol of the reverse, but the forms issuing from each elbow of the god appear very distinctly to be serpents, a symbol pertaining characteristically to Śiva and not to Vishṇu. There appears to be some confusion between the two.[2]

The copper money now current in Cochin consists entirely of Dutch pieces, most of which exhibit dates from 1731 to 1792 A.D.[3]

Canter Visscher (p. 82) describes a base coin struck at Cochin which he calls *Boeserokken*,[4] an alloy of lead and tin, with the arms of the Dutch East India Company on one side, and something like a harp on the other.[5] They are cast in a mould, and sixty of them are equal to a Cochin fanam. Some further remarks on the fanams will be found in the concluding section.

## LIST OF THE COCHIN RULERS AS FAR AS KNOWN.

| | End of reign. | | End of reign. |
|---|---|---|---|
| Víra Kéraḷa I. | 1549 | Ráma Varmá I. | 1746 |
| ———— | 1565 | ———— | 1750 |
| ———— | | ———— | 1760 |
| ———— | | ———— | 1775 |
| ———— | 1565 | ———— | 1790 |
| ———— | 1601 | Virolam Tamburan | 1798 |
| Víra Keraḷa II. | 1615 | Ráma Varma II. | 1805 |
| Rávi Varmá I. | 1624 | Ráma Varmá III. | 1809 |
| ———— | 1637 | Víra Keraḷa III. | 1828 |
| ———— | 1645 | Rama Varma IV. | 1837 |
| ———— | 1646 | Rama Varma V. | 1842 |
| Víra Arya | 1665 | Rama Varma VI. | 1851 |
| ———— | 1697 | Víra Kérala IV. | 1853 |
| ———— | 1697 | Ravi Varma II. | 1864 |
| ———— | 1722 | Ráma Varmá VII. ascended the throne in 1864. | |
| ———— | 1742 | | |

1 Land of the Permauls, p. 577.

2 Dr. Gundert observes in a private letter, "I think in the whole of Malabar attributes of Śiva and Vishṇu are not very carefully kept distinct." I have already adverted to a similar discrepancy with regard to some of the Durgi pagodas found in the valley of the Krishṇa.

3 Land of the Permauls, p. 575.

4 The last part of this word is probably *rúka*, Hindi, a small piece of money. But the etymology is very obscure. The name (*basaruco*, etc.) is found from the beginning of Portuguese coinage in India; and it was also a denomination of the earliest English coinage at Bombay.

5 See a full account of this and the earlier coinage in his Letters, p. 82.

## SECTION IV.

# CONCLUDING REMARKS.

The great number and diversity of coins now found in all parts of the country have been accounted for by the right of striking money assumed by so many provincial, and even by village authorities in later times. I have several small groups in my collection, to which I am unable to assign either authors or localities. An exception, however, must be made with reference to the remark at the end of sub-section 9, Part II. (page 99), regarding the assumption of the royal style and titles on the decay of the Vijayanagar empire along its eastern and southern frontier. Three principal types are conspicuous. One of these has the standing figure of Vishṇu, with or without his two wives, on the obverse, and a granulated reverse, and prevails chiefly along the east coast southwards. Another, having the seated figure of Durga, with, as before stated, the Vijayanagar reverse of Srí Pratápa Kṛishṇa, much affected by the Zamíndárs of the Ceded Districts (Kadapa and Bellary), and those of the neighbouring Carnatic provinces along the valleys of the Tungabhadra and Kṛishṇa. Thirdly, the effigies of Śiva and Parvatí seated, in Ikkeri, Bednur, and the north-west parts of Maisur, which has been already noticed in treating of that province. But they were not confined to one locality. Sir Thomas Munro states that in the Ceded Districts alone "the currency consisted of thirty-two different kinds of pagodas, and fifteen of rupees, issued by Nawábs, Rájas, and Polygars," giving rise to endless fluctuations of value in exchange, so that the saráfs or money-changers reaped a rich harvest, realizing sometimes as much as 12 per cent. on a single transaction.[1] It would answer no useful purpose to enter into a minute description of these, as they have no historical value, and are gradually disappearing. A few only survive as objects of curiosity.

i. The type of the first class appears to have been derived from the favour in which the Vaishnava tenets were held by the later Vijayanagar princes of Chandragiri, the chiefs of Venkatagiri, and at the sacred shrine of Tripati. It thus came to be adopted by the European factories and by the Nawábs of the Carnatic. Conspicuous examples of these are found in the *Star pagoda* of the English East India Company at Madras, and in the *Porto Novo pagoda*, believed to have been first coined by the Portuguese at Porto Novo or Feringhipet, and at

[1] *Letter from the Collector to the Board of Revenue, 25th January, 1806.*

Arcot under the Nivayat Nawábs of the Carnatic.[1] The *húns* of Sa'adut Ulla Khán, of this type, who succeeded Nawáb Dáwad Khán, and died in 1731, are recognized by the Persian letters الله (*illah*) on the granulated reverse, which is replaced on those of his relative Safdar 'Ali Khán by the letter ع (*ain*). On his murder in 1741, the office of Nawáb was conferred by the Nizám on another family that of Anwar-ud-dín Khán, but his son Muhammad 'Ali, received his investiture direct from Delhi, with the high-sounding title of Walajah Nawáb-ul-Hind in 1766. In 1858 I received some information regarding his coinage with extracts of the mint accounts from the Dewan of the late Nawáb. By these it appears Walajáh struck coins at other places besides Arcot, viz. Porto-Novo, Trichinopoli and Tiruvamur, and among the coins named are the *Walajáhi, Kuruki, 'Umdat-ul-Múlki, Star* and *Feringhipet.* Some of these I have not seen. The *Kuruki* is not uncommon. It has the three standing figures strongly marked, and a plain granulated reverse. It and the *Star*, so called from the star impressed on the granulated reverse, were probably coined at Tiruvamur, beyond the precincts of the English Factory, at which place the mint was said to be still standing in 1858.[2] According to the Imperial Gazetteer[3] the Madras mint was built within the walls of Fort St. George in 1723. But the Factory must have exercised the right of coining at a much earlier period, for the Madras Public Records state that consignments of bullion despatched to Fort St. George on the appointment of Sir George Winter as governor in 1661, were coined

[1] In all these the figures are erect, but there is a smaller coin in which the figures are represented as seated, with an obscure Nágari reverse, probably belonging to the last princes of Vijayanagar, as may also the pretty little coin known as the *Lakshmi mdda*, in which the goddess is also seated. A friend at Madras was so fortunate as to purchase a sapphire ring on which the three seated deities had been beautifully and deeply cut as a seal, perhaps the signet of a Vijayanagar prince or noble. It is now in the possession of Mr. Franks of the British Museum.

[2] The Dewán states that from the mint records of Hijri 1207 = A.D. 1792, Walajáh is shown to have coined.

| | |
|---|---|
| *Arcot rupees* .. ... ... ... ... | 55,772 |
| *Pondicherry rupees* ... ... ... | 66,772 |
| Total ... .. ... | 1,22,544 |

The accounts of Hijri 1198 = A.D. 1783 show that the annual coinage at the Porto Novo mint was 300,000 pagodas, on which the profit to the state (Sircar), including mint charges, fees (*rusúms*), at the rate of 10½ *Feringhipet pagodas* per thousand, was 3,150 pagodas.

The mint records of Hijri 1186 = A.D. 1772 show that the gold coinage was—

| | |
|---|---|
| *Walajáhi pagodas* ... ... ... | 1,370 $\frac{1}{4}$ |
| *Kuruki* do. ... ... ... ... ... | 22,654 $\frac{1}{16}$ |
| *'Umdat-ul-Múlki* do. ... ... ... | 995 $\frac{3}{4}$ |
| *Star* do ... ... ... ... ... | 3,81,052 $\frac{1}{16}$ |
| *Feringhipet* do. ... ... ... ... | 15,098 $\frac{7}{16}$ |
| Total ... ... ... | 4,21,171 ½ |

The silver coinage for the same year was—

| | | | |
|---|---|---|---|
| *Arcot rupees* ... ... ... ... | 7,230 | 12 | 9 |
| *Tiruvamur* do. ... ... ... ... | 2 | 3 | 0 |
| *Old Pondicherry* do. ... ... ... | | 10 | 6 |
| Total .. ... ... | 7,233 | 10 | 3 |

The mint records of Hijri 1216 = A.D. 1801 show that under *'Umdat-ul-Umara* there was coined in gold—

| | |
|---|---|
| *Kuruki pagodas* ... ... ... ... | 17,200 $\frac{89}{256}$ |
| *Star* do ... ... ... ... .. | 1,21,287 $\frac{123}{256}$ |
| *Feringhipet* do. ... ... ... ... | 16,970 |
| Total ... ... ... | 1,55,458 $\frac{22}{256}$ |

In silver—

| | | |
|---|---|---|
| *Arcot rupees* ... ... ... ... | 803 | 0¾ |
| *Tiruvamur* do. ... ... ... ... | 745 | 2½ |
| Total ... ... ... | 1,548 | 2¼ |

The Dewan adds that the rupees struck at Tiruvamur did not bear the name of that mint, but that of Arcot, and that the heathen mint officers, to distinguish them, added to the die a mark like that on their foreheads, probably the triple *náma* of the S'ri Vaishnava sect. On the establishment of the English mint at Madras in the time of Azim-ud-Daula, the same mark retained its place in the die first used; but when this was superseded by the new die, a flower mark was substituted. A person I sent to examine the dies in the Nawáb's palace at Chepak found two, one having the figure of Hanumán, the other three standing figures and the word والا (*Wala* which was always used by Walajáh) on the granulated reverse. I cannot learn that coins were ever struck with them, but their existence showed that some such design had been in contemplation.

[3] Vol. vi. p. 165.

into pagodas in the Fort mint, of what denomination, however, is not stated.[1] Also that in 1688 a proclamation was issued forbidding the introduction into the Factory of a counterfeit pagoda, fabricated at the Dutch mint of Pulicat, "of the same stamp, but not three-quarters the value of ours, which has raised great doubts and scandals upon our coin, . . . . to the great prejudice and discredit of our pagodas and the loss of our mint custom."[2] Still later, at the siege of Fort St. George in 1702, among other conditions of surrender, Nawáb Dáwad Khan demands the surrender of the Mint.[3]

The preceding remarks appear to refer to the gold coinage, but in 1725 the attention of the Factory was attracted to the coinage of the rupee. It appears that the profits gained at the Madras mint on the coinage of silver had encouraged the issue at the native mints at Arcot, St. Thome, and Covelong of rupees inferior in standard, but of the same nominal value, so as to divert the flow of bullion from the Company's mint to their own. This led to stringent regulations prohibiting the export of bullion from the Factory, and to a reduction of the mint charges.[4] In 1730 the Factory pagoda was found to have become much depreciated, and it was resolved "that a new pagoda be coined, of equal weight and fineness with the *Negapatam pagoda*, with the same stamp, only distinguished with the letter 'M' on each side the image."[5] From these extracts compared with the information of the Dewan, it appears that these Vaishnava *húns* were struck at the same time by the English, the Portuguese, and perhaps the Dutch, as well as by the Nawábs of Arcot, and though bearing the same name, were not confined to the same mints. Thus the *Star, Kuruki* and *Porto Novo* were struck equally at the Factory and the Nawáb's mints, the latter being situate, according to the Factory records, at Arcot, St. Thome, and Covelong, but according to the Dewan at Arcot, Tiruvamur, and Porto Novo. By St. Thomé and Covelong are probably meant the obscure village of Tiruvamur. The *Porto Novo húns* I apprehend to have been first produced by the Europeans at that place, whence it came to be also designated as Feringhipet. When the influence of the Portuguese on the Coromandel coast was circumscribed by the Dutch and the Muhammadans, the mint appears to have passed into the hands of the Nawáb, who continued to issue *húns* under the name of *Porto Novo, Feringhipet, Negapatam* (where had also been a Portuguese Factory), and afterwards of *Scot pagodas.* Buchanan found in 1800 that at Palghat "the accounts were kept in *Feringy* or *Porto Novo pagodas* or *varahuns; pudameni*[6] commonly called *vir raya* fanams and *cash,*" and that there was a profit in bringing *Porto Novo pagodas* from Dharapuram in Coimbatore to Palghát, and carrying back *vir ráya* fanams.[7]

ii. The *Durgá pagodas* constituted the bulk of those current in the Ceded Districts at the time they were brought under British administration as mentioned above. They are known by the names of *Durgá, Gurramkonda, Harpanhalli* old and new, *Chitakdurgi, Dhárwári, Sravanore,* etc., etc. They were all much alike, presenting only slight differences recognizable by the

[1] Wheeler, Madras in the Olden Time, vol. i. p. 32.
[2] *Ib.* p. 208.
[3] *Ib.* p. 393.
[4] *Ib.* vol. ii. pp. 387-8.
[5] *Ib.* vol. iii. p. 92.
[6] *pudameni*, signifying new coinage, so called in contradistinction to the *palaya* and *kalaya mani*, or ancient coinage. (See Gundt. Dict. p. 859.)
[7] Buch. Journ. vol. ii. pp. 353-4.

money-changers, which enabled them to assign them to the localities where they were said to have been struck. I have got thirty specimens, which I do not consider worth while to distinguish by attempting to describe them separately. All have the Nagari reverse except one, which is granulated. Several have Vaishnava emblems of the *ṣankha* and *chakra*.

iii. The third class having the figure of Siva and Parvati, sometimes called *Uma Maheswara pagodas*, were, as has been stated, coined at Ikkeri and afterwards at Bednur. They were current chiefly in Maisur, under which head, at p. 105, they have already been mentioned. I do not therefore, purpose to notice them further, but will leave them to be dealt with by local numismatists, who will have opportunity for determining their origin on the spot. Descriptions of them would form suitable adjuncts to the volumes of the districts to which they belong in the series of Manuals in preparation by the orders of the Indian Government.

I wish before closing this paper to add a few words on the many varieties of gold fanams. Though no longer current, they are still found in considerable numbers, many of them having curious devices, without legends, which are difficult to explain, and afford little clue to the discovery of their origin.

These small gold pieces, representing the tenth part of the *kaḻanju*, weigh from 5 to 6 grains, and might be taken for the unit of the system,[1] as indeed they are in the case of the *Kanthiráya fanams*, which were in use long before a metallic *Kanthiráya pagoda* was struck. They appear to have been much esteemed by the people in their small dealings, and are found in every part of the country. Those connected with the principal dynasties already discussed generally exhibit the same devices as the *húns* and *pagodas*, of which they are the multiples. Such are those of the Kulachuris, the elephants of the Koṅgus, the Choḷas, the boar, fish, and fish and tiger fanams of the Chola-Chalukyas, the lion or *sinha* from Kadapa and Bellary, some with the lion looking back, the device of the Kadambas, others are not so distinguished. Others with a *nága* serpent called *subramanya*, or, according to Marsden, *subcrau*;[2] the *S'ri Vaishnava* three-pronged sectarian mark, probably struck at Venkatagiri or Tripati; the *Getti* fanam with the figure of a dagger identified with the Mahraṭṭas of Tanjore; the bull, which may be related either to Kondaviḍ, Woraṅgal, or perhaps to the later Choḷas;[3] the seated *Lakshmi fanam* connected with the *Lakshmi máda* or half *pagoda*, etc., etc. Besides these there are great numbers which have no resemblance to any other, the devices on which are unintelligible. A very common type is that which passes among the sarafs as the *vir ráya*, *rati val*, single or double plough, etc., fanams, and deserves special notice. In the latter part of the section on Travancore and Kéraḷa coins I have assumed, on grounds therein stated, that they derive their origin from the rulers of the small principalities on the Malabar coast

[1] See p. 47, *ante*.

[2] Num. Or. vol. ii. 747. *Subramanya* was the son of S'iva to whom the serpent was sacred. These, according to Colonel Hawkes, were coined by the Polygar of Kudikonda in Bellary in three forms, recumbent, erect with hood expanded, and also with three heads, when it is called *suruyada* (Madras Exhib. Cat. 1856). I have specimens of the two former, but not of the last.

[3] Since the above was in type General Pearse has shown me two gold fanams, weighing respectively grains $6\frac{4}{10}$ and $6\frac{5}{10}$. He calls them Western Chalukyas, which I consider doubtful. The obverse is a front standing four-armed figure Vishṇu (?), the reverse the same in profile before a lamp.

who first rose to eminence on the partition of Kera!a, amongst whom the Zamorin was conspicuous. In this view I am supported by Buchanan, who states that they were struck at Calicut,[1] the capital of that prince, a more correct explanation than that of Marsden, who attributes them to the Rája of Kodagu or Kurg (Coorg).[2] Accepting this assignment of the origin of the gold *vir ráya* fanams, a greater difficulty is found in accounting for their general distribution over all parts of Southern India, often in spots far distant from the place of their origin. But here, too, the careful observation and exact record of Buchanan comes to our aid. He says, when dealing with the money of Pálghát and Cherakal *táluks* of Malabar, that "the exchange of the *pagoda* for the *pudameni* or *vir ráya* fanams is very variable, fluctuating between 11¼ and 11¾ per cent.," so that a profit of from 11 to 12 per cent. is gained by bringing pagodas from the Carnatic into Malabar and carrying back *vir ráya* fanams.[3] The number of the latter still found in the eastern districts is thus explained. But it is by no means improbable that their prevalence in the eastern districts may have led to their being imitated there to facilitate local currency, which would account for the variations observed among them. Without seeking for them, but on the contrary refusing to purchase, I find that my cabinet contains between sixty and seventy, insensibly accumulated during a course of years by my collectors, or sent by persons who knew I was inquiring for coins. They weigh generally from 5 to 6 grains.[4] The obverse sometimes presents an indistinct curved line or lines, which may possibly be the remnant of an effaced *sankha*, or a sort of oblong or elongated mark, which I take to be the remains of a degraded standing figure, and the reverse a device which has defied, and still continues to defy, all attempts to give it an intelligible meaning. That it pertains especially to Malabar may be inferred from its appearance on the *rási*, the oldest coin there extant, as well as repeated on many of the later pieces. It exhibits a transverse bar, sometimes with the end turned up like the letter *J*, or simply elongated something like a crocodile or saurian; at other times with one or two dependent lines, which have given rise to the money-changer's name of single or double plough fanams. Above this is always a number of dots arranged in two or three lines over each other. Marsden has compared this symbol to a *jinjál* or wall piece of ordnance with its pile of shot.[5]

These refer only to the gold fanams, but Marsden describes a silver *vir ráya* or *Mangalore* fanam, weighing 5¾ grains,[6] having the same symbols and devices as the gold *vir ráya*. I have not met with it, but have little doubt that the *tárés* mentioned at p. 57, and weighing from 1 to 2 grains, are just the fractional parts of that piece. From the greater distinctness of the symbols on these, especially that of the standing figure on the obverse, an inspection of the full-sized silver fanam may throw further light on the device of the gold *vir ráya*.

[1] Buch. Journ. vol. ii. p. 310.
[2] Num. Or. vol. ii. p. 744.
[3] Buch. Journ. vol. ii. p. 353-4.
[4] 10 *vir ráya* fanams weighed ... ... ... $56\frac{1}{10}$
Heaviest ... ... ... ... ... ... ... $6\frac{8}{10}$
Lightest ... ... ... ... ... ... ... $3\frac{6}{10}$
10 others ... ... ... ... ... ... ... $59\frac{7}{10}$
Heaviest ... ... ... ... ... ... ... $6\frac{3}{10}$
Lightest ... ... ... ... ... ... ... $5\frac{8}{10}$
[5] Num. Or. vol. ii. p 744.
[6] *Ib. ib.*

It might have been thought that the small size of the fanam would have rendered its general use inconvenient; but so far from this being the case, they were still further minimised, as appears from minute pieces, of which I have a considerable number, weighing from 1 to 2½ grains. These may be taken to represent half and quarter fanams in the same manner as the *tares* have been taken to represent fractional parts of the silver *vir ráya*. Some of them are distinguished for their great purity, from which circumstance they are called *Aparanji* fanams. They are found on old sites after heavy rains, and were brought to me on several occasions from Dráksharam, Waddáda, Kalingapatam, etc., in the Rájamahendri district.

The trouble of reckoning and carrying about such small pieces might have been thought to prove adverse to their popularity, but the modern practice of Travancore shows that this is not found to be an obstacle in transacting business. Of the two coins in popular daily use there, viz. the silver *chakram* and the *cash*, the former being "small and globose is exceedingly difficult to count or handle, so much so that it slips out of the fingers and runs over the floor, and is only discovered again with difficulty. £100 sterling amounts to 28,500 *chakrams*, weighing 24 pounds avoirdupois, and hours would be wasted in reckoning this number of small coins. They are therefore measured or counted by means of a '*chakram* board,' a small square wooden plate with a given number of holes the exact size and depth of a *chakram*. . . . A small handful of coins is thrown on the board, which is then shaken gently from side to side so as to cause a single *chakram* to fall into each cavity, and the surplus, if any, is swept off with the hand. A glance at the board, when filled, shows that it contains the exact number of coins for which it is intended. The rapid manipulation of this simple but ingenious implement requires some practice, but the Government clerks and native merchants are exceedingly expert and exact in its performance."[1] Although the use of this expedient does not appear to have extended beyond Malabar, its employment in that district to the present day exemplifies the partiality of the natives for such small pieces of money.

[1] Land of Charity, p 111, where a figure of the *chakram* board will be found.

# APPENDIX.

## RECENT DISCOVERIES OF ANCIENT RÁSHTRAKUTA COINS (p. 77).

I have been informed by Mr. James Campbell, since the foregoing was printed, that besides the coins found at Nasik in 1872, three other hoards have been discovered, namely, at Karad in Sátárá; in 1882, at the village of Malgaon near the Kanduti caves, four miles east of Andheri station in Salsette; and in Bombay Island in excavating a drain in Cavel Street, Kalbadevi Road. All these were silver, similar to those above described in Nasik, weighing about 33 grains, having the head of the king on the obverse, and a bull couchant on the reverse, with the legend, as read by Professor Bhagwanlál, "Parama Mahesvara Mátapitṛi-padanudhyata Srí Krishṇarája," meaning, "The illustrious Krishṇarája, the great lord, meditating on the feet of his mother and father." General Cunningham's ascription of these coins to Krishna Rája Ráshṭrakúṭa is thus confirmed. It is probable, as has been surmised, that he was father of that Indra who was overcome by Jayasimha Chalukya on his first invasion of the Dakhan, and that his dominions extended over the western half of Kuntala and the Konkan, forming the ancient kingdom of the Ráshtrakúta or Raṭṭa Kuta *kula* race. On this assumption his date may be placed in the latter half of the fourth century, or from 360 to 400 A.D., and this explains why his coins have no relation to the South Indian monetary system, either as regards their value or execution, then in a very rude and primitive condition, but were formed on the elegant Greco-Parthian model which at that time characterized the circulation of his western neighbours in Gujarat.

## CORRECTION OF EASTERN CHALUKYA GENEALOGY (p. 87).

Since the above was printed I have found a memorandum, and copy of a translation of the Chelur copper-plates, made for Colonel McKenzie, which enable me to clear up, in some degree, the confusion found in the latter part of the genealogy of this family as given in the text. The succession, as therein stated, agrees as far as Amma Raja I. and his immediate successors. I therefore transcribe the remainder of the dynasty, from that prince, according to the translátion now found. Amma Rája reigned seven years, when he was expelled by a usurper named Taḍapa (other accounts say that it was the son of Amma, who was of tender years), but he only maintained himself in power one month, when he was driven out by Vikramaditya, the son of Chalukya Bhima, who only reigned for eleven months. He was dethroned by Yuddha Malla, the son of Tadapa, who reigned seven years, and he in turn was conquered by Rája Bhima, the brother of Amma, who reigned for sixteen years. His son, Amma Rája II., succeeded him, and reigned for twenty-five years, and after him his step(*sic*)-brother, Dana Nripa, ruled for three years. After his death there was an interregnum of twenty-seven years. Saktivarmá, the son of Dana Nripa or Danarnava, restored the monarchy and reigned for twelve years. He was succeeded by his son, Vimaladitya, who ruled seven years, and he by his son, Rája Rája Narendra, who ruled for forty years His queen is stated to have been a princess of solar race, the daughter of a Choḷa named Rajendra, and their son was Rajendra Chola, "who became the head of Rajas, and ruled over Vengi, Kéraḷa, Páṇḍya Kuntala, and likewise occupied the throne of the Chola Raj, where he resided." He married a princess of solar race, named Madhurantari, the daughter of Rája Rajendra Déva, by whom he had several sons. One of them, named Rája Raja, was deputed by his father to be Viceroy of Vengi, vacant on the death of his father's uncle, Vijayaditya, who had administered it for fifteen years. In this post he only remained for one year, when, disliking the duty, he returned to his parents at the Chola capital, and his brother, Vira Chola, was sent in his stead.

Notwithstanding the further light thrown by this inscription upon the Eastern Chalukya succession, it is still involved in considerable doubt. That Rajendra Chola was the next illustrious prince of the Chola line, and ruled over the greater part of Southern India from 1064–1113 A.D., seems to be certain. By a rough calculation of the number of years assigned to each of the Vengi princes in the *ṣasanam*, the period from Kubja Vishṇuvardhana, or 605 A.D., would bring the close of Rája Raja Narendra's reign to 1058 or 1060 A.D., which tallies pretty nearly with the ascertained date of Rajendra (see pp. 120–21). But the inscription refers to previous relations existing between the Chalukya and the Chola families, and even calls Rajendra Chola the son of Raja Raja Narendra. Dr. Burnell's chronology, as given in his Palæography (p. 40), agrees with this, but makes the latter to be a Chola and not a Chalukya prince. The confusion has apparently arisen from intermarriages between the lunar Chalukya princes and the solar Chola princesses. It may be inferred from the language of the *sasanam* that Vijayaditya was the first viceroy appointed by Rajendra to administer the government of Vengi, and that he was a Chalukya, but I find no mention of him elsewhere. On his death, about 1077-8 A.D., Rajendra deputed his own son, Rája Rája, to succeed him, but he only retained the office for one year, when he was replaced by his brother, Víra Déva Chola, Kulottunga Chola or Saptama Vishnuvardhana, who appears to have been a ruler of great ability, and to have had a long tenure of power.

But here another doubt arises in the identification of Rája Rája, who could not be the Rája Rája of the Ceylon type of coins. The difficulty may be accounted for by the multiform nomenclature of these princes, who were sometimes called by one name, sometimes by another. Thus we find in the list given by Burnell, p. 131 *ante* (who from his situation in Tanjore had exceptional means of ascertaining the truth), that the prince whom I have considered throughout as the great Rajendra, is Vira Chola, alias Kulottunga Chola I., Rájarajendra (Rája rája) Koppakesarí Varmá, with the date 1061-1113 A.D. (see also p. 42 *ante*).

# DESCRIPTION OF PLATE I.

[The contents of the accompanying 4to. Plate represent the reproductions, by lithography, of specimens selected from the series of six 8vo. copper plates, engraved by native artists in Madras, to illustrate Sir W. Elliot's original articles on South Indian coins, published in the Madras Journal of Literature and Science. No attempt has been made to recast the order in which they now appear—they simply follow the old arrangement of the 8vo. Plates. The selection having been mainly made with a view to preserve some of the more artistically accurate copies of the originals, in preference to a resort to modern autotype illustrations, which do not always so clearly show the more minute details of coins of lead or copper which have chanced to suffer from age and oxydation.]

No. 1.—Primitive spherule of copper, probably the normal form. p. 58.

No. 2.—Spherule of gold. Normal form. p. 53 and note 1,

Nos. 3, 4, 5, 6.—Silver. *ṣalákás*, puraṇas, or eldlings. impressed with the symbols of various attesting authorities, whether dynastic or commercial. p. 45 and note 8, also pp. 50, 51.

Nos. 7, 8.—Gold. *padma-ṭankas* or *kamala mudras* of the natives. From Banawasi. pp. 54, 66.

No. 9.—A true die-coin. 66 grains. Eight-rayed figure, *chakra* or Sun. *Rev.* plain. From South Mahratta country. Early Chalukya? (Fig. 31 of Glean., p. 233.)

No. 10.—58 grains. Similar to 7 and 8. Centre (?)—At either side the archaic form of the word *S'rí*, below a vase, above the word *Vijaya*. From Malabar. (Fig 32 of Gleanings, p. 232.)

No. 11.—54 grains. The same class as above. From Karnul. (Fig. 33 of Gleanings, p. 232.)

No. 12. — 53 grains. Ditto. Centre has Kṛishṇa piping, on either side the old form of the word *S'rí*, sun and moon above. From Tanjore. (Fig. 35 of Glean., p. 233.)

Nos. 13, 14, 15.—Ditto. 58 grains. Kadamba dynasty. From South Mahratta country. p. 66.

No. 16.—63 grains. Ditto. From Hewli. p. 66.

No. 17.—63 grains. Die-coin. From Hewli. Kadamba dynasty. p. 66.

No. 18.—60 grains. Standard floral reverse. p. 55.

Nos. 19, 20.—Like 7, 8. With boar symbol, early Chalukya. From South Mahratta country. 55 to 58 grains. pp. 54, 66, 67, 70.

No. 21.—Early Chalukya. p. 70.

No. 22.—From Bellary. 58 grains. p. 70. (Gleanings, pp. 88–90.)

**Obverse.**

Boar with trappings.

**Reverse.**

*Chakra.*

No. 23.—Like the above, but ruder. From South Mahratta country. p. 70. (Gleanings, pp. 88–90.)

Nos. 24, 25.—Andhra coins from Dipaldinni.

**Obverse.**

Horse.

*Broken Legend, No.* 25. . सतकणस रञ

*. Satakaṇisa Raño.* p. 34.

**Reverse.**

Ujjain symbol. p. 22.

Nos. 26, 27.—Ditto. 70–90 grains. pp. 22–3.

**Obverse.**

Chaitya.

**Reverse.**

Ujjain symbols. pp. as above.

No. 28.—Unique coin of Gautamíputra. See Ind. Ant. vol. vi. p. 276, No. 5. (p. 32 of this work).

*Legend.* रञ गोतमिपुतस सिरि यञ सतकणस

*Raño Gotamiputasa Siri yaño Satakaṇasa.*

Nos. 29, 30.—p. 23.

**Obverse.**

Elephant.

*Legends*, No. 29. . सतक

*. Sataka.* p. 34.

No. 30. . . सतक

*. . Sataka.* p. 34.

**Reverse.**

Ujjain symbol.

---

**Kurumbar or Pallava Coins of the Coromandel Coast.** p. 35.

No. 31.—Bull and curious device, surrounded with sun-rays.

No. 32.—Ditto, and sun.

No. 33.—Ditto, and Maltese Cross (sun).

*Legend.* म्पतक

*(Kuda) mpa taka.*

No. 34.—Bull and sun.

*Legend.* . तक

*. taka.*

No. 35.—

No. 36.— **Reverse.**

Crab.

No. 37.— **Reverse.**

Fish.

No. 38.— **Reverse.**

Two-masted ship like the modern coasting vessel or *d'honi*, steered by means of oars from the stern.

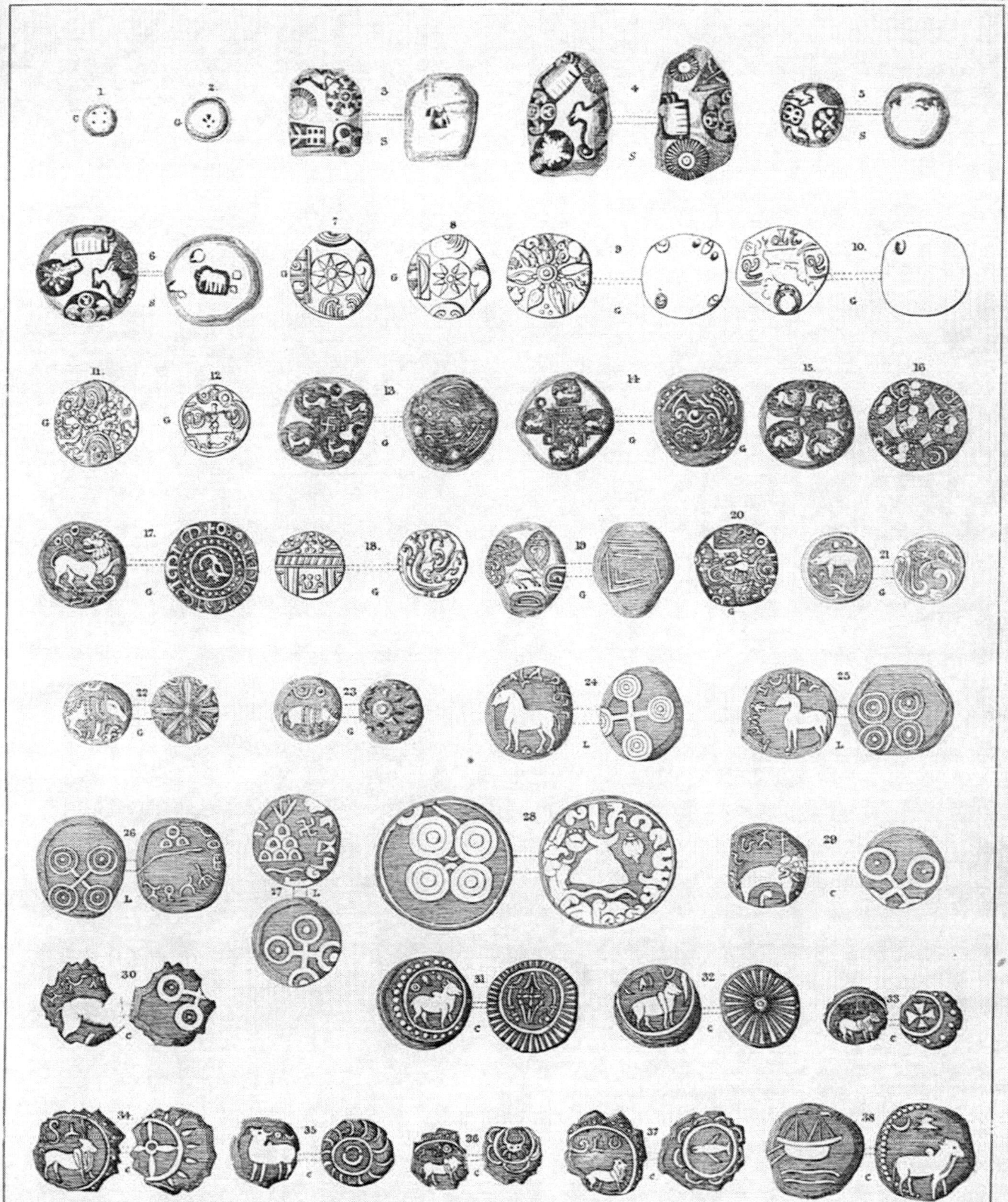

## EXPLANATORY NOTE TO PLATES II. III. IV.

More than a twelvemonth has elapsed since the completion of Plate I., owing to the difficulty, caused by my loss of sight, of selecting the coins required for the Autotype process. General Pearse undertook this task, but after four or five days succumbed to illness while preparing the Catalogue. The opportune arrival, at this juncture, of Mr. Robert Sewell, Madras C.S., who kindly proffered his aid, has enabled the work to be finally completed.

The rough Catalogue, thus hastily prepared, has now been revised in the absence of the coins (left in London). The diction has been altered considerably, several coins have been omitted as irrelevant, and a very few added. In some instances the arrangement has also been altered, involving a change in the order of the numbers. The result, though not so satisfactory as could be desired, exhibits examples of the most typical varieties described in the memoir, references to which are given in the descriptions.

The whole was placed in the hands of Prof. Percy Gardner, who kindly undertook to superintend the execution of the Autotype Plates. To him, and to Mr. Fleet for his readings of some of the legends, as well as to the two gentlemen first mentioned, viz. General Pearse and Mr. Sewell, the latter of whom has conducted the Catalogue through the Press, my most grateful acknowledgments are due.

W. E.

*December*, 1885.

# PLATE II.

## ANDHRA COINS.

[To this series belong Nos. 24-30 of Plate I.]

No. 39.—Lead. From Kolhâpur. *Obv.* Bow and arrow. Legend around reading *Rañô Gôtamiputasa Vilivâyakurasa.*[1] *Rev.* Rail, *chaitya*, and tree. Codrington's Collection. (*Bombay Journal*, xiii. 303.)

No. 40.- Copper. From Kolhâpur. *Obv.* Bow and arrow. Legend around reading *Rañô Gôtamiputasa V[i]l[i]r[â]yakurasa.*[1] *Rev.* as in No. 39 (?). Codrington's Collection.

No. 41.—Lead. Weight, 250 grains. From Kârwar. *Obv. Chaitya* with two rows of inverted semicircles at the base, and a larger open or cupola-arch above. Legend, *Rañô Mala(?)na ....* *Rev.* The sacred tree in a square pedestal, emblems at the side. Pearse's Collection. (p. 31, *ante.*)

No. 42.—Lead. Weight, 278 grains. From Kârwâr. *Obv.* Central device similar to No. 41. Legend (?). *Rev.* similar to N . 41, with the *taurus* symbol. Pearse's Collection. (p. 31.)

No. 43.—Lead. From the Kṛishṇâ district. *Obv.* Elephant to right with legend below, reading *Rañasa S[i]r[i]yañasa .....*[1] *Rev.* Ujjain symbol. (p. 23.)

No. 44.—Lead. From the same place. *Obv.* Horse to right, moon above. Legend reading *Satakaṇasa Raño.*' *Rev.* Plain.

No. 45.—Lead. From the same place. *Obv.* Two-masted ship. *Rev.* Ujjain symbol. (*Madras Journal*, iii. N.S. 243, fig. 74.)

No. 46.—Lead. From the same place. *Obv.* Maneless lion. facing right; in front a tree. *Rev.* *chaitya* (?). p. 23.

No. 47.—Lead. Weight, 602·3 grains. From the same place. *Obv.* Maneless lion facing left, above legend (?). The letter *sa* alone is legible *Rev.* Plain. (p. 23.)

No. 48.—A rock-crystal seal bearing the letters *salâ*, followed by the symbol for "2," which Gen. Pearse refers to Sálivâhana. (*See p.* 19, *note.*)

## PALLAVA COINS.

The coins which have the effigy of a maned lion, as mentioned on p. 23, were originally assigned, doubtfully, to the Pallava dynasty of Vengi (Madras Journal, iii. N.S. 237, figs. 48, 49, 50, 52). The tract of country in which they occur, and the statement of the late Dr. Burnell that "the tiger banner of Vengai is quoted in a Chola inscription of the eleventh century at Tiruvaḍaimarudûr in Tanjore" (South Ind. Palæography, 106; conf. Ind. Ant. v. 50), confirms me in the accuracy of my first impression.—W.E.

No. 49.—Alloy (coarse silver ?). *Obv.* Lion with ample mane, facing right. Some examples have a sword above or in front of the animal. *Rev.* Vase on a stand, between two tall trifid lamp-stands or standards (?), the whole within a broad circle of radiating lines.

No. 50.—Alloy. Design on both sides very similar to No. 49.

No. 51.—Gold. Whence not known. Mionnet's scale, 2½; weight, 72·7 grains. *Obv.* Lion to left, paw upraised, within a circle around which is the legend *S'rî Simganasannâ* (?) *pra* (?). *Rev.* Three-storeyed edifice or temple (?); below, a word not read. A doubtful coin.

No. 52.—Gold fanam. Weight, 7·5 grains. From Râjamahendri. *Obv.* Lion with paw uplifted. *Rev.* The letter *Ma* with another imperfect letter under it.

No. 53.—Gold. Weight, 5·7 grains. *Obv.* Lion to left. *Rev.* The syllable *La* or *Bi*, according to the date of the alphabet.[1]

No. 54.—Gold. Mionnet's scale, 3; weight, 59·5 grains. *Obv.* Maned lion to right. *Rev.* Apparently a three-storeyed building with pillars (?) below.

---

## KURUMBAR COINS.

No. 55.—Silver (?). Mionnet's scale, 4. Weight, 39·6 grains. From the Arcot District. *Obv.* Horse facing right, with a pellet in front; above, a very doubtful inscription in characters which have been read *Sirma Râja* (?). *Rev.* indistinct. This is one of the two coins mentioned on p. 36, supposed to have been lost. It was discovered in arranging the present series, but the other is still missing.

The remaining coins of this series are thin copper, as are also Nos. 31 to 38 of Plate I., all from the sea-shore south of Madras. The obverse of all is the same, an elegantly shaped bull facing right, except in No. 35, where it looks to the left. (p. 35.)—W.E.

[1] I am indebted to Mr. J. F. Fleet for these readings.—W.E.

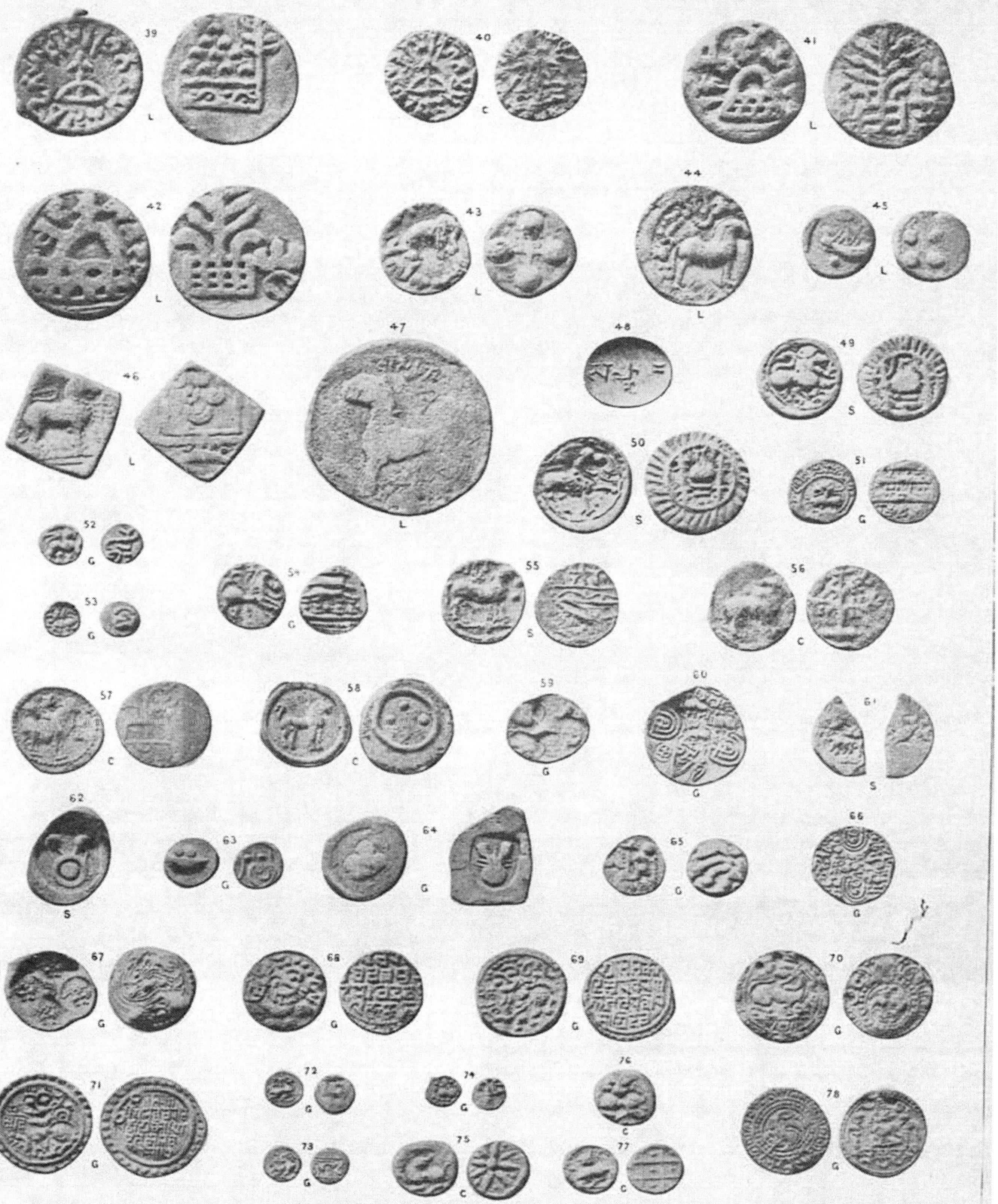

No. 56.—*Rev.* A tree. (*Conf.* "*Gleanings*," fig. 80.)

No. 57.—*Rev.* A tree.

No. 58.—Copper. Weight, 43·9 grains. *Obv.* An animal like a dog. *Rev.* Four dots or bosses within a circle. ("*Gleanings*," fig. 103.) This unique specimen may perhaps belong to the preceding or Pallava section, and the reverse suggests that it may possibly have been a weight. (Conf. Prinsep, in J.A.S.B. iv. 627–8, figs.34, 35, 36.)

### Earliest Punch and Die Coins.

Under this head fall the coins figured in Plate I. Figs. 1–6.

No. 59.—Gold. Weight, 58 grains. Very early rude punch-marked coin, from the Ahmadnagar District. *Obv.* None of the punch-marks give any distinct design. *Rev.* Plain. Gibbs' Collection. (p. 55.)

No. 60.—Gold. Weight, 57·2 grains. *Obv.* Various punch-marks, amongst which appears twice the word *S'rî*. *Rev.* Plain. Gibbs' Collection.

No. 61.—Silver. Weight, 12·8 grains. Transition punch-coin, found with others in the Konkan, with a bull, erroneously called a lion at pp. 50 and 66, superimpressed on the punch-marks. Received from Dr. Codrington.

No. 62.—Silver. From Sultânpur, near Wai. *Obv.* and *Rev.* As described at p. 55. Received from Dr. Codrington.

No. 63.—Gold. Described at length at p. 56, *q.v.* From zinc impressions, there being originals in the British Museum.

No. 64.—Gold. From zinc impressions sent by Dr. Codrington. (p. 55.)

No. 65. Gold. Weight, 55·4 grains. *Obv.* Seated figure with umbrella, chowrie, sun and standard. Floral reverse. Gibbs' Collection. In connection with this see Tavernier's coin, and Fig. 18, Plate I. and p. 55. Origin of all three unknown.

### Kadamba Coins.

Nos. 7, 8, 10, 11, 13 to 17, of Plate I. belong to this Series. (Conf. "Gleanings.")

No. 66.—Gold. Weight, 54·5 grains. From Sunda. *Obv.* Indistinct figure of a lion in the centre, with four punch-marks, two being the word *S'rî*, the third a word which has been read *Bhujaṁ* (?), the fourth an *aṅkus*. *Rev.* Plain.

No. 67.—Gold. Weight, 58·525 grains. From Sunda. *Obv.* The emblem called a *padma* in the centre, with some punch-struck retrospectant lions round it. *Rev.* Scroll ornament and two indented marks. (*Conf. Plate I. figs.* 13, 14, 15, *and p.* 66.)

No. 68.—Gold. Weight, 66·3 grains. From Bombay. *Obv.* Apparently the front face of a lion. *Rev.* A Nágari legend, unread. Gibbs' Collection.

No. 69.—Gold. *Obv.* Lion passant to left. *Rev.* Four lines in Nágari, *S'rî-Saptakôṭîs'vara-charaṇa-labdha-vara-vîra-Sôyidêva,*[1] i.e. "The brave Sôyidêva who has obtained boons from the feet of the holy Saptakôṭîs'vara." Sôyi, or Sôvidêva, or Sômês'vara, was a prince of the Goa branch of the Kadamba family. (From an electrotype of the original coin in the Bombay Museum.)

No. 70.—Gold. *Obv.* Lion looking backwards, with Canarese legend below, which has been read *Seluga* (?). *Rev.* An indistinct object in the centre surrounded by a circle of dots, and that again by an outer circle in which an ornament resembling an omega or a circular buckle alternates with a trefoil. From zinc impression of the original coin in the Bombay Museum. (See *Bombay Journal*, ii. 65, *plate xii. fig.* 3; "*Glean.*" fig. 37.)

No. 71.—Gold. *Obv.* Lion looking to the front, and in old Nâgari the word *Pramôda*, i.e. the cycle-year of coinage. *Rev.* Legend, *S'rî-Saptakôṭîśa-labdha-vara-vîra-Jayakâ(ke)śidêva-Malavaramâri*,[1] i.e. "The brave Jayakês'idêva, the destroyer of the Malavas, who obtained boons from the holy Saptakôtîsa." Jayakês'i was one of the Kadambas of Goa. From zinc impression of the original in Bombay Museum. (*Bombay Journal*, x.; *Proc.* xxiv. liii.)

Nos. 72, 73.—Gold fanams. Weight, 2·9 grains. From the Southern Mahraṭṭa country. *Obv.* Lion regardant, similar to No. 71. *Rev.* Legend undecipherable.

No. 74.—Gold fanam. Weight, 5·9 grains. Imperfect. *Obv.* A lion. *Rev.* An *aṅkus*.

No. 75.—Copper. From Maisûr. *Obv.* Lion looking backwards. *Rev.* A star of eight rays. Pearse's Collection.

No. 76.—Copper. *Obv.* Lion passant and regardant. See Nos. 71, 72, 73. *Rev.* Indistinct. Pearse's Collection.

No. 77.—Copper. From Bangalore. *Obv.* Lion passant, regardant. *Rev.* Crossed lines, with pellets in the squares. Probably of late date. Pearse's Collection.

No. 78.—Gold. Weight, 65·1 grains. *Obv.* Lion within a floral border (?), like that on No. 70. *Rev.* Hanumân, seated between two chowries, and below him an old Canarese word *Nakara*, referring possibly to the god Nakarês'vara, of Baṅkâpur. An electrotype of a similar coin has been received from Bombay.

[1] See note to p. 152B.

# PLATE III.

### Chalukya Coins.

Nos. 19 to 23 of Plate I. belong to this series. (Conf. "Glean." pp. 88-90, figs. 1-5.)

No. 79.—Gold. Weight, 65$\frac{1}{10}$ grains. A large thin plate, having on the *Obv.* the figure of a boar in the centre under an umbrella, and two chowries with the *taurus* symbol, and a lamp in front of and another behind the animal; around, impressed by separate punches, old Canarese letters, reading *S'rî Châlukya Vallabha.* The last word doubtful. *Rev.* Plain. Another specimen has been figured by Lieut. Latter in J.A.S.B. xv. 240, fig. 6.

No. 80.—Gold. Weight, 66$\frac{1}{10}$ grains. *Obv.* Similar to the above, the separate letters reading *S'rî Râja Râja,* and a doubtful letter which has been read *ndra* or *rya* (pp. 51, 54, 66, 67, 70). With these compare Nos. 19, 20, of Plate I.

No. 81.—Copper. *Obv.* A boar, facing right, sun and moon above. *Rev.* A *śaṅka.*

No. 82.—Copper. *Obv* same as above. *Rev.* Indistinct.

No. 83.—Copper. *Obv.* Boar facing right. *Rev.* Lion looking backwards. This perhaps refers to the conquest of Banawâsi by the Chalukyas.

No. 84.—Copper. *Obv.* Boar facing left, with sun and moon above. *Rev.* Indistinct.

No. 85.—Gold fanam. Weight, 6·7 grains. From Râjamahendri. *Obv.* Boar facing right, above him an *aṅkus.* *Rev.* The letters *sa,* under which is the number 11 in decimal figures. From the locality this probably belongs to the Eastern Chalukya branch.

No. 86.—Gold fanam. Weight, 6·2 grains. *Obv.* Boar facing right, enclosed in a circle. *Rev.* A lion, above him the sun.

### Kalachuri Coins.

No. 87.—Gold. Weight, 54$\frac{6}{10}$ grains. From the Sattârâ province. *Obv.* Figure advancing to the right. *Rev.* Three lines of Old Canarese, in the second of which is the name *Murari.* From the locality, and the name Murâri, this may be assigned to the second prince of the Kalachuri dynasty of Kalyân. (p. 78.)

### Coins of the Yâdavas of Devagiri.

No. 88.—Gold. Weight, 52·2 grains. *Obv.* A figure like that of an anthropoid garuḍa with head covered, nose somewhat pronounced. *Rev.* Three lines of Old Canarese, which have been read *Râja S'ivabaṭa,* for *-bhaṭa.* From Bijapur. The cognizance of the Yâdavas of Dêvagiri being a garuḍa, I attribute this coin, though with doubt, to that family.—W.E.

No. 89.—Silver, small. Weight, 4·2 grains. *Obv.* figure of garuḍa, like the preceding. *Rev.* Apparently letters, unread. Two of these coins, found in the bund of a tank at Seotur, on the Pûna Road, eight miles from Sattârâ, were sent me by Sir Bartle Frere, the Resident.—W.E.

No. 89½.—Copper. *Obv.* Garuḍa. *Rev.* A legend, *Veṅkaṭa* in the centre.

### Coins of the Yâdavas of Dvârasamudra.

The only coins of this dynasty which I know (but have not seen) are those procured by Gen. Pearse in Maisûr.—W. E.

No. 90.—Gold. Weight, 61·75 grains, size 2½. *Obv.* Maned lion before an altar; above him a smaller one, with the sun in front; both lions face to the right. *Rev.* Three lines of Old Canarese, reading *S'rî Talakâḍu goṇḍa* (as now read, not *-dona*), i.e. "He who took the glorious Talakâḍu," namely, Vishṇuvardhana, the fourth prince. (pp. 80, 82, *note* 1, 115.)

No. 91. Gold. Weight, 63 grains. *Obv.* Same as above. *Rev.* Three lines of Old Canarese, reading *S'rî Noṇambavâḍi goṇḍan,* i.e. "He who took the glorious Noṇambavâḍi." (p. 82, and *note* 1.)

No. 92.—Copper. *Obv.* Elephant facing right, above *S'rî,* in Canarese. *Rev.* Legend not legible. This refers, perhaps, to the Nâyaks of Tonnûr. (p. 81.)

---

### Coins of the Kâkatiyas of Woraṅgal and Vêma Reḍḍis, of Koṇḍavîḍ (?).

No. 93.—Gold fanam. From Rêwâda. Weight, 6·6 grains. *Obv.* Bull couchant to right. *Rev.* Doubtful. (pp. 85, 102.)

No. 94.—Copper. *Obv.* Bull couchant to right, over his back a lingam. *Rev.* Legend in Telugu. (pp. 85, 102.)

No. 95.—Copper. *Obv.* Like the last. *Rev.* Legend in Telugu. (pp. 85, 102.)

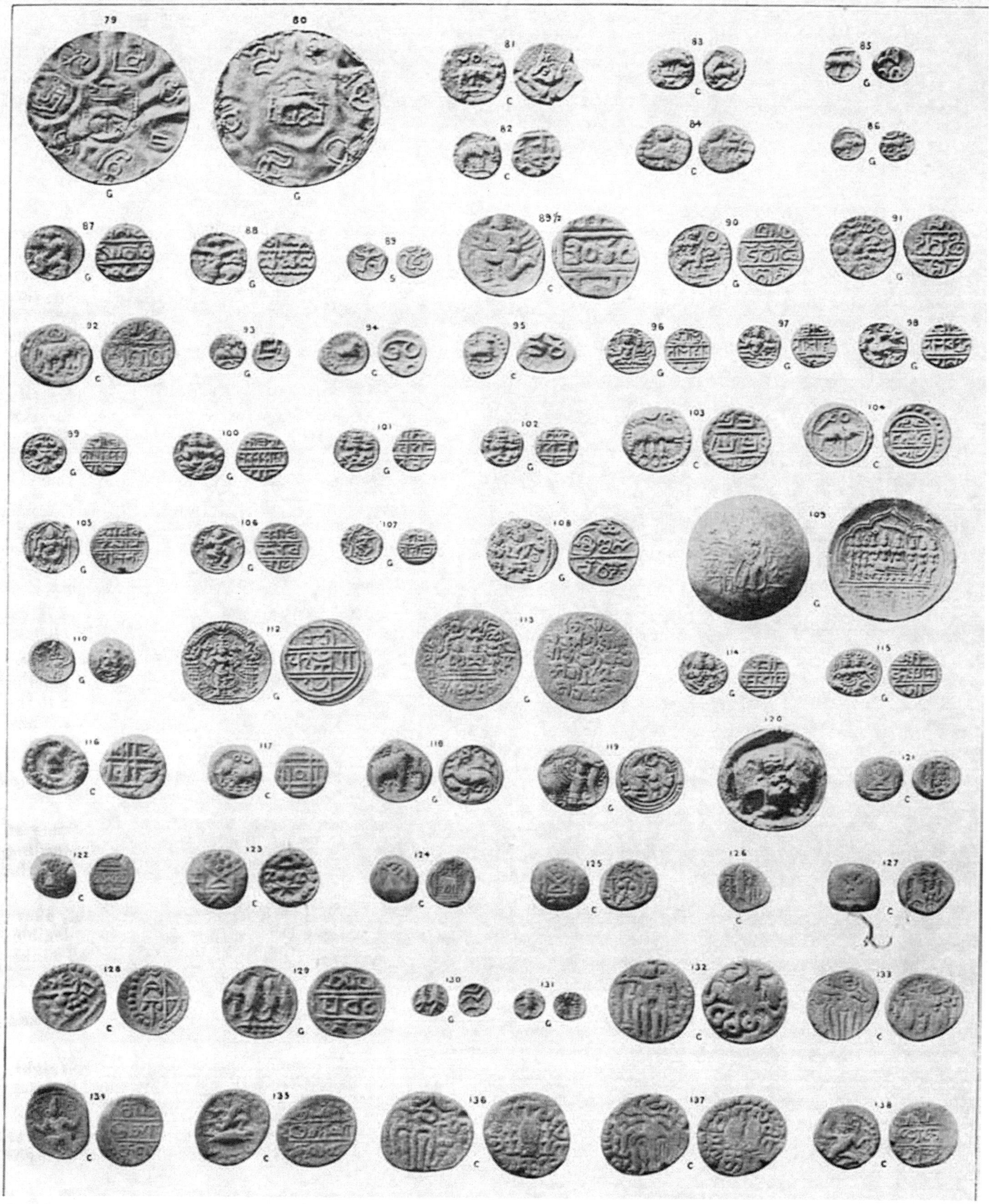

### Vijayanagar Coins.

For the description of coins Nos. 96 to 106 we are indebted to Mr. Thomas, who has described them in note 1 to pp. 97–98. It is remarkable that the gold coins should be of a S'aivite character, while the symbols on the copper coins and on the seals of the dynasty, probably through the influence of the minister, are Vaishṇavite. But the Kuruba princes generally bore names derived from S'iva, while those of the succeeding dynasty, except the last, were adopted from Vishṇu. (p. 92.)

No. 96 (Thomas's No. 1).—Gold. Weight, 25·2 grains. *Obv.* S'iva and Pârvati seated. *Rev.* Nâgari legend श्री प्रताप हरिहर *S'rî Pratâpa Harihara*, the second king of the first or Kuruba dynasty.

No. 97 (Thomas's No. 1).—Gold. Weight, 25·4 grains. Same as the last.

No. 98. (Thomas's No. 2).—Gold. Weight, 24·2 grains. *Obv.* Two-headed fabulous bird called Gaṇḍabhêruṇḍa walking to the left (*conf. note* 3, p. 96), like a heraldic spread-eagle, holding elephants in each beak and each claw. *Rev.* (See No. 99.)

No. 99 (Thomas's No. 2).—Gold. Weight, 26·4 grains. *Obv.* Two-headed insessorial Gaṇḍabhêruṇḍa, with elephants as above. *Rev.* of Nos. 98 and 99, the Nâgari legend श्री प्रतापाच्युत राय *S'rî Pratâpa Achyuta Râya*, i.e. the third king of the Narasimha line, the ninth from Bukka.

No. 100 (Thomas's No. 3).—Gold. Weight, 52·6 grains. *Obv.* Same as No. 96. *Rev.* श्री प्रताप सदासिवा राय *S'rî Pratâpa Sadâsivâ Râya*, i.e. the fourth of the Narasimha line, and the tenth from Bukka.

No. 101 (Thomas's No. 4).—Gold. Weight, 25·7 grains. *Obv.* Same as No. 96. *Rev.* Indistinct legend, possibly श्री कंव त्ररमल राय *S'rî Kanva Triramala Râya*, for "Tirumala Râya," the brother of Râma Râja of the third dynasty, who removed to Pennakoṇḍa. (p. 93.)

No. 102 (Thomas's No. 4).—Gold. Weight, 26 grains. Same as above.

No. 103 (Thomas, No. 4).—Copper. Mionnet's size 3; weight, 55 grains. *Obv.* Boar facing right, sword and sun above. *Rev.* Three lines of Nâgari चलम त्ररमल तक *Chalam* (*Chalan*) *Triramala taka* for (*taṅka*). (See remark on No. 101.)

No. 104. *Obv.* Boar to right, sun and moon above. *Rev.* Legend unread.

No. 105 (Thomas's No. 5).—Gold. Weight, 51·2 grains. *Obv.* Vishṇu. *Rev.* श्री वेंक ईस्वराय नमः *S'rî Veṅka Îsvarâya namah.* Probably one of the Veṅkaṭas in the list on p. 93.

No. 106 (Thomas's No. 6).—Gold. Weight, 52·7 grains. *Obv.* The youthful Kṛishṇa trampling on Kaliya (the dancing Kṛishṇa). *Rev.* A legend read as श्री चिकदेव राय *S'rî Chikadêva Râya.* Mr. Thomas doubts whether this belongs to the Vijayanagar series (note, p. 98). I am also doubtful (see p. 97). It may belong to a Maisur sovereign named Chikkadeva.—W. E.

No. 107.—Gold. Weight, 25·9 grains. *Obv.* The youthful Kṛishṇa again. *Rev.* Nâgari legend, indistinct, (?) *Veṅkadêva.*

No. 108.—Gold. Weight, 58 grains. *Obv.* Râma and Sita seated, sun and moon above, a figure (Hanumân ?) standing before them. *Rev.* In Old Canarese *S'rî Îsvara.* This coin appears to be connected with the *Râma-Ṭaṅka* medals, attributed to the second dynasty. (pp. 95, 99.)

No. 109.—Gold. Weight, 174 grains. The third-sized *Râma-Taṅka*, cup-shaped. Convex side, Hanumân to the left, with Nâgari letters. Concave side, Râma and Sita seated, with attendants. Nâgari legend below. (p. 99.)

No. 110.—Gold (spheroid). Weight, 18 grains. *Obv.* Hanumân. *Rev.* S'iva and Pârvati (?), indistinct. (p. 99.)

No. 111.—Cancelled.

No. 112.—Gold. Weight, 119·7 grains. *Obv.* Vishṇu under an arch. *Rev. S'rî Kṛishṇa Râya.* (*Conf. Nos.* 174 to 178.)

No. 113.—Gold. Flat. Weight, 123·4 grains. *Obv.* Râma and Sita seated, with attendants; around, and on *Rev.*, Nâgari legend not read. A modern *Râma-Tanka*, of no value. (p. 99.).—W. E. (Pearse's Collection.)

### Maisur Coins.

No. 114 (Thomas's No. 3*a*.)—Gold. Weight, 53 grains. *Obv.* S'iva and Pârvati seated. *Rev. Sadâsivâ*, adopted from the Vijayanagar type by Sadâśiva, the first Nâyak of Ikkêri. (pp. 97, 105, 106, 146; *conf.* J.A.S.B. lii. 45, 93.)

No. 115.—Gold. Weight, 52·8 grains. *Obv.* S'iva and Pârvati seated. *Rev. S'rî Kṛishna Râja.* Later Ikkêri type, afterwards adopted by Haidar 'Alî. (p. 105.)

No. 116.—Copper. *Obv.* A Canarese number (?). *Rev.* Lines crossing at right angles. (p. 105.)

No. 117.—Copper. *Obv.* Elephant to left, sun and moon above. *Rev.* Double lines crossing at right angles with a circle in the centre. In others, *Rev.* various, often smooth from attrition. This is the *âne paisa*, or "Elephant Cash," so common in Maisûr, referred to at p. 105.

### Chêra or Kongu Coins.

No. 118.—Gold. Weight, 52·3 grains. *Obv.* Elephant. *Rev.* Floral design.

No. 119.—Gold. Weight, 58·5 grains. *Obv.* similar to the above, but here the animal is caparisoned.

These two coins, attributed to the Chêras, have been frequently reproduced in the south-west. I have fanams of the same type. The figure on the seal of the Koṅgu copper-plates is exactly similar. See next number.—W. E.

No. 120.—Seal, having the figure of an elephant, attached to the copper grants of the Koṅgani princes. From an electrotype impression.

Nos. 121-127 —The seven following characteristic copper coins are difficult to describe. They all have on the reverse the same symbol, which may be compared to an altar or drum-shaped object? The obverse has generally a bow, and one or more five-pointed posts or standards, in one instance together with an elephant, in others a weapon like a sacrificial bill or axe. (p. 117.)

No. 128.—Copper. *Obv.* Seated figure, Ceylon type, with *aṅkus*. *Rev.* Bow with arrow strung, and umbrella. It is doubtful if this is a true Koṅgu coin, but I once had an example with the Ceylon sitting figure on one side, and the true Koṅgu altar on the other.—W. E.

### Pâṇḍyan Coins.

No. 129.—Gold. Weight, 57 grains. *Obv.* Two fish under an umbrella, flanked on right by lamp and on left by chowrie, sun and moon above. *Rev.* legend in Nâgari, uncertain. (*Conf. As. Res.* xvii. 592–3; pl. iv. fig. 81.)

No. 130.—Gold. Weight, 6·5 grains. *Obv.* Two fish. *Rev.* Unrecognizable.

No. 131.—Gold. Weight, 6·2 grains. *Obv.* A fish. *Rev.* Figure before an altar.

These two coins, Nos. 130, 131, with several others having one or two fish, or a boar, were found in Râjamahendri, and may be connected with the Choḷa-Chalukya period.—W. E.

No. 132.—Copper. *Obv.* Standing figure, Ceylon type. *Rev.* A mountain; below, the Tamil word *Ketu.* *Ketu*, being synonymous with *dhvaja*, I attribute this, with hesitation, to Malayadhvaja, the second name in the Purâṇic lists. (pp. 125-6.)—W.E.

No. 133.—Copper. *Obv.* Similar standing figure. *Rev.* Fish on either side of sceptre or crozier, flanked by lamps. Above, in Tamil letters, *Vîra Páṇḍiyan*, the fourth or fifth king in the lists. (p. 126.)

No. 134.—Copper. *Obv.* Anthropoid Garuḍa with *Sankha* and *chakra* above. *Rev. Samara Koláhala*, the forty-first king in the lists. (*Compare* No. 137.)

No. 135.—Copper. *Obv.* Similar, Garuḍa kneeling on the fish. *Rev. Samara Koláhalan.* (p. 126.)

No. 136.—Copper. *Obv.* Standing figure with two characters to right. *Rev.* Fish between lamps; in margin *Samara Koláhala.* (p. 126.)

No. 137.—Copper. *Obv.* Same as above. *Rev.* Two fish surrounded by legend *Samara Koláhala.*

No. 138.—Copper. *Obv.* Anthropoid Garuḍa carrying a bow, *Sankha* above. *Rev. Bhuvanêka Vîran.* (p. 126.)

# PLATE IV.

### Pâṇḍyan Coins (*continued*).

No. 139.—Copper. *Obv.* Standing figure. *Rev.* In old Tamil, *Korkai Âṇḍār,* i.e. "Ruler of Korkai," a title of the Páṇḍyan princes. Sewell's Collection.

No. 140.—Copper. *Obv.* Similar standing figure. *Rev.* Seated figure, and legend *Kúna Páṇḍya*, the last name in the lists. (pp. 121, 126, 128–9.)

No. 141.—Copper. *Obv.* Sceptre between two fish under a crescent *Rev. Sundara Páṇḍiya,* in Tamil. (p. 127.)

No. 142.—Copper. *Obv.* Horse galloping to right, under three symbols indistinguishable. *Rev.* Fish on either side of sceptre; above, a bull to left with chowries. (p. 127.)

No. 143. Copper. *Obv.* Standing figure. *Rev.* A crocodile to left; above, the legend *ke* (or *se*?), and a scorpion (*Makara ketu* or *dhvaja* (?), could such a name be found); below, two fish looking inwards. Gen. Pearse's gold coin I have not seen.—W.E. (p. 127.)

No. 144.—Copper. *Obv.* Standing figure, with two fish and sceptre to right. *Rev.* Seated figure with legend, which has been read *Terumalai* (?). (p. 127.)

# SOUTH INDIAN COINS.

Pl. IV.

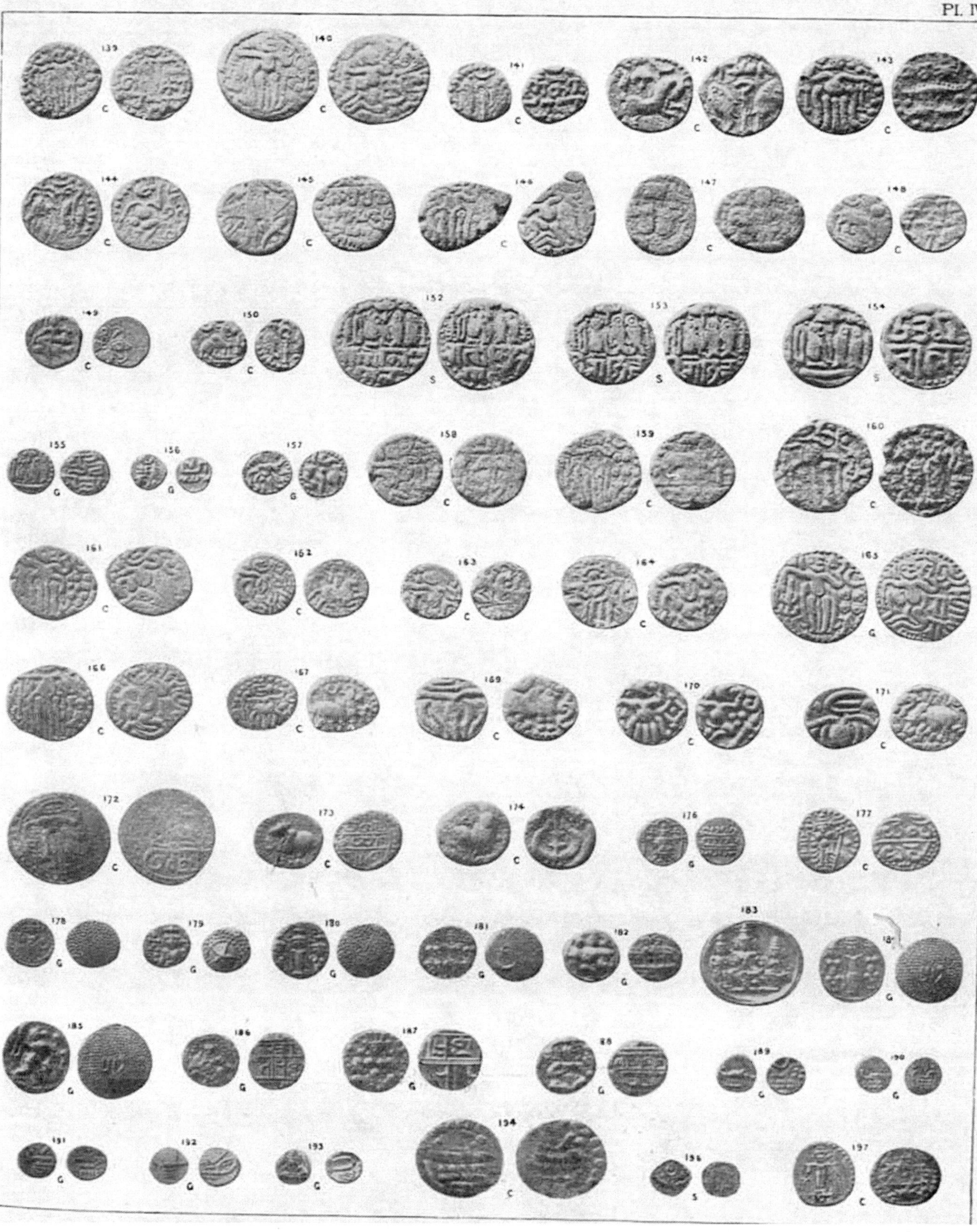

No. 145.—Copper. *Obv.* Two fish crossed; in the angles a crescent and *triśula*. *Rev. Kacchi Valungum Perumán*, i.e. "Conjeveram-bestowing chief or prince." (p. 122, note 2.)

No. 146.—Copper. *Obv.* Standing figure. *Rev.* Seated figure and sceptre between two fish.

No. 147.—Copper. *Obv.* Two feet (or *Vishnu-páds* ?) under sun and moon. *Rev.* Legend which, according to Dr. Caldwell, reading from another coin found at Káyal, is *Káyal*. (pp. 124–5.)

No. 148.—Copper. *Obv.* Boar to right, under sun and moon. *Rev. Sundara Pándiyan*, above two fish on each side of the sceptre. This belongs to what has been called the Chola-Chalukya period, in which the relations between the Pándyans and the Cholas have not been clearly ascertained. (pp. 121, 134.)

No. 149.—Copper. *Obv.* Figure, with halo round the head, seated on the fish. The right arm rests outstretched on the knee, the leg pendant, the left leg is doubled, and the left arm akimbo. This is a doubtful coin, its only connection with the Pándyans being the figure of the fish.

No. 150.—Copper. Bull to right, sun and moon. *Rev.* Sceptre between two fish.

---

## Chola Coins.

No. 151.—Gold. Coin lost; facsimile in woodcut. Weight, 50 to 60 grains. *Obv.* and *Rev.* Exactly the same, viz. a tiger seated to the proper left, opposite it a fish, over the head of each an *aṅkus*, and behind the tiger four characters unread. (p. 132.)

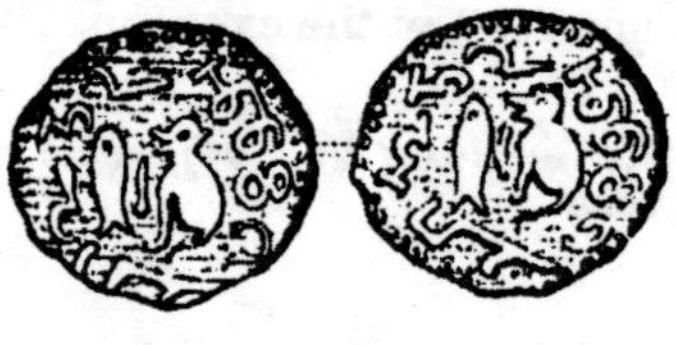

No. 152.—Impure silver. Weight, 62 grains. *Obv.* and *Rev.* The same, viz. a tiger seated under a canopy, chowrie on either side, opposite it two fish, behind it a bow, and below all the Nágari legend *Rachô Koṇu Choḷa*. (pp. 124, 132.)

No. 153.—Impure silver. Weight, 52·2 grains. *Obv.* and *Rev.* Same as above, legend *S'ri Râjêndraḥ*. (pp. 124, 132, *note* 2.) Pearse's Coll.

No. 154.—Impure silver. Weight, 62·6 grains. *Obv.* The same group of symbols occupying the whole field. *Rev. Uttama Chola* in Nágari. (pp. 132–3.)

No. 155.—Gold. Weight, 7·2 grains. *Obv.* Same as above. *Rev. Yuddha Mallâḥ*. (p. 134, *note* 1.) This coin was received since the note was written.

No. 156.—Gold. Weight, 6·7 grains. *Obv.* Fish and tiger seated under a crescent. *Rev.* Legend not legible.

No. 157.—Pale gold. Weight, 8·2 grains. *Obv.* Standing figure. *Rev.* In old Nágari *iraka* (?) or *daraka* (?) under a chowrie. (Doubtful coin.) (p. 133.)

No. 158.—Copper. *Obv.* Seated figure with apparently the legend *Rája Rája* under the arm. *Rev.* Boar to left, legend above and below illegible. The letters above seem to be in Tamil and to read *Vira*. (pp. 133–4.)

No. 159.—Copper. *Obv.* Standing figure, crescent to right of head. *Rev.* Boar, sun, moon, and lamp, above a scroll. (p. 134.)

No. 160.—Copper. *Obv.* Standing figure. *Rev.* Two fish surrounded by an obscure legend, *Raja Rája* (?). (p. 134.)

No. 161.—Copper. *Obv.* Same as above. *Rev.* Seated figure with fish and sceptre where the legend *Rája Rája* usually appears. (p. 134).

No. 162.—Copper. *Obv.* Seated figure with legend *Rája Rája*. *Rev.* A horseman between two umbrellas galloping to right. (p. 133.)

No. 163.—Copper. *Obv.* Seated figure. *Rev.* Two horses and rider, umbrellas above. (p. 133.)

No. 164.—Copper. *Obv.* Standing figure of *Krishna* as *Muralidhara* (the flute player). *Rev.* Seated figure and legend *Rája Rája*. (p. 133; *conf. Pl. I. Fig.* 12.)

No. 165.—Gold. *Obv.* Standing figure, crescent in field, and fish below four dots. *Rev.* Seated figure and name *Rája Rája*. (p. 133.)

No. 166.—Copper. *Obv.* Standing figure, and *Rev.* Same as No. 165. (p. 133).

No. 167.—Copper. *Obv.* Very rough, same as above. *Rev.* Bull erect to right, sun and moon. p. 134.

No. 168.—*Cancelled.*

No. 169.—Copper. *Obv.* Same as the last. *Rev.* Bull to right, crescent above. (p. 134.)

No. 170.—Copper. *Obv.* Same as above, with a lozenge having dots in the angles and one in the centre. *Rev.* Seated figure having an axe to his proper right. (p. 134).

No. 171.—Copper. *Obv.* Same as above. *Rev.* An elephant to left, above his head a *sankha*. and an illegible legend.

No. 172.—Copper. *Obv.* Same as above. *Rev.* Bull couchant to left, with crescent in the field, below, in Tamil letters, *Setu*. (p. 134.)

No 173.—Copper. *Obv.* Standing bull facing to left, lamp in front. *Rev. Kónéri Ráyan*,—who he was, not known.

No. 174.—Copper. *Obv.* Standing bull facing right. *Rev.* A large three-leaved symbol, or fleur-de-lis? *trisula?* This coin, examples of which are not infrequent, closely resembles one figured by Sir A. Phayre as struck in Arakan about the eighth century A.D. (p. 134.)

### Modern Coins.

No. 175.—Woodcut of coin accidentally omitted. Gold. Weight, 26 grains. *Obv.* Lakshmi seated, with *ṣankha* and *chakra*. *Rev. S'ri Pratápa Kṛishṇa Ráya* in Nágari. Not very rare. The *Lakshmi-máda* of the saráfs, of elegant design. It appears to me to be connected with the series of Kṛishṇa coins, Nos. 106, 107, pp. 97, 144, *note* 1.—W.E.

No. 176.—Gold. Weight, 26 grains. *Obv.* Vishṇu standing under an arch. *Rev.* Like Nágari cut by one ignorant of the character. This coin, which should have been omitted instead of the preceding, is the *Veṅkaṭapati Naiḍu pratápa*, or half pagoda of the saráfs, very common, often made into ornaments.—W. E.

No. 177. Gold. *Obv.* Same as the last. *Rev. Venkaṭ Ráya* in Telugu. (Pearse's Coll.)

No. 178.—Gold. *Obv.* Vishṇu standing. *Rev.* Granulated.

No. 179.—Gold. *Obv.* Same as the last. *Rev.* Granulated charged with a star. (p. 143) This is the Madras star-pagoda. This and the preceding numbers came into use on the fall of the Vijayanagar dynasty, and were adopted by the local chiefs of Raidrúg, Venkatagiri, Tripati, etc. (pp. 98, 143), and by the European factories. Nos. 180, 181, 182, like the above, were struck on the east coast, some by the Nawábs of the Carnatic, others by Zamíndárs (p. 143). The same remark applies to No. 183, only the figures are seated.—W.E.

No. 180.—Gold. *Obv.* Vishṇu and his two wives standing. *Rev.* Granulated, known as the *Kuruki* pagoda, struck by the Nawábs of Arcot. (p. 144.)

No. 181.—Gold. *Obv.* Same as above. *Rev.* Granulated, with the Arabic letter *ain* (ع) struck by Safdar 'Alí, of the family of the Arcot Nawáb. (p. 144.)

No. 182.—Gold. *Obv.* Same as above, but the three figures are seated. *Rev. S'rí Pratápa Kṛishṇa.*

No. 183.—Sapphire ring with same figures as on the last. (p. 144, *note.*)

No. 184.—Gold. (Spurious.) *Obv.* Vishṇu and his two wives standing. *Rev.* Granulated, with the Arabic letters والا, *Wálá*, for the Nawab Wálájáh. (p. 144, *note* 2.)

No. 185.—Gold. (Spurious.) *Obv.* Hanumán. *Rev.* Same as the last. (p. 144, *note* 2.)

No. 186.—Gold. *Obv.* Durgâ seated. *Rev. Pratápa Kṛishṇa* in Nágari. The same coin as No. 7 in Mr. Thomas's note, p. 98, undoubtedly belonging to one of the Ceded District Polygars. (pp 105–6, 143, 145–6.)

No. 187.—Gold. *Obv.* and *Rev.* Same as the last.

No. 188.—Gold. *Obv.* Same as the last two, with Vaishṇava emblems of *S'ankha* and *Chakra*. *Rev.* Same as above. (pp. 99, 142, *note* 2, 143, 145–6.)

Nos. 189, 190, 191, 192.—Gold. *Víraraya* fanams. *Obv.* Transverse bar with three lines of dots above. *Rev.* A design not explained. (p. 146–7.)

No. 193.—Silver. The Malabar *táré*. *Obv.* A deity. *Rev.* Similar to above. (pp. 57, 147.)

No. 194.—Copper. Mionnet's scale, size 4½. Weight, 172 grains. *Obv.* and *Rev.* Like the *Víraráya* fanam, of which it is apparently a multiple. Not common.

No. 195.—*Cancelled.*

No. 196.—Silver. Weight, 11·6 grains. Double *Chakram* of Travancore. *Obv. S'ankha* shell. *Rev.* Hexagonal diagram interlaced. The *S'ankha* shell is the cognizance of the Travancore state, and the diagram is seen on many of their coins. (p. 139.)

No. 197.—Copper. A *duḍḍu* of four *kasus*. Weight, $39\frac{7}{10}$ grains. *Obv.* Vishṇu or Kṛishṇa with a sprig or branch under the arm, and the Malayálam numeral 4 in the exergue. *Rev.* Hexagonal diagram. (p. 139.)

N.B.—The last two Nos. (196, 197) are added as examples of Western Coast coins.

# INDEX.

## C.



## D.



## E.



## F.



## G.

H.



I.



J.



K.

L.



M.



N.



O.

P.



R.



S.

T.



U.



V.

THE END.